THE WARREN BUFFETT PATH
TO YOUR FINANCIAL FREEDOM

THE WARREN BUFFETT PATH
TO YOUR FINANCIAL FREEDOM

THE BUSINESS INVESTOR

A step-by-step guide
from mindset
to methodology

PETER GUSTAFSON

Cover and Layout Design: Glen Edelstein

Contact & Requests:
www.peter-gustafson.com
E-mail: peter.gustafson.dk@icloud.com

'Life can only be understood backwards,
but it must be lived forwards.'

—*Søren Kierkegaard, Danish philosopher*

To my parents, children and grandchildren

Preben and Else
Amalie and Fanny
Liva and Leonardo

Looking backwards and forwards – I am truly grateful.

CONTENTS

FOREWORD

by Robert P. Miles

This book is a true pleasure to read – at last, a guide to investing that speaks to both newcomers and seasoned professionals alike. Peter Gustafson delivers fresh perspectives on Warren Buffett's essential benchmarks for investment returns, paired with clear explanations of key financial terms crafted by someone who is not only a skilled business journalist, but also an accomplished entrepreneur, business owner and successful private investor. So successful that he has found financial freedom to do with his time as he wishes and is now passing along just how he did it.

Most books about Buffett either analyze his methods without being written by successful investors, or are produced by investment managers to attract clients. This book is different.

The Business Investor builds on the platform of Benjamin Graham's *The Intelligent Investor* and adds on top the Warren Buffett's principles of owning great companies – run by excellent management – and investing only when you have the odds in your favor of achieving an attractive return based on the company's earnings. Everything is laid out and systematically explained.

Peter began his journey in Denmark, where he graduated from Copenhagen Business School with a master's in finance, but immediately made his way to financial and business journalism, reporting on European businesses and capital markets. After becoming business editor at Denmark's leading newspaper, his career evolved as he founded and grew his Nordic consulting company, PROSPECT, helping management in Nordic and European listed companies and global private-equity funds enhance their strategic and financial communications and navigate the complexities of corporate governance. This experience inspired him to start building a private investment portfolio and between 2007 and 2009 Peter spent two years studying Warren Buffett, giving him the perspective of approaching each investment decision with both a journalist's curiosity and a business owner's strategic vision and mindset.

I first met Peter when I began teaching an Executive MBA course focused on Warren Buffett at the University of Nebraska, Omaha. Peter eagerly joined my class, determined to understand more about the world's leading investor. Passionate about learning all he could about Warren Buffett and Charlie Munger, he took part in university-sponsored programs like mine and absorbed knowledge from books, transcripts, videos, and audio content. I felt very fortunate when he came upon the unique Genius of Buffett program.

Shortly after meeting Peter, I found myself in Copenhagen after a memorable Baltic Sea cruise. Thanks to his media and business connections, he arranged for me to appear on Danish television and other media to discuss the brilliance of Buffett. This opportunity opened the door for me to teach outside Omaha and beyond the United States.

When I created the Buffett program, I did not anticipate the significant advantages of connecting with a community of like-minded, self-selected lifelong learners such as Peter. Each spring, prior to the Berkshire Hathaway annual meeting weekend, participants convene from six continents and up to seventeen countries. Although attendees differ in appearance and speak various languages, they share a common investment philosophy. The exchange of insights, experiences, and strategies among some of the leading investment professionals has fostered a global network, attracted repeat participants and, most importantly, cultivated lasting friendships.

After Peter had attended more sessions than any other participant, I invited him to present the final wrap-up of the multi-day course that offers a deep introspection of Buffett's principles. He brought his own story – how he achieved financial independence by investing in companies across continents, outside the familiar territory of Buffett's choices, and focusing solely on intelligent stock selection for his personal portfolio rather than managing money for others.

Peter has spent years mastering the art of business investment, which he now passes on to all those interested in market-beating performance. He invested more than 2,200 hours in writing and refining this book, sharing his hard-won knowledge in these pages. Readers can expect to spend about ten hours with this book to discover valuable insights that may lead to a lifetime of extraordinary returns.

Remarkably, through his dedication, Peter uncovered a unique aspect of Buffett's philosophy – Buffett's personal hurdle rate, or the minimum return he demands before making any investment. It's an insight I have not seen discussed elsewhere. As an added benefit, Peter has tapped his global network of like-minded investors to review his manuscript and offer professional insights.

Whether you're at the start of your investing journey or already an experienced professional, I urge you to read Peter's book. You'll find wisdom that can enrich your understanding and potentially reward you with a lifetime of impressive returns using the power of investing like a business owner.

—*Robert P. Miles, author, executive in residence, University of Nebraska, Omaha, College of Business, program creator and instructor of: The Genius of Warren Buffett: The Science of Investing and the Art of Managing.*

INTRODUCTION

Warren Buffett is one of the richest individuals in the world, and his track record as an investor spans more than seven decades. Every year, thousands of passionate and skilled investors from around the globe gather in his hometown of Omaha, Nebraska, to learn from Buffett and from one another during the annual meeting of his company, Berkshire Hathaway.

For several years now, I've had the privilege of being invited to Omaha to teach Buffett's investment method in the days preceding this event. During these sessions, I've systematically examined Buffett's principles, highlighting the business characteristics he looks for and his emphasis on the fact that investing is, above all, a test of character. Being a successful investor is a lonely pursuit, not a democratic process. *You*, as an investor, are in the starring role – and if you don't invest rationally and don't understand yourself as an investor, you'll simply have no chance of outperforming the stock market.

My twenty years of studying Warren Buffett's investment approach, my Omaha teaching and my thirty years' experience as a business owner and full-time investor are the foundations for this book. The words are my own, but they're inspired by the greatest investor and business mind in history.

Writing the book has been a challenge. My goal is to help the millions of active investors out there who don't just want to chase the latest media 'hot tip'. This book is for investors who don't want their decisions swayed by market euphoria or fear, but who instead seek a rational framework based on sound principles and a structured, robust approach. In short, it's for those who want to adopt Buffett's principles and thinking and become successful investors themselves.

Many books have been written about Buffett and his extraordinary success, and I've read nearly all of them – the best ones several times. But

I've never come across a book that directly translates Buffett's investment principles and practices into a clear guide for self-directed investors, showing exactly *how* to apply his approach to improve their own results and significantly increase their chances of beating the market.

I've been immersed in Buffett's investment philosophy and investment strategy for two decades and used them as the foundation for my own investing. His approach works – regardless of where you live, how much money you invest, or whether you're a beginner or a seasoned investor. This book provides you with the essential principles and the practical guidelines you need to invest rationally and ultimately achieve financial freedom.

If you are an investor – young or experienced – eager to learn and improve your investment skills, you will learn from the book and gain insights that will drive your thinking deeper. If you are an asset manager handling 'other people's money', this book will serve as an inspiration and show you how to distinguish yourself from other asset managers. It is well known that asset management – or money under management – is very much a marketing game, where standing out from your competitors is crucial. This book offers you a very clear way to do so.

Unfortunately, many investors believe that success on the stock market requires mastering complex formulas full of Greek letters. Equally unfortunate, many investors treat the stock market like a casino – viewing stocks as chips they throw onto the table, hoping for a quick win.

That's not how it works. And I can assure you: Warren Buffett doesn't use a single Greek letter in his investment calculations or decisions. Nor does he treat the stock market like a gambling table. So why should you?

This book explains what stock investing is *really* about. When you buy a stock, you're buying a piece of a business. You are a business investor – nothing more, nothing less.

Of course, you need to be able to do some basic math to be a successful investor, but you don't need anything beyond addition, subtraction, multiplication and division.

To help you focus on what really matters – which is understanding the business you're becoming part-owner of and envisioning what it might look like five to ten years from now – I've made the book as readable and accessible as possible. To that end, I've intentionally minimized the focus on numbers and calculations.

You'll find the most important financial metrics and valuation formulas gathered in the Appendix. This is to emphasize that the most critical element in successful investment is your understanding of the business: its leadership, its market, how its customers think and how it is likely to evolve over the next decade. If you get that analysis right and act accordingly, it doesn't matter much if you pay 5% more or less for your ownership stake.

The truth is, if you can select and invest in three to five great businesses, run by excellent management teams, and if you have the patience to hold them for many years, you won't need to do anything else. You're almost guaranteed to get rich.

This book is designed to help you successfully pursue that path.

Let me begin with the five questions you must be able to answer with a confident 'yes' in order to reach this goal:

1. Are you investing based on sound investment principles?
2. Are you investing in a great business and will the business also be great in ten to twenty years?
3. Are you confident that your company is led by excellent management?
4. Have you invested at a price that offers an attractive expected return?
5. Do you have the temperament and knowledge to keep acting rationally over the long run?

If you can truthfully answer 'yes' to all five questions – and if your answers are based on sound judgement – then your biggest remaining challenge is patience. And if you have that, it's hard *not* to become rich!

*　*　*

Before we move on to the main sections, let's look at what lies behind the investment principles and the essential characteristics of the companies you should focus your investments on.

MASTERING THE THREE MOST IMPORTANT INVESTMENT PRINCIPLES

To be frank (which I'll be throughout this book), if I hadn't studied the writings of Benjamin Graham – the legendary author of *The Intelligent Investor*[1] and Warren Buffett's mentor in his early years – it's unlikely that this book would have been written.

And if I hadn't spent two full years, back in 2007 and 2008, intensely reading and internalizing Buffett's own writings and investment principles, it's unlikely that I would have had the opportunity to become a successful investor myself.

I stand on the shoulders of giants, and I am deeply grateful.

Your first task as a rational stock-market investor is to understand and apply the three core investment principles that Warren Buffett learned from Benjamin Graham – principles he has used consistently for over seventy years.

Investment principle 1: think like a business owner

This is a phrase I'll use many times in the book.

In 1996, I became the founder and owner of a well-regarded Danish consultancy firm, PROSPECT. Then, in 2009, after thirteen years of hard work, I decided it was time for a change. Rather than continuing to own and run a single business, I chose to become a part-owner of several companies through stock-market investment.

As I transitioned into the role of full-time investor, I naturally brought with me the mindset and discipline of a business owner. What I didn't fully realize at the time – but quickly came to understand – is how crucial that mindset is for anyone investing on the stock market. Unfortunately, it's a mindset that many investors never adopt.

But it makes perfect sense. As both Benjamin Graham and Warren Buffett have emphasized repeatedly: when you buy a stock, you are buying a piece of a business. In other words, you become a business owner.

---

1 Benjamin Graham, The Intelligent Investor (Harper Brothers, 1949).

From my years running PROSPECT, I knew that success required a constant focus on improving customer experience, ensuring product and service quality, streamlining internal and external operations and managing the company's financial health. I'd never once thought about the 'stock price' of PROSPECT, because it wasn't a listed company – there was no stock price to follow.

You've likely already grasped the key message here: the only real difference between a private business and a publicly listed one is that the latter has its stock price quoted every weekday – hour by hour, minute by minute, even second by second.

But following the stock price and the short-term swings on the stock market won't make you successful. What matters is following the development of the business and answering the most important question: what will this company look like in five or ten years?

So, investing successfully requires you to think like a long-term business owner.

Investment principle 2: take advantage of 'Mr. Market'

This principle is easy to understand but often very hard to live by. You must take advantage of the stock market – what Benjamin Graham called Mr. Market – and not be its slave.

Don't let the stock market shape your investment decisions. It does *not* have deeper insight than you, nor does it possess wisdom about the long-term value of businesses. When the stock market moves dramatically over a short period of time, it is simply reflecting the mood swings of its participants.

When the market drops sharply and panic sets in – when there are more people desperate to sell than to buy – you may be tempted to follow the crowd and convince yourself it's 'smart' to sell to avoid further losses. Conversely, when markets are booming and everyone seems eager to buy, you might get swept up in the enthusiasm and jump in as well.

Don't.

Instead, you need to make Mr. Market your servant, not your guide. Sometimes, he will offer you outstanding buying opportunities – when panic and pessimism drive prices below the intrinsic value, or the 'real' business value. At other times, he will offer you excellent selling opportunities – when prices become irrationally high due to overexuberance.

This book will explain how to make use of those moments and avoid letting Mr. Market's emotions dictate your actions.

Investment principle 3: invest with a margin of safety

We all make mistakes, and the third principle is about protecting you from the consequences of those mistakes.

Investing is about putting our capital to work based on our analysis of the company's expected future. At the end of the day, our investment is based on a guess – but we want this guess to be as informed as possible. Qualifying our investment is what our work as investors is all about. But we can all reach incorrect conclusions or act without having all the facts and make mistakes – this is part of being human.

Imagine if every time you read a crime novel you were forced to guess the killer's identity by page fifty. Sure, you might be right from time to time – but often you wouldn't. The same goes for investing: even with solid analysis, you will sometimes be wrong.

That's why this principle is essential. In simple terms, investing with a margin of safety means having a buffer. Build in room for error. Give yourself the equivalent of both belt and suspenders.

That way, even if your estimates aren't perfect (and they rarely will be), you've still protected yourself from catastrophic outcomes.

* * *

With these three investment principles in place, you can answer 'yes' to the first of the five critical questions above.

To answer 'yes' to the remaining four, you'll need to apply the following investment guidelines. These will help you evaluate whether you're truly on the right path as a rational, long-term investor.

INVEST IN GREAT BUSINESSES

Achieving attractive investment returns – where your wealth grows at a good speed year after year – is far easier when the companies you invest in show a similarly steady progression in their revenue and earnings.

Therefore, you must make sure you are investing in great businesses that will actually do the heavy lifting for you. If the company becomes increasingly profitable and valuable over time, your investment in it will inevitably follow suit.

This thinking helps you identify the essential characteristics a company must possess to qualify as a 'great business' – one that compounds value at an attractive speed over the long run.

INVEST IN EXCELLENT MANAGEMENT

Poor management is one of the most common reasons why a company fails to realize its full value potential. Put plainly: if management lacks operational focus or capability, the business won't perform optimally – even if the underlying fundamentals are strong.

Equally important is management's capital allocation. Managers often fail to allocate the company's earnings and financial resources rationally – and poor capital allocation is one of the top two reasons investors fail to achieve attractive returns.

As I will outline in this book, your job is to assess whether a company's management is excellent – and whether it meaningfully contributes to maximizing the business value (and thereby your investment) over time.

USE WARREN BUFFETT'S INVESTMENT HURDLE RATE

Once you've confirmed that you're using the right investment principles and are looking at a great business run by excellent management, the next crucial factor the book will unlock is how to buy the company's stocks at a price that gives you the potential for attractive returns.

Your 'hurdle rate' is your demand for returns – the absolute minimum return you will accept – and must be sufficiently high that you get attractive results and your capital grows at a good clip. There are not that many great businesses led by top-tier managers – and these companies are quite often so expensive that investing at such prices won't deliver the returns you're hoping for.

There are also many cheap companies listed on the stock exchange and pricewise they look attractive. But they are most likely cheap for a reason. These companies are often not great businesses run by excellent management – and consequently they don't offer a long-term attractive investment.

I've worked with Warren Buffett's investment hurdle rate for two decades. I will explain in this book how to understand and apply the hurdle rate to ensure that – providing your analysis of the business and its management is correct – you're investing at a price that maximizes your chances of earning attractive long-term returns.

Let me offer you an alternative way to look at the task you're facing.

If your company is better than average – if its earning power over the next ten to twenty years improves more than the average, if its management is stronger and more financially shrewd than the average, and if you can invest with the conservative expectation of more attractive returns than the market average – then you will almost certainly achieve a better return than the market. In other words, the key is to be an investor – or co-owner, as I prefer to call it – in companies that offer you more than average across all dimensions. But it all truly comes together only when you ensure that your own investment work and decisions are also better than average.

UNDERSTANDING YOURSELF IS THE MOST CRUCIAL FACTOR

Ultimately, investing is first and foremost about temperament. To become and remain a successful investor, you must learn to master yourself and maintain mental balance.

It simply doesn't work if your mood or emotions influence your decisions. That's why you need to analyze yourself and your investments.

This book will show you how self-analysis can help you uncover your strengths and weaknesses and define your investment profile clearly. This will in turn enable you to assess whether you're truly a suitable and capable co-owner of a given business.

However, it's important to remember that just as the world changes constantly, so do you. Your knowledge and emotional resilience evolve over time. You should use this knowledge to regularly recalibrate your self-awareness as an investor.

SOME ENCOURAGING FACTS

First of all, I want to stress that Warren Buffett's principles and investment logic work all over the world, on every continent and in every country. You can use the framework wherever you invest and – providing you have the patience – you'll significantly improve your chances of getting rich and achieving financial freedom!

Even though you'll make plenty of mistakes – and you will – the stock market is surprisingly generous. If you approach it with the right mindset, principles and methodology, it will still offer excellent opportunities to reach outstanding returns long-term despite your mistakes.

I've personally made just about every investment mistake you can imagine. In Part VII, 'Learning from my biggest successes and failures', I'll share some of those errors so you can avoid repeating them in your own investment work. Hopefully, you'll also feel inspired to read about my biggest successes and will manage to replicate them – again and again.

Despite the mistakes, I've achieved an average annual return (before non-related costs) over the past fifteen years that has outperformed relevant benchmarks with a meaningful margin and have become much wealthier than I was when I started as a full-time investor in 2009.

This has been possible only because I have consistently applied the three important investment principles and tried to concentrate my investment on great businesses run by excellent management. Most of the mistakes I've made – both big and small – have occurred when I've drifted from these rational investment principles and paid the price.

Investing is simple, yet not easy – but if I can do it, you absolutely can too.

Happy reading!

PART I:

Why Is It So Difficult to Become a Successful Investor?

1.

Everybody Wants Action on the Stock Market

Over the years, I've spent a great deal of time thinking about why the stock market functions the way it does, and why 95% of investors behave more like speculators than investors.

I've asked myself why stock prices of listed companies fluctuate so much – sometimes moving up and down by large percentages within a month, a week, or even a day. It's not uncommon for a company's stock price to swing 50% over the course of a year, from its highest to lowest point, without any clear explanation or evidence that the company's long-term underlying value has changed so drastically. Why is the number of stocks traded every day so huge? Some companies have their entire share capital traded more than once a year.

This is because nearly every participant on the stock market is focused on the short term, making quick, emotional decisions based on stock-price movements. Everyone but you wants action on the stock market. This, of course, cannot happen with non-listed companies.

Two important factors drive this behavior. The first is the human desire to make money and get rich – the faster the better. Humans are wired for instant gratification; and if that gratification can come with minimal effort, even better.

The second factor is crucial to understand if you want to think independently and outperform the market. Aside from the independent and rational investor, everyone else working in or around the stock market makes their money from trading stocks, advising on stocks, managing other people's money, handling securities administration, or writing about the market.

The stock market is influenced and driven by many different groups of 'advisors' or administrators, all with one objective: to make money from the activity itself. And if activity is the goal, then the market's focus must necessarily be short term.

Brokers make money from buying and selling stocks – the more trades, the better. Analysts generate revenue for brokerage firms by producing equity research that predicts whether a stock will go up or down by a meaningful percentage in a brief period of time, giving investors reasons to buy or sell. Asset managers gather capital from investors who are willing to let someone else manage their money. As a money manager, you're usually paid a percentage of the assets you manage annually, rather than given a salary based on your performance relative to the market. However, as a manager, you can't come back to your clients year after year and say, 'The best investment decision this year was – again – to do absolutely nothing and just let our great companies run.' So, as an asset manager, you need to be seen as active and decisive – which is fine for the manager, whose pay is based on the assets they manage rather than their own performance.

Additionally, the securities market – including the stock market – is run by an enormous administrative service industry that slowly but steadily takes a small cut of the capital held in the system or flowing between accounts. Again, if all companies were non-listed and ownership could change hands only once a year, this entire administrative industry would quickly go out of business.

Finally, the raison d'être of the financial press (print, online and TV) is to report on financial markets – including the stock market. Journalists in the financial media crave stories and excitement about what's happening in the market, as well as predictions of potential disasters or fortunes waiting to be made. If stocks weren't constantly moving up and down, there'd be very little for them to write about.

If all companies were privately owned and their owners met just once a year to rebalance their holdings, the stock market as we know it would cease to exist.

The stock market gets its blood and oxygen from short-term activity, while most investors – who *are* the market – are driven by the human desire for instant gratification. Together, these two forces have created the greatest financial-speculation machine in the history of mankind, powered by the strongest drug ever invented: the desire to get rich – *quickly*!

As a rational, independent investor who wants to do something different than the market, it's only logical to *invest over the longer term* rather than *speculate for the short term,* using the big swings in the market or in individual companies as your servant – not your guide. If the average investor is driven by the urge to take shortcuts and impatiently jump the line to get rich quickly, you should focus on doing the opposite: working with discipline and persistence to become rich slowly – step by step.

2.

The Difference Between Speculation and Investment

Most investors don't realize that to take advantage of – and outperform – the market, they need to think and act differently than everyone else investing in it. Instead, most investors think like the market, talk about the market and act like the market – they *are* the market.

But if you don't do something different, how can you expect to achieve a different outcome than the market?

I'm sure this sounds logical – and perhaps relatively easy for an intelligent, rational person to do. Yet, for many if not most investors on the stock market, it is almost impossible to act differently than the market.

I have already argued why the stock market has a short-term speculative focus; and if you act like the market there is a good chance that you are a speculator and not an investor.

So, let's start by defining what speculation and investment are and how they differ. This is a good first step towards thinking independently and laying the groundwork for what we must understand and digest during the rest of this book.

SPECULATION

Speculation is a very simple game – and it is a game!

You buy an asset – a stock, a painting, a gold bar, or perhaps cryptocurrency – with one objective: to profit from the difference between what you paid for it and what you can sell it for. The speculator is largely indifferent to the size of the earnings – assuming there are any – generated by the underlying asset (which in the case of a stock is the underlying business). As a speculator you are interested only in the potential profit from selling at a higher price than you paid. All you hope for is that the price of your asset goes up as fast as possible and then you can sell it and jump to the next 'bet'.

You have probably already rightly concluded that it is possible to speculate only if there is an organized market where you can constantly buy and sell. It would be very difficult to speculate on a non-listed company because there is no stock price to follow and it would be impossible to buy and sell every day – or every hour or every minute.

INVESTMENT

A true long-term investor works with a totally different mindset.

Imagine that you want to use your hard-earned money to buy a small business operating in an industry you know something about. The company is not listed on the stock exchange; but you don't really care, because your plan is to own the company for many years – perhaps for the rest of your life. Before you buy the company, you will need to review all the historical financial data, interview the management team and current owners, research the industry and the competitive landscape. Your aim is to understand how the business will perform in the future – how much money it will earn in five or ten years. Based on this, you assess the price you must pay for the company and estimate the return on your investment, both in the short and long term. Then you ask yourself: 'Does it look like an attractive investment? Yes or no?'

If your answer is 'Yes', you can write the cheque and become a business owner. Afterwards, you can use the annual profits to pay yourself a dividend or reinvest the money to buy more businesses. If your company is successful, it will grow sales and earnings every year, becoming more profitable and valuable as time passes.

That, in a nutshell, is investment. Investment means laying out money and getting your returns from the earnings of the underlying asset (the company) and benefiting from its growth over the years – whether you buy the whole company or a part of it, and whether or not the company is listed and traded on a stock exchange.

3.

How to Get Returns on Your Stock Investment

Before we dig deeper into the principles of sound investment, let's spend a few minutes on how you actually get your return on investment as a long-term stock investor – or business owner.

As you know, the speculator's sole focus is to profit by selling an asset at a higher price than it was purchased for. But the long-term business owner and true investor let the company earn the returns for them in a different way. This distinction is very important to keep in mind.

There are three return drivers that together make up the long-term return for a stock investor:

1. Dividend payments – and any other kinds of 'payouts' to the owners
2. Appreciation in company valuation as earnings grow and prospects improve
3. Changes in the general valuation of the company or the stock market

Let's begin by reviewing these three factors at an elevated level and exploring what creates the investor's 'return on investment.' It's important to understand what these three elements include – and equally important what they do not. When we have done that, we will use the rest of the book to better understand how to maximize the returns on your investment.

DIVIDENDS – AND ANY OTHER KINDS OF 'PAYOUTS' TO THE OWNERS

Most (though not all) companies regularly distribute capital to shareholders – often as dividends or sometimes by share buybacks, where the company buys shares that reduce the number of outstanding shares and make the remaining shareholders own a bigger part of the company. In the United States, it is common to receive either quarterly or annual dividends. In this way, a stock can resemble a bond, where the company's management determines the amount to be paid out. Management can choose to distribute all or some of the earnings as dividends, or not to distribute any of the earnings but to instead use the profits for other investments.

We will later examine when it is rational for company leadership to decide to distribute dividends. For now, it is sufficient to note that dividends often fall in the range of 1.5–3% annually. In other words, the company distributes 1.5–3% of its total value (stock price multiplied by the number of outstanding shares) as dividends.

If you purchase stocks at (say) US$100 each, it wouldn't be unusual to receive between US$1.50 and US$3.00 per stock in dividends in the first year.

At first glance, this may not seem like a substantial return on your investment – and unfortunately, many stock investors tend to overlook the importance of dividends. This is understandable. When a stock's price can easily fluctuate by 5–10% in a single day – equal to several years' worth of dividend payments – it's easy to become distracted by short-term price movements instead of focusing on long-term dividend income.

In fact, it's often easier for investors to maintain focus on a company's fundamentals – its earnings and dividend payouts – when the company is privately held. Without a stock-market listing, there's no daily share price to distract attention.

However, for the long-term and rational business owner, dividend payments often represent a significant portion of the overall return on investment – regardless of whether the company is publicly traded or privately held.

It is not uncommon for dividends to increase steadily over time and eventually represent a substantial portion of the original investment made.

APPRECIATION IN COMPANY VALUE

You will see this point repeated throughout this book: over the long term, stocks follow earnings per share. The more a company's revenue and earnings grow — measured on a per-share basis — the more valuable its shares become, all else being equal. This does not mean that a stock's price at any given moment accurately reflects the company's real value — the so-called intrinsic value. The current stock price merely mirrors what investors think of the company right now, and those opinions can be heavily influenced by short-term factors and emotions such as nervousness, fear, optimism, or even euphoria.

However, in the long run, a company's share price generally follows its present and future earnings power per share.

For simplicity, let's assume a company grows its revenue and earnings at an average rate of 6% annually — both now and in the future. Without delving into the capital requirements needed to support that growth, you can expect the company's share price to increase by around 6% per year over the long term.

Of course, the opposite can also happen. If a company's future outlook deteriorates and earnings are expected to decline, its value will likely fall accordingly. In this case, the investor can expect a decrease in value — or in other words, a negative return on investment.

It's essential to distinguish between *genuine* changes in a company's long-term earnings potential, and therefore the potential increase in the stock price, and short-term market sentiment driving stock-price fluctuations.

If a company pays a dividend of about 3% and its earnings and intrinsic value grow at approximately 6% annually, then the investor is looking at a baseline expected return on investment of around 9% per year.

But there's one more important layer to the valuation component.

If, for one reason or another, a company undergoes a fundamental shift in its future earnings potential — or in how management allocates capital

– investors may re-evaluate the quality of the business. For example, the company may gain access to new and lucrative markets that significantly enhance expectations for long-term revenue and earnings growth. Alternatively, management might realize they can allocate the company's earnings and financial resources far more effectively than they have in the past.

Such fundamental improvements can lead to a broad re-evaluation of the company's worth. As an illustration, investors might previously have valued the company at fifteen times its after-tax earnings. But if the business achieves clear competitive advantages or management demonstrates more rational decision-making, investors may start valuing it at twenty times its earnings.

This 33% increase in valuation (from fifteen to twenty times earnings) doesn't happen overnight – it occurs over time. But it reflects a genuine improvement in business quality. That improvement is recognized in a higher market valuation, and therefore constitutes an additional component of the investor's long-term return on investment.

Naturally, if the opposite occurs – if the company's quality permanently declines, whether because of a worsening earnings outlook or poor management – investors may similarly reduce the valuation multiple. For instance, they may no longer be willing to pay fifteen times its earnings and instead reduce the multiple to twelve, resulting in a permanent loss in value of 20%.

With this understanding, investors are better positioned to analyze and evaluate whether a company's prospects and the capabilities of its management team provide a solid basis for expecting an attractive return on investment.

CHANGES IN THE GENERAL VALUATION OF THE STOCK MARKET

The final factor influencing an investor's return on investment is entirely outside of one's personal control, so while you should understand how it works it isn't something you should spend too much time on. The stock market – and the overall sentiment driving it – can, over very long periods, be shaped by forces that either support a broad rise in stock prices or the opposite.

Interest rates, for example, are a fundamental driver in how all types of assets – stocks, bonds, real estate, or anything else – are priced. Interest rates act as a kind of gravitational force on asset valuations: the higher the interest rate, the less valuable other assets become, because they must offer returns that can match or exceed that rate. Conversely, the lower the interest rate, the more valuable other assets appear.

In other words, when interest rates decline, asset prices – stocks included – tend to rise. When interest rates increase, the value of those assets – again, including stocks – tends to fall.

It's no secret that over the past forty years, the yield on the ten-year US Treasury Bond – which is commonly used as a benchmark for the 'market interest rate' – has declined from about 13% to around 4–5%. While this book doesn't seek to explore the underlying causes of this long-term decline, we can conclude briefly that the current interest-rate environment provides a basis for significantly higher valuations across all asset classes – including stocks – compared with forty years ago.

However, as an investor, it is important to remember one key principle: in financial markets – and particularly on the stock market – anything can happen and everything is possible. That includes a scenario where interest rates rise significantly and remain elevated for many years.

For the long-term owner of a non-listed company, this market-fluctuation factor really doesn't make any difference. You own your company and focus on running the business whether interest rates are 4% or 7% without thinking about the market price of your company. But for most investors focusing on investing in listed companies, the market-fluctuation factor can become very disturbing.

My advice to you is simple: focus on your company and what its business can generate for you in returns on your investment over the long run. Leave the 'market speculation' to all the other investors. But keep in mind that today's interest-rate levels are not historically high. The low interest rates of the past ten to fifteen years are not a reliable guide for how rates will behave over the next ten to fifteen years.

YOUR RETURN ON INVESTMENT

The long-term return on your stock investment can be defined as:

return on investment = growth in long-term earnings (per share) % + dividends (per share) + other payouts including buybacks (per share)

This return can be increased or decreased further by a fundamental change in the valuation of the company (change in P/E-ratio) due to changes in the 'quality' of the company and its management.

Later in the book we will discuss what an attractive return on investment is, but for the moment we can conclude that we aim to generate an attractive return on our investment by focusing on the factors we can understand and analyze.

Key takeaways from Part I

- Almost everybody on the stock market has a short-term focus and wants action.
- You must think differently than the market to get a different outcome than the market.
- Speculation is buying an asset with the sole purpose of selling it again at a higher price.
- Investing is buying an asset and letting the earnings the asset produces become your return.
- Return on a stock investment comes from dividends and long-term growth in earnings.
- Over the long-term, stocks follow earnings per share.
- When evaluating your potential return on your investment, focus on the company, its management and the factors you understand.
- Forget about analyzing macroeconomics and don't try to guess how the stock market will develop in general.

PART II:
Mastering the Three Most Important Investment Principles

4.

Why It's So Important to Master and Apply Investment Principles

Sound investment principles are like the foundations beneath a house. Without solid foundations, the house becomes wobbly and unstable – unable to withstand a storm.

The stock market is an extremely heterogeneous environment where all investors are essentially trying to outsmart one another in their efforts to gain economic advantage and build wealth. Unlike the bond and currency markets, the stock market does not revolve around a single short-term underlying factor that aligns all stocks. In the short term, the price of each publicly traded company – as well as the broader market – can unpredictably fluctuate due to many different factors.

Investor focus and sentiment often shift rapidly and unforeseeably, leading to wild swings in confidence or uncertainty, which in turn cause large price movements and a constantly changing market mood. Likewise, an individual company's stock price can fluctuate much more than the market overall. In these cases, investors' attention and perceptions of a company's situation and prospects can change quickly – often because of a single press release or news headline.

As outlined earlier, it's only by acting differently than the market that you can expect to outperform it and do better than average.

For the individual stock investor, the best way to meet this challenge and avoid blindly following the whims of the market is to master and consistently apply sound fundamental investment principles.

Some investors will already be working with these principles – and if that's you, then you can choose whether to skim through this part of the book or take the opportunity to brush-up your existing knowledge. But if you are new in investing, or unfamiliar with the principles described, you should carefully read and digest these chapters.

When you master the principles and understand the ways they interconnect, you will have exceptionally strong and resilient foundations on which to build your investment 'house'.

5.

Investment Principle 1: Think Like a Business Owner

When you buy a stock, you are purchasing a share of a company and in doing so becoming a business owner. The secret to outperforming the stock market largely depends on your understanding of this concept. As a business owner, you focus on the business itself and its long-term future opportunities and challenges, whether the company is listed or not. You don't waste your time following the short-term swings in the stock price.

The principle of thinking like a business owner when investing in a business was introduced by Benjamin Graham in his iconic work *The Intelligent Investor*[2]. Having read Graham's book, Warren Buffett realized the importance of adopting this mindset rather than simply studying and following stock prices and has applied it to his own investment work over the last seventy or more years. This fundamental principle – that you're not just investing in stocks but buying businesses, or parts of businesses – is among the main reasons Buffett has become one of the wealthiest people on Earth.

To most stock-market investors, it probably seems obvious that when you invest in a stock you become a co-owner of a company. But moving from understanding the idea to actually incorporating it into your investment philosophy and your investment work can be a significant mental challenge.

Nevertheless, it is the key to your outperformance as stock investor.

Even when given this key, the vast majority of market participants – both professionals and private investors – never understand its importance or what to do with it, and instead maintain a stock-price mindset throughout their entire investing journey, treating stocks like chips and the market like a casino. They continue to speculate, obsessively watching prices, often checking daily – or even multiple times a day.

---

2 Graham, 1949.

Many such stock 'investors' jump from one stock to another over relatively short periods, hoping to sell each stock at a higher price than they paid and then move on to the next. The average investor is far more impatient and short-term-oriented than a business owner. Most investors think in terms of weeks or months, while a committed business owner must think in terms of years or even decades.

Good business owners are not particularly focused on short-term capital gains. Instead, they think about what the business will look like five or ten years down the road. They focus on how the company, its customers and its competitors are likely to evolve, and they consider the opportunities and risks that must be managed in both the short and long term.

This fundamental difference in mindset – between the price-focused investor (or speculator) and the business-focused owner – was not clear to me when I decided to become a full-time investor in 2009. Nor was it clear how difficult it is for so many investors and money managers to embrace the business-owner concept when managing stocks.

By 2009, PROSPECT – the Danish consultancy firm I'd founded in 1996 and still owned – was well-established. But, after thirteen years of hard work, I decided to transition and become a co-owner of a small number of businesses rather than 'just' owning and running my own. So, I entered the stock market as an investor, bringing with me all the lessons I'd learned from being a business founder and operator. I became a business investor.

I didn't initially understand that thinking like a business owner was going to be essential if I were to succeed on this new path. But when I read and listened to what Warren Buffett repeatedly emphasized in his writings and annual meetings, the idea that owning a stock means owning a part of a business began to make complete sense.

From running and owning PROSPECT, I knew that success required constant attention to improving customer experiences, the quality of our products and services, operations and finances. I had to focus on the market, the competition and the strategic and operational risks involved in running the company. I never thought about stock-price movements, as PROSPECT was not publicly listed – there was no stock price to follow.

When you think like a business owner, it doesn't matter whether your company is publicly listed or not. The only difference is that a listed company has its stocks quoted every weekday – hour by hour, minute by minute, second by second. But the path to success isn't about following the stock price day by day or week by week. It's about following the development of the business and answering the most important question: what will this company look like in five or ten years?

If you think like a business owner, you know that if the company performs well over the next five to ten years, then so will you. Over the long run, stock prices follow company earnings per share – not the other way around. If you understand and follow the company's long-term development, you can let the stock price take care of itself.

This first investment principle of thinking like a business owner will take you much closer to your goal of achieving financial freedom.

6.

Investment Principle 2: Take Advantage of 'Mr. Market'

Once you start thinking like a business owner instead of a stock speculator in a casino, the large price swings on the stock market – both generally and in individual companies – take on a completely different meaning. Instead of following stock prices daily and worrying about sharp drops or celebrating sudden spikes, the stock market takes on a servant role for you.

What do I mean by that? When you focus on the company's future earnings potential and the expected returns on your money, a large price decline becomes an opportunity to invest on even more attractive terms. Conversely, if prices rise sharply, it may mean that the stock price no longer aligns with the company's financial condition and future earnings outlook. In that case, the rise becomes an opportunity to sell your shares at an attractive price relative to their future value.

In other words, the market – or Mr. Market, as Benjamin Graham called it – offers you the opportunity, every weekday and every hour, to buy or sell shares at the current price. The investor who thinks like a business owner can look at Mr. Market's offers each day and ask: *Does this price allow for an attractive long-term return based on the company's earnings potential?* If the answer is yes, you can buy. If the offered price is so high that it can't be justified by the company's expected earnings, it might be time to sell.

Mr. Market can play a lot of tricks on you, if you let him. But if you are smart you will recognize the patterns and the underlying reasons behind his fluctuations. Some notable examples of this are the IT-fueled market bubble of 1998–2000, the financial mania leading to the financial crisis of 2008–09, the European EURO crisis around 2015, Brexit in 2016 and then the COVID-19 crisis exploding in early 2020. Last but not least, as I write this book it looks like we might have another IT bubble – this time fueled by AI.

But the smart investor will notice what it is Mr. Market is doing: **making most investors walk in the same direction, driven by emotion and short-term focus.** And that gives the intelligent and rational investor a great chance to take advantage.

The key thing is that you are always free to decide whether to act. Mr. Market doesn't care if you trade today – he'll be back tomorrow with a new price list. But many investors trade because everybody else is trading and they buy or sell what everybody else is buying or selling.

If you think like a business owner – and aren't forced to sell for financial reasons – you can afford to remain largely indifferent to price declines as long as the company's fundamentals remain intact. In fact, as suggested above, big price drops may be welcomed as chances to invest on better terms. This is the complete opposite of how most investors react, because most fear market downturns and cheer rising markets.

Remember: thinking like a business owner means you'll automatically welcome price declines and prefer to buy when prices are low and sell when they become too high relative to the company's expected future earnings.

In other words, as a rational investor, the only purpose of the stock price is to help you determine whether an attractive long-term return can be achieved, based on the company's future earnings. And it doesn't take a genius to realize that your return increases when the price you pay decreases. If the company's earnings can support (or improve on) the return you require then it makes sense to invest, regardless of what happens to the stock price afterwards. If not, it's rational to wait until the stock price has fallen further.

Since your focus is on the company's earnings, it's also logical to conclude that any prediction about short-term stock-price movements – whether for an individual stock or the market as a whole – is speculative and of no use to you. Yet ironically, short-term predictions are what dominate the discussions among media, analysts and most investors.

Understanding that Mr. Market is your servant – not your speculative guide – is the second essential investment principle. It helps you further separate yourself from the average investor and increases your odds of long-term outperformance.

Let me stress one more point. I completely understand that you may be used to checking stock prices daily – even multiple times a day. Changing that habit can be tough. But try. Start by reminding yourself that a company's real value does not change day by day. It typically takes months or years for a business's intrinsic value to shift in a meaningful way. So why check the stock price every day? Unless you're actively buying or selling, checking once a week – or even every two weeks – should be more than enough.

You can set yourself up to focus only on meaningful updates too. Make sure you automatically receive notifications when there's real news, like quarterly reports or other significant events. That's the time to dig in and evaluate the company. At those moments, reassess your view of the company and compare it with the current price and your return expectations. It might be time to buy more – or possibly to sell.

You should also remind yourself that if your investments were in *non-listed companies* – and there are far more of those than there are listed ones – you wouldn't have the option to check stock prices daily. And guess what? The owners of non-listed companies get by just fine without knowing the minute-by-minute value of their ownership stakes.

Another way to convince yourself to stop checking prices daily is to ask: *Do I really need the emotions that come from seeing a 1% rise or fall today when no new information has been released?* Why should you care? You know what your company is worth, so you know the fair value of its stock.

If you know that your estimate of fair value is around US$100, and the stock trades at US$80, it shouldn't matter whether the price is US$79 or US$81 today. But if the price rises above US$100, then it's time to evaluate whether to sell; and if it falls further from US$80, it may be time to buy more.

As a rational business owner and investor, you've already grasped the key idea: you focus on the company's real value and use Mr. Market as your servant – not the other way around. This principle will serve you extremely well over the long run.

Let me conclude this chapter with some essential advice for those of you who want to master the impatient Mr. Market and become a successful investor. Your most powerful tool is the opposite behavior: you must have a lot of patience. This is a big challenge for many investors.

7.

Investment Principle 3: Invest with a Margin of Safety

There is no practical method by which you can precisely determine what a company is worth. Even in the mergers and acquisitions (M&A) market, where entire companies are bought and sold by professional investors and private equity funds in auction processes, buyers cannot be certain that the price paid for a company will turn out to be the right one. Similarly, it often happens that a company buys a competing firm that fits within its business model because it has interesting technology or maybe complementary products. But even when both the buyer and the seller are in the same industry, you can never be completely sure that the purchase price is 'correct'.

Really, there is no such thing as the 'right' purchase price. There will always be a greater or lesser degree of uncertainty regarding the pricing. This is partly because buyers naturally do not know the company they are buying as well as the seller does. There is also always uncertainty surrounding the future development of the business. And any price the buyer calculates as being fair and appropriate will undoubtedly be based on the analysis they have done and the assumptions they have made.

The same analysis and reasoning must be applied when you as a stock investor consider buying a piece of a business. A company's stock trading at US\$50 with 1 million shares in circulation does not guarantee that the company's true value is US\$50,000,000. Yes, it is the value at which the company is trading today; but tomorrow the stock price might rise to US\$52, and then the company's market value would correspondingly rise to US\$52,000,000. Is this new price any more accurate than yesterday's value, if the company has not delivered any new information that justifies a change in price?

As a rational investor with the goal of outperforming the stock market, you must invest with a margin of safety that ensures you a 'safety belt' in case your analysis of the company is slightly off or the company's future development turns out to be less positive than you initially assumed.

Like the first two investment principles, the margin of safety was developed by Benjamin Graham in *The Intelligent Investor*[3]. In general, there are two different ways of applying it when you invest.

DISCOUNT TO FAIR VALUE AS A MARGIN OF SAFETY

The first way of applying the principle is to follow Benjamin Graham's example and figure out what the fair value of the company is within a particular range. As an example, let's assume you calculate the fair value of the company to be between US$90 million and US$100 million. Applying the margin of safety indicates that you will invest only if you can do it at a market valuation of, say, US$70 million. That will give you a margin of safety of at least US$20 million at the bottom end and maybe even US$30 million at the top end. If the true value is US$90 million, your margin of safety becomes 22% (20/90). If the true value is US$100 million, your margin of safety is 30% (30/100).

The value at which you buy the shares should ensure that if you have made an error in your valuation, or misunderstood the company's true earning power, your margin of safety will protect you from significant losses. A good margin of safety can save an investment, making it acceptable instead of leading to disaster.

For the rational investor, it is natural to think that the value of a company – and, consequently, the valuation of its shares – depends on several assumptions about the company's situation and expectations for future development. Therefore, the opportunity to analyze and understand how the margin of safety can be calculated lies in addressing the assumptions for the valuation and not in the 'discount' on the purchase price relative to the company's true value.

---

3 Graham, 1949.

Let me expand using the above example. In the valuation of a company, you have used the right – albeit conservative – assumptions to the best of your ability and have concluded that the company's value is about US$95 million – or, better, somewhere between US$90 and US$100 million. Therefore, you do not want to pay more than US$70 million for the company. With 1 million shares outstanding, you would therefore be willing to pay US$70 per share, assuming that the true value per share is between US$90 and US$100. You can conclude that you can invest with a nice and comfortable margin of safety – which in this case is simply a discount relative to what you have calculated the company's 'true value' to be.

You could also achieve your margin of safety by making very conservative assumptions about the company's future earnings. For example, you might calculate the company's value based on a projected annual growth rate of 5% over the next five to ten years, rather than a more optimistic growth rate of, say, 8%.

Similarly, you might simply decide that the company you are analyzing will not be able to maintain its historic profit margin, or **earnings before interest and taxes (EBIT) margin.** If the company has historically achieved an EBIT margin of, say, 15%, you could build another margin of safety into your valuation by using 12% in your analysis of anticipated future earnings.

MARGIN OF SAFETY BY DEMANDING A HIGHER EXPECTED RETURN THAN THE MARKET RETURN

The second way of implementing a margin of safety is to look at the company's present and future earnings and, based on your knowledge that your return on investment is made up of dividends and growth in long-term earnings, decide that you want the company to reward you with a higher return on your money than the market average.

Historically, the market has been able to give investors a return based on dividends and growth in annual pre-tax earnings of about 8% to 10% on average. So, applying your margin of safety might lead you to demand a return on your investment of let's say 15% before tax annually over the long run. A company giving you pre-tax earnings of 10% on your money and that is able to increase these earnings by 5% per year on top of that will in practice give you a 15% return on your investment. Here you have to be a little careful. Not all earnings can or will be paid out as dividends. Some companies can actually both grow and pay out all earnings as dividends if management choose to do so. Other companies cannot pay out the earnings as they must be used to finance growth. So, keep a close eye on what management decides to do with the 'free' earnings and how much is paid out as dividends. We will discuss this in more detail when we look at management's capital allocation.

Demanding attractive returns in this way is actually how Warren Buffett thinks about investing within a margin of safety, whether he buys 100% or just a small fraction of a company.

The advantage of basing your margin of safety on the required returns supports the investment principle of thinking like a business owner. After the investment is made, this way of thinking reduces the focus on stock-price development and instead increases attention on the company's financial performance. You get the returns from the company's earnings, not from the movement in the stock price. The financial statements and future earnings of the company become your starting point for reviewing your investment success – not the stock price you invested at and the following development in its price.

Let me end this chapter about the third investment principle by analyzing how big the margin of safety needs to be to protect you against mistakes and unforeseen negative future developments for your company.

The answer is quite obvious. As an investor, you want the margin of safety to be as big as possible. But the more foreseeable and predictable the company's future is, the smaller the margin of safety you need.

Generally, a stock investor should aim for a margin of safety of no less than 20% – whether using a price-based or return-based calculation method. However, it is important to remember that a 20% or even 40% margin of safety is in itself insufficient justification for investment. You must always consider what other investment opportunities are available to you at any given time. It is not rational to invest just because you can achieve a big margin of safety in a great company run by excellent management if there are other, better investment opportunities available that meet your investment principles and return requirements. It is rational to invest only if a great investment opportunity with the required margin of safety is available and *better than the best alternative.*

Key takeaways from Part II

- Using the three investment principles will create a solid platform for your work as an investor and significantly improve your chances of outperforming the stock market.
- Think like a long-term business owner – not as a gambler on the casino using stocks as chips to bet on winners and losers.
- The business owner is always focused on how the business will look in the future – that is much more important than how the stock price is doing right now.
- Don't let Mr. Market instruct you – use him as your servant.
- As a business owner, you want to buy at low prices, so you should welcome big declines on the stock market as opportunities to make great purchases.
- Always make sure you have a comfortable margin of safety.
- The more stable and predictable the company's future, the smaller the margin of safety you need.
- Demand an attractive return – including a margin of safety – on your money based on the company's future earnings growth.

PART III:

Invest in Great Businesses

8.

What is a Great Business?

Deciding to invest in great businesses is a cinch if your objective is to outperform the market over the long run.

Stop and think about this statement for a moment.

If you are the owner of a great business that performs better than average businesses do, you as an owner have a big chance of sustainably outperforming the market over the long run – if you make your investment in the company at a reasonable price.

But not only are the odds that you'll outperform the market over the long run in your favor; by owning the same great company for a very long time, you'll also avoid doing what most stock investors do – buying and selling regularly and jumping from company to company based on movements in the general stock market or changes in the stock prices of individual companies.

If you own your companies much longer on average than most stock investors do, you'll end up knowing your companies much better than the average investor knows theirs and you'll need to make fewer costly transactions. This reduces your risk of doing something wrong.

But what is a great business? How do we define it? And how do we ensure that what looks like a great business right now will still be great in five, ten or twenty years' time?

Let's start by defining what characterizes a great business and why it's essential to invest in such companies instead of in various mediocre businesses. The best and simplest explanation comes from Warren Buffett's late partner, Charlie Munger:

> **'Over the long term, it is difficult for a stock to earn much better returns than the business that underlies its**

> **earnings. If the business earns 6% on capital over 40 years and you hold it for that period, you won't achieve much more than a 6% return, even if you initially buy it at a significant discount. Conversely, if a business earns 18% on capital over 20 or 30 years, even if you pay a seemingly high price, you will end up with an exceptional result.[4]**

[fo]In other words, investing in companies with sustainable high returns on capital, and holding on to them for many years, will almost certainly give you exceptionally good results and bring you closer to financial freedom.

As I mentioned in the Introduction, you will find all the key figures you need to understand and how to calculate the key metrics in the Appendix. However, as it is so important to understand what is meant by a high return of capital, how it is calculated and what conclusions we can draw based on what we find, we're going to look at the relevant numbers here.

As we go through the calculations and work out the return on capital, you need to remember two things:

- First, and most important, if we define the strict capital the company needs to run its operational business, and calculate the return on this operational capital, we get vital information about how good – or profitable – the business has been *so far!*

- Second, we are also able to calculate the return on all the capital that has been invested in the company, and not just the capital invested in the required operational assets. This return on (total) invested capital will give us important information about how well management has invested and allocated all the capital in the business. The numbers are an essential part of evaluating management and how excellent it is, which we will examine in the next part of the book.

In the following section, I'll introduce three interconnecting concepts that are crucial to this process and will become familiar to you as you work

---

4 Charlie Munger, 'A Lesson on Elementary, Worldly Wisdom as It Relates to Investment Management and Business' (speech made at the USC Marshall School of Business, 14 April 1994).

through this book. First, we define the earnings measurement we need to use when we calculate return on capital: **net operating profit after tax (NOPAT)**. Then we define what invested capital we are talking about: **return on invested capital (ROIC)** tells us the return on *total* invested capital; and **return on unlevered net tangible assets (ROUNTA)** tells us the return on the capital needed to run the business and its operations. As will quickly become clear, NOPAT, ROIC and ROUNTA should all be considered together.

NET OPERATING PROFIT AFTER TAX
(NOPAT)

The analytically correct earnings figure to use when calculating ROIC and ROUNTA is what's known as the net operating profit after tax, or NOPAT.

As a starting point you should understand an unfortunate fact: when equity analysts, company executives and investors in general talk about a company's earnings and profits, they often refer to whichever earnings figure looks the most favorable or is easiest to use.

Your task, as an independent investor and a rational, analytical business thinker, is to always be aware of which earnings figure you are using and why you are using it, and to apply the same perspective consistently across the companies you analyze. In other words, compare apples with apples and pears with pears.

It is not very difficult to calculate NOPAT when you have the company's income statement in front of you. You locate the item 'operating profit' – which on some financial statements is listed as 'earnings before interest and tax' (EBIT) – and from this figure deduct the tax the company (again, all other things being equal) would pay on that operating profit.

Let's assume our example company's operating profit amounts to US$25 million and the tax rate is 20%. Then we arrive at a NOPAT of US$25 million × (100% − 20%) = US$20 million. This is the NOPAT-earnings figure we will use throughout the calculation of ROIC and ROUNTA.

With time, your experience will make these calculations easy to carry out. However, if you have even the slightest doubt, it is a good idea to spend time improving your accounting knowledge.

RETURN ON [TOTAL] INVESTED CAPITAL (ROIC)

ROIC tells you the return on all the capital that management has invested in the company. Total invested capital is defined as equity + debt (including leasing debt) minus excess capital.

ROIC = NOPAT / (equity + debt – excess of cash)

Equity is the capital the owners have invested in the company and the debt is the capital the company holds in the form of loans and loan-like obligations. You can easily find these figures in the company's financial statements, on the liabilities side of the balance sheet.

Let's assume that our company's total invested capital is US$100 million, made up of equity totaling US$60 million and debt totaling US$40 million. We also see that the company holds an insignificant cash position of US$1 million, so we keep the US$100 million as the amount of totally invested capital.

We can now easily calculate the ROIC as (20/100) = 20%.

There are a few things to note about evaluating the cash position and why excess cash should be deducted from the invested capital. If the company has a lot of excess cash on the balance – that is, cash that isn't needed to run the business – we must adjust the amount of total capital. This is because it is possible for management to simply use the cash to pay down debt or pay a dividend to the owners, thereby reducing the equity in the company. There is always a judgement call involved in deciding how much cash is needed to run the company's daily activities and how big the cash pile should become before some of it should be deducted from the total invested capital. However, as a rule of thumb, if the company has a cash position of more than 2–3% of total assets, you should start thinking about adjusting the invested capital.

In Part IV of the book, alongside other important management factors, we will explore ROIC further as an indicator of how effectively management allocates capital. For now, let me remind you of what Charlie Munger said: 'If the long-term return on invested capital is 18%, you will achieve a very attractive investment result, while a 6% return on invested capital – well, that's nothing to write home about.'[5]

RETURN ON UNLEVERED NET TANGIBLE ASSETS (ROUNTA)

While ROIC tells us the return on the total capital the company has invested, the return on unlevered net tangible assets, or ROUNTA, tells us the return on the company's operationally invested capital and therefore more about the quality of the business. In simple terms:

ROUNTA = NOPAT / (equity + debt – goodwill [or other non-operational intangible assets] – excess of cash)

This might sound and look complicated, but it is not. You use the same number for capital in ROUNTA and ROIC, but for ROUNTA you deduct goodwill and other non-operational intangible assets.

Let's look at our imaginary company and develop the ROUNTA. When we study how the capital has been invested in assets, we notice that some capital has been invested in fixed long-term assets, such as property, plant and equipment, as well as in short-term assets like inventories and accounts receivable. These assets total US$60 million and are **tangible assets** assumed to be necessary for operating the business.

However, under long-term assets we also see that the company has an item listed as 'goodwill' to the amount of US$40 million. This is an

---

5 Munger, 1994.

intangible asset – an accounting asset that is not used in operations. In fact, goodwill exists only because the company's management previously acquired another company and paid more than the value of the tangible assets included in the purchase.

Because our company does not use the US$40 million in goodwill for any operational purpose, and goodwill constitutes only an accounting entry, we *exclude* goodwill when calculating ROUNTA – the capital invested in the company's operations.

We therefore conclude that US$100 million is the total capital invested in the company, but that only US$60 million of the capital has been allocated to operational assets.

We are now able to calculate ROUNTA = 20/(60 + 40 – 40) = 20/60 = 33,33%.

In other words, we can conclude that (all else being equal) our imagined company is capable of earning 33.33% annually on the assets it uses to run the business. This is an exceptionally attractive return and signals that the company could very well be a great business. As a rule of thumb, you can assume that a company showing a ROUNTA of 20–25% or higher is a highly attractive, strong business; a ROUNTA of 12–20% can be considered a mark of a relatively good business; while a ROUNTA below 12% is considered poor.

Later in this chapter – and throughout this part of the book – we will explore ROUNTA in greater depth and examine what characterizes a great company.

A FEW EXTRA THOUGHTS ABOUT NOPAT, ROIC AND ROUNTA

In Part V, we will take a closer look at how to calculate a company's earnings and determine which measure of earnings is most appropriate to use when we think as a business owner and look for attractive returns on our money.

Before then, we need to clarify a few details related to NOPAT and the calculation of ROIC and ROUNTA.

As outlined, NOPAT is calculated as operating income minus the associated taxes. This means that interest expenses on the company's debt are not deducted. Of course, debt is not free – companies must pay interest to their lenders every year. In other words, NOPAT represents the company's after-tax operating profit as if it were financed entirely with equity and carried no debt.

This also means that NOPAT is the same number whether a company is 100% equity-financed or entirely debt-financed, and is used identically when calculating both ROIC and ROUNTA.

Consequently, it's critical for investors to assess how much debt a company is using in its capital structure. The more debt involved, the more financially risky the business becomes. High debt levels make companies vulnerable to changes in lending terms. All else being equal, companies with no debt or very low debt are always preferable. As a rational investor, you should generally avoid investing in highly leveraged companies – unless the business generates such strong and consistent earnings that management can confidently repay (not merely refinance) the debt when necessary.

There are a few more technical points to address. By itself, ROIC does not tell us much about the quality of the business we're investing in. Rather, as indicated, ROIC tells us the return on the total capital the company – and by extension its management – has invested. That's why it's essential to understand *how* and *why* management has allocated capital in the way it has, and to be clear about the differences between ROIC and ROUNTA. We'll explore this further in Part IV.

As discussed, to properly assess the quality of the business, we must look at ROUNTA, which focuses only on the capital invested in operational assets. But even ROUNTA can hide risks in the details.

Let's illustrate this hidden risk with a simplified example based on our definition of ROUNTA:

ROUNTA = NOPAT / (equity + debt – goodwill [or other non-operational intangible assets] – excess cash)

Let's assume that management decides to acquire a company that consistently earns US$20 million in NOPAT, and they pay US$200 million for it. For simplicity, assume that the acquired company has no tangible assets – so the entire purchase price is recorded as goodwill. The acquisition is funded entirely by borrowing US$200 million.

After the acquisition, the ROUNTA for the newly combined company would look like this: ROUNTA = (20 + 20)/(equity = 60 + debt = 240 – goodwill = 240) => ROUNTA = 40/60 = 66.66%.

At first glance, the ROUNTA has doubled, which appears to be a positive development. The combined company seems to be a better business than the original, with the ability to generate 66.66% return on operational assets, compared with 33.33% before the acquisition.

However, there's a hidden danger behind that impressive ROUNTA figure. Management has now created a company with US$240 million in debt – up from US$40 million – while equity remains unchanged at US$60 million. This significantly increases the financial risk of the company. If the acquired business underperforms and earns only US$5 million instead of the expected US$20 million, the company could find itself in serious trouble, with lenders concerned about the US$200 million they have loaned.

This less attractive investment structure is captured by ROIC, as we will see. Prior to the acquisition, our calculation was: ROIC = 20/(60+40) = 20%. Let's now calculate the post-acquisition ROIC for the entire company. The NOPAT has increased to 20+20 = 40. Equity remains unchanged at 60, while debt has increased from 40 to 240. Since goodwill is not deducted, ROIC is calculated as 40/(60 + 240) = 40/300 = 13.33%.

In other words, ROIC reveals that management's investment has reduced the ROIC from 20% to 13.33%.

The conclusion is fairly straightforward: ROUNTA and ROIC must be interpreted together. ROUNTA helps us assess the quality of the underlying business, while ROIC reflects the quality of management's capital-allocation decisions. As an investor, it's also your responsibility to examine the company's debt levels and financing structure – topics we will explore in more detail later.

Crucially, you must always remember that the numerator – NOPAT – is based on the assumption that the company carries no debt. Related to this, I need to add a point that may initially seem confusing, but that doesn't actually complicate the overall picture.

The ROUNTA concept was developed by Warren Buffett himself as the best indicator of a company's quality. However, rather than using NOPAT alone, Buffett recommends in his annual letters to shareholders that one should use net profit – meaning after-tax earnings, the so-called 'bottom line' – when calculating ROUNTA. Fundamentally, the difference between NOPAT and net profit largely comes down to financing costs on debt. But since Buffett's companies typically carry little to no debt – especially the companies he uses as examples in his ROUNTA calculations in his annual letters – net profit and NOPAT are practically identical in those cases. The more debt a company has, the higher its financing costs and, therefore, the lower its net profit relative to NOPAT. Conversely, the less debt, the lower the financing costs and the closer the alignment between net profit and NOPAT.

My recommendation is that you can use either NOPAT or net profit in calculating ROUNTA (and ROIC). The key is to maintain a clear focus on whether the company is conservatively financed without excessive debt. Ultimately, when evaluating whether a company qualifies as a great business, it's essential to remember that a company can be considered great only if it consistently generates high returns on the capital invested in its operating assets – regardless of how that capital is financed.

In the beginning, you might find it difficult to remember and work with NOPAT, ROIC and ROUNTA, but it should be only a matter of time before you get comfortable with the numbers and calculations. My advice is to keep a financial dictionary or online reference close at hand. That way, as and when necessary, you can simply look up the terms and concepts you want to better understand and spend a few moments studying how they are used and what they actually tell you.

In short, you can think of accounting and financial statements as the common language of business – but be aware that it is a language of many dialects!

✦ ✦ ✦

With that, we're ready to take a deeper look at ROUNTA and reveal how it can help us gain a clear overview of the different categories of businesses, from the bad to the acceptable and all the way to the truly great and the exceptional. In other words, we've reached an exciting stage: learning how to use ROUNTA as an investment filter, allowing us to screen out less attractive companies and concentrate on identifying outstanding ones.

A quick reminder: when analyzing ROUNTA – or any other financial metric you pull from a company's financial statements – you're looking only at *historical* data. These figures reflect the past and offer no guarantees about the future. We'll address that uncertainty in a later chapter. For now, let's explore the different categories of businesses based on their ROUNTA performance.

ANALYZING ROUNTA COMBINED WITH GROWTH RATE IN EARNINGS

Using ROUNTA – the return on the capital invested in *operational* assets – in combination with a company's earnings growth enables us to categorize the type of business we're analyzing. It is useful to divide the landscape into six categories. Based on the category a company falls into, we can form a general view of its long-term potential as an investment – assuming, of course, that our assessment of its prospects and management is accurate.

GROWTH IN EARNINGS AND RETURN ON CAPITAL (ROUNTA)

	ROUNTA <12%	ROUNTA 12%-20%	ROUNTA 20%-25%
HIGH GROWTH (6%-8%)	VALUE DESTROYER	GOOD BUSINESS	GREAT BUSINESS
LOW GROWTH	BAD BUSINESS	ACCEPTABLE BUSINESS	CASH COW

Many management teams focus more on revenue growth than on earnings growth. Over the long term, earnings growth naturally requires revenue growth, but very few companies can sustainably achieve more than 6–8% organic growth annually. The same applies to ROUNTA, which is the best indicator of whether a business is truly great – but remember, when you look at high ROUNTA you should also review the company's ROIC and debt financing.

The boundaries between the individual categories should be taken with a pinch of salt, but a company with a high ROUNTA – say, 25% – and solid growth operates in an entirely different universe than a company with a low ROUNTA – perhaps 6% – and little or no growth.

Let's walk through the six categories, starting with the least attractive types of businesses and working our way up the 'quality ladder'.

The bad business

This category includes companies that consistently generate a low ROUNTA. If a company can only generate a return on operationally invested capital of, say, 5–6%, it becomes difficult to see how any meaningful return on investment can be achieved. Of course, the assets that drive revenue and earnings must be maintained; but each time the owners are required to make new investments or upgrade production facilities, these investments will clearly also yield unattractive returns.

Since revenue growth is also minimal, the investment outcome is simply disheartening. Over time, such companies often fail to generate returns exceeding inflation, meaning they effectively destroy shareholder value.

For management in bad businesses, there is essentially only one sound decision: distribute as much capital as possible to the shareholders, who are highly likely to find better investment opportunities elsewhere.

It's difficult to pinpoint exactly where bad businesses are found, but certain patterns tend to repeat. Industries characterized by intense competition – where customers have little preference between a company's product and that of its competitors and where price is all that matters – are often problematic. If, on top of that, the business is operating in a mature industry with low growth, and its product requires a large, costly production setup, then you're likely in the right neighborhood to identify a bad business.

The value destroyer

The difference between a bad business and a value destroyer is straightforward: the latter experiences sustained revenue growth, and this expansion must be supported by capital-intensive investments in the production setup.

However, because the company lacks the ability to convert sales growth into proportional profit growth, the dollar you invest is almost immediately worth less. In other words, management is forced to invest capital at very low returns and destroy shareholder value to stay in the game. Quite simply, it would be more attractive to invest the same capital in bonds.

To make matters worse, companies operating in low-return industries that experience high growth are often locked in fierce competition for customers. These sectors are also frequently cyclical, suffering from downturns that place additional pressure on pricing and margins.

Management in value destroyers are often caught between a rock and a hard place. In many cases, the most rational course of action would be to liquidate the company and preserve the capital shareholders still possess. Unfortunately, history shows that value destroyers are rarely wound down while solvent. Instead, owners often continue to inject capital into the business, clinging to the eternal hope that *this time it will be different*.

The airline industry is a perfect example of where to look for a high population of value destroyers.

The acceptable business

This is the category where most companies fall. Acceptable businesses typically grow at an average rate of 4–6% per year and can generate a ROUNTA of approximately 12–15%, which is not bad.

This reflects a solid, average-quality business – the growth is sufficient to outpace inflation and deliver a modest real return year after year. However, the company continues to require a relatively large production base, which must be regularly expanded to support revenue growth.

Still, the higher the earnings generated from the capital invested in production assets, the more attractive the business becomes. As Charlie Munger noted, an 18% return on capital sustained over time can produce an exceptionally attractive overall return. Unfortunately, companies in this category often lack real pricing power and must follow market prices rather than set them. Nevertheless, they can remain acceptable businesses

– where long-term shareholder returns are largely determined by how effectively management allocates earnings and capital.

Most mature industries are populated by companies in the acceptable category – these businesses make up the vast majority of the corporate landscape.

The good business

If a company can maintain a reasonably strong return on invested capital while also growing at a solid pace over many years, it qualifies as a good business. A good business will often be working within an industry that has yet to mature and where growth is still good; but it will also have competitors and no real pricing power, so earnings only grow in tandem with sales. This is often enough to justify investments in more production equipment, as the ROUNTA of 12–20% is acceptable or good. Consequently, the company continues to generate a healthy and value-creating return on capital over time with a solid growth in earnings. The quality of your investment will ultimately depend on how long the company can sustain the situation and how effectively management allocates the company's earnings and capital resources.

The cash cow

Now we arrive at the first of two categories defined by the company's ability to generate very high returns on capital invested in operational assets. Later, we will examine what enables a company to achieve sustainably high ROUNTA; for now, it's important to note that this first high-ROUNTA category typically sees very little revenue growth. Often, this lack of growth simply reflects the fact that the company offers a product for which demand increases slowly. However, because the company has established a competitive moat – a sustainable market advantage that effectively keeps competitors at bay – customers continue to buy and are willing to pay the asking price. At the same time, management does not need to make significant ongoing investments in additional production capacity, which contributes to a very high and sustainable ROUNTA.

Management may attempt to significantly grow revenue and earnings by making substantial investments, but these investments repeatedly fail to deliver the necessary increase in sales. Instead, invested capital rises while earnings stagnate – resulting in a declining ROUNTA. Not a good idea.

This often leads to strong cash flow that management has nowhere to reinvest, and the only rational capital decision management can take is to return the earnings to shareholders. In some cases, management may have the skill to reinvest surplus capital in other attractive businesses, but this is very rare.

In financial jargon, cash-cow companies are often referred to as 'dividend stocks' because they tend to distribute a large portion – sometimes all – of their profits to shareholders in the form of dividends. But a cash cow in our definition needs to have high ROUNTA.

A cash-cow investment is about as close as a stock investor can get to a bond-like investment: earnings grow, but slowly, and all the cash is sent back to the owners.

The great business

Finally, we reach the most exceptional category – the kind of business that allows shareholders to quickly compound value. A company that combines a very high ROUNTA with strong growth in both revenue and earnings is a truly great business.

These companies are rare, but they do exist – in every country and in virtually every industry, although some sectors have a higher concentration of great businesses than others.

If you can identify and invest in just a few great businesses at a reasonable price, you likely won't need to do much else. It is often a mistake to take further action after making such an investment. Simply holding on can, over time, prove sufficient to achieve financial freedom.

We will explore these kinds of investments in depth from various angles in the coming chapters, but let me briefly mention a few of the challenges involved with investing in great businesses.

First, the company must be able to sustain its high ROUNTA for many years to come. Second, no business can maintain high growth in revenue and earnings forever. At some point, growth will slow and the company will likely transition into the cash-cow category.

Finally – and critically – your long-term investment success depends on whether the company's management can continue to allocate earnings rationally.

There are countless examples of great businesses whose management squandered profits in disgraceful ways. We'll dive deeper into this issue when we explore what defines excellent management in the next section of the book.

Now that we have established the quality landscape in which different kinds of businesses operate in terms of ROUNTA and growth, let's look at what happens over the long run when a company is able to compound value at different speeds.

9.
Owning Great Companies for the Long Term

Let's try to really understand the power of owning a great business for the long term. The secret to this is to understand the power of compounding, or, as Albert Einstein expressed it: 'Compound interest is the eighth wonder of the world. He who understands it, earns it; he who doesn't, pays it.'

Let's compare three companies from three different categories in our business landscape.

Company A: a bad business. This company has a low ROUNTA and grows at a modest rate of just 3% per year. There is a high risk that most or all of its annual earnings must be reinvested just to maintain its market position. Consequently the 3% annual growth is likely all investors can expect.

Company B: an acceptable business. This company has a reasonable ROUNTA and grows at a normal pace. Management has decided to reinvest all earnings back into the business, which results in a total annual growth rate of 7.5%. Investors don't receive dividends but benefit from a steady 7.5% compounding in value.

Company C: a great business. This company has a very high ROUNTA, meaning it doesn't require much additional capital to finance its organic growth. Furthermore, because the management team is excellent at capital allocation, they are able to reinvest profits in attractive opportunities. Consequently, shareholders can expect earnings to grow by as much as 15% annually.

Let's set aside taxes and other factors that may be relevant to individual investors, and focus purely on the raw compounding effect.

	ROUNTA	Growth	Start US$	5 years	10 years	20 year	30 year
Company A	LOW	3%	100,000	115,927	134,392	180,611	242,726
Company B	MEDIUM	7,5%	100,000	143,563	206,103	424,785	875,496
Company C	VERY HIGH	15%	100,000	201,136	404,556	1,636,654	6,621,177
B compared to A				24%	53%	135%	261%
C compared to A				74%	201%	806%	2,628%

The real insight from these figures is the power of long-term compounding. If you own a high-quality business with sustainable, durable earnings growth, let it run.

As shown in the table on the previous page, the difference in value growth is already significant after just five years. Company A's value has increased from US$100,000 to approximately US$116,000, while Company C's value has more than doubled. It's also evident that although Company C has 'only' double the growth rate (15%) of Company B (7.5%), its value grows at more than twice the pace. After ten years, Company C's value has more than quadrupled, while Company A has delivered a total return of just over US$34,000, or 34%.

The difference becomes truly striking over thirty years, with Company A growing from US$100,000 to US$242,726, while Company C rises from the same starting value to over US$6.6 million.

Investing in just a few truly great businesses that remain so over many years and can consistently grow their earnings year after year can make a world of difference – and may offer a straightforward path to achieving financial freedom.

We can see how this plays out by looking at some of the wealthiest people in the world and how they managed to become extremely wealthy. Think for example of Bill Gates with Microsoft, Jeff Bezos with Amazon and Sam Walton with Walmart – they all achieved their wealth by establishing and owning their business for many years. The chances are that if you had invested in one of these companies when it was small, and continued to be a shareholder until today, you would have enjoyed a highly enriching journey and achieved significant wealth too.

While the people who have built some of the world's most valuable companies may well share some common psychological personality traits, it is much easier and more important to identify the decisive common traits of the valuable companies themselves. Almost without exception, these businesses have been able to maintain a solid growth rate in earnings and high return on capital invested – be it ROIC or ROUNTA – over many years. Just as Charlie Munger said, high return on capital and solid growth opportunities over a long period of time are the foundations for creating some of the largest companies in the world owned by some of the wealthiest people in the world. Long-term investments in great companies are where you want to have your money on the stock market. This is where you maximize your chances of outperforming the market. And if you can find such companies at a fair price while they are still small and growing, you are on the expressway to being wealthy.

10.

How Can a Company Maintain High Return on Capital for Many Years?

In the real world, where businesses are fiercely competing for the same customers, you might ask how one company in a particular industry is able to grow profits like weeds and create enormous amounts of wealth for its owners. So, let's try to find out how a very profitable company maintains a high return on capital for many years. Why are competitors or new startups allowing the great company to earn so much money, and why do they not 'steal' some of its profits?

The answer to this question is crucial if we're to understand what makes great businesses.

All companies want to make as much profit as possible, and no director would voluntarily allow a competitor to take over the entire market and hoover up all the profits in a particular industry. Neither competitors nor customers will give a great business free rein to make a lot of money and maintain a high return on invested capital. Instead, the company with high returns on invested capital creates and builds a competitive moat – a protective barrier – around its business and earnings. This moat prevents competitors from simply stealing revenue and profits. It also stops customers pressuring the company to lower the prices of the products or services it sells.

Very often a company with a secure moat around its revenues and earnings sells a product or a service that customers really need or want. The customer needs or desires to buy this product or service and the alternatives are few or close to none. In other words, either the company or the product has captured the customer's awareness and occupied a share of their mind.

This addiction, desire or preference for the product or service makes the customer less price sensitive and more loyal. The moat keeps the customers inside the company's business area.

From the competitor's point of view, the moat prevents the competitor from selling their products and services to the same customers. The moat keeps the competitors outside.

Your job as a stock investor and an owner of businesses is to identify the moat and understand why the company can produce high return on capital. You do that by looking at the product your company is selling and figuring out why its customers are addicted to or prefer it to the products competitors are bringing to the market. When you have identified why the customers prefer the product and why they stay loyal, you have identified the moat.

Sometimes, analysis and understanding of the moat is very simple and straightforward. In other situations, it can be harder to uncover or understand why the company has a solid grip on the customers and is able to prevent them from buying competitors' products.

Once you have identified the moat and understood the customers' preferences and loyalty, your job is simply to monitor customers' and competitors' behavior over time and judge whether the moat will become stronger or weaker.

As a rational investor, you have certainly identified the challenge. A great business can maintain its position only for as long as it can maintain the moat that protects its revenue and earnings. As soon as the moat disappears – for whatever reason – the foundation for producing high ROUNTA erodes, which also reduces the returns for its shareholders. A company without a moat is a mediocre company or maybe even a bad company. It is vulnerable to attacks from competitors and unable to withstand price pressure from customers.

As a stock investor with the aim of outperforming the market, your most important job when you have become a co-owner of a great company is to keep track of the company's moat and ensure that it protects the company's earnings and growth opportunities. On a regular basis, you must assess whether the moat is becoming deeper and wider or is being eroded. The biggest risk for you as an owner is the company losing its protective moat. If a company does not maintain the moat, it becomes a mediocre company that cannot maintain high return on capital and no chance of compounding its value fast. If that happens, you as an owner of the company will lose your chance of outperforming the stock market.

If you invest in great companies with a strong moat and high return on capital, and spend your time analyzing and thinking about how the situation will most likely look five to ten years from now, you have an excellent opportunity to differentiate yourself from the stock market's short-term focus as driven by speculative-oriented investors and commentators fixated on momentary stock-price fluctuations.

11.

How to Find Great Businesses with a Protective Moat

When it comes to finding great businesses to invest in, the smartest approach is systematic. You can either do this automatically, using an online stock screener, or manually, by reviewing the annual reports or factsheets for publicly traded companies, such as those published regularly by Value Line or Morningstar.

The advantage of factsheets is that they will quickly provide you with a clear overview of the company's development over the past ten years, so you can immediately assess whether the company's current position is in line with its historical trend or if the present financial circumstances are special. If you find a company with a secure moat and observe that it can deliver high returns on capital, there's a pretty good chance you are looking at a great business.

Once you have identified a company with a high ROUNTA – or with clearly increasing returns on capital – you can begin studying it more closely.

You will always find exceptions, but generally speaking there are four characteristics that indicate a company might be something special and have a strong moat protecting its earnings. Let's look at these characteristics, while keeping in mind that having a strong moat is all about keeping the customers inside and the competitors outside.

The four kinds of moat relate to:

1. Intangible assets
2. Switching costs
3. Network effects
4. Cost advantages

If a company has a business model with a moat built on one or more of these characteristics, there is a good chance that it is also a great business with high ROUNTA. If you can also conclude that it is run by excellent management and you can purchase a stake in it at an attractive price, then you have a very good chance of making a highly rewarding investment over the long term.

STRONG AND PROTECTIVE INTANGIBLE ASSETS

Most companies have some kind of intangible assets, such as software, goodwill, patents, licenses, brands and so on. Some of these intangible assets are of little value in protecting the company's earnings in both the short and long term. Goodwill, for example, holds no value in your analysis of the long-term competitive strength of the business and its business model.

But consider the value of the brand for a company like Coca-Cola or Apple. Think about the value of patents for companies like Eli Lilly or Novo Nordisk, two of the world's largest manufacturers of insulin for diabetes and dominant players in the rapidly growing industry of weight loss medicine. Consider the importance of licenses for an airport, a toll bridge, or a national TV provider.

If the customers prefer the product or service, and if the company's intangible assets provide some form of protection that prevents competitors from producing and selling the same product or service, then there is a moat around the business. This moat enables the company to charge a good price and thereby generate attractive returns on the capital invested. Of course, this is true only as long as the customers genuinely need the product or service or like it so much that they choose it over anything similar.

It is easy to understand that the strength and durability of a moat based on intangible assets can vary. A moat based on a brand can be very strong, but can also very quickly disappear if for any reason customers suddenly come to dislike the product or the company behind it.

A patent for a pharmaceutical product is stable until it expires, taking the moat with it, because competitors are then allowed to sell generic imitation products. There is also a risk that competitors will successfully develop a similar and possibly better product that is protected by another patent. If customers start buying this new product, the first company may be left without a moat despite still having a valid patent.

EXPENSIVE SWITCHING COSTS

A company can also be a great business if it is difficult, expensive, or time-consuming for customers to switch to a product or service offered by a competitor. How often do you switch your bank or insurance company? How many times do you switch from an iPhone to a Samsung? What happens if a car manufacturer decides to start buying critical autoparts from a new supplier and something goes wrong with the new parts that necessitates the manufacturer to recall millions of cars? It's probably better to stick with the existing supplier, even though switching might save a dollar or two per unit.

Think about the machines you have installed in your house or your company. These machines use 'consumables' every time you use them. Think of coffee machines, printers, vacuum cleaners, the heads for your shaver or electric toothbrush and so on. You've already made the main purchase, and while you could probably find a cheaper option you likely just keep buying the consumables that fit your existing equipment.

Customers may not be very price-sensitive when switching to alternative products or solutions is difficult or effortful; often, risk avoidance is more important than saving money.

Combined, this characteristic and the business's relationship with its customers make it possible to charge a premium price and, often, secure a high return on the company's invested capital.

Let's consider an industry where customers are very price-focused and have no brand loyalty – in other words, where the customer experiences no cost or inconvenience switching from one product to the other.

The companies in this industry also have a lot of assets involved in the production and selling of their products or services and therefore a lot of capital is invested in the industry. The airline industry is a great example, because companies have a lot of assets (planes and employees) and customers just want to buy flight tickets as cheaply as possible.

We all know that since the airline industry's inception, the demand for flying has gone only one way – up! We also know that the demand for flying will likely continue to rise in the future, so it's fair to say that it has been and will probably continue to be a 'growth industry'.

But airlines sell a very simple product or service. They safely transport customers from point A to point B – a flight is just an airborne taxi ride. Many flights are available for customers to choose from and it's very easy to go online and figure out which ticket is cheapest. Perhaps you flew Delta Airlines last time but this time it's American Airlines and next time it might be Lufthansa or British Airways. There are absolutely no switching costs and offering the lowest price is the only game in town.

Meanwhile, all the airline companies must commit billions of dollars in capital. No wonder, then, that almost all airline companies have been lousy businesses since the entire industry was deregulated many years ago.

Let's look at the opposite situation, at the other end of the same industry. While all airplanes fly in and out of airports, only a small number of the world's cities are large enough to support more than one airport. In most cases, airports operate like local monopolies, facing little or no direct competition.

Consequently, airports often have significant pricing power and are largely free to set prices for their customers – which comprise both the airlines using their facilities and the shops and restaurants that serve travelers passing through.

As a customer, you might find a cheaper flight to your destination if you depart from an airport that's a five-hour drive away – but for you, the switching costs are enormous. The same goes for airlines: they may be able to secure lower fees at that other airport, but if passengers must then arrange transportation for a five-hour transfer they'll likely just choose a different airline operating from the more convenient location.

Airports are often excellent businesses with strong moats created by high switching costs.

NETWORK EFFECTS

Sometimes a company can build a business that creates a customer network. This network is of great convenience and value for the customers, who become 'members of the club'. The network allows customers to act in a certain way or perhaps to work easily with other members. The company providing the customer network can reap extraordinary profits without fearing that customers will leave the club and start using another – especially if there are no competing networks to switch to.

Some of the best network businesses are credit-card companies, where both the customers and the sellers of products or services (shops, restaurants and all other consumer-oriented companies) agree to use the same payment card. MasterCard, Visa and American Express are all great examples of such businesses.

Stock exchanges also benefit from network effects. Listed companies pay an annual fee for having their shares listed and traded on the stock exchange, and brokers and investors, buyers and sellers agree to use the same trading system provided by the exchange. Any business built on the need for people to share information and trade with each other in a closed system has the potential to become a business with great network effects.

Perhaps Microsoft has the strongest network moat of all companies. Microsoft's software programs enable its customers all over the world to work efficiently together and share documents with each other. It doesn't really matter what you pay per month or per year; you don't want to work without these programs. Similarly, social-media companies like Facebook (Meta) and LinkedIn use a slightly different business model but with the same purpose: to enable the users to easily share information within the network.

COST ADVANTAGES

It is no surprise that companies able to maintain a permanent cost advantage over their competitors can sometimes generate attractive returns on the capital invested in the business. It should also be obvious that it is easier to find companies with cost advantages in industries where the production costs make up a large portion of the final product's sales price. In such cases, a company may earn more on a product if they can produce it at a lower cost than their competitors, or they can make their product more attractive to customers by selling it at a lower price than their competitors – or both!

Let's look at a couple of examples.

Perhaps a company can exclude certain production elements or has easier or cheaper access to the commodities needed for production. It could also be that the company's location and logistics are superior to its competitors.

Or maybe the company is much larger than its competitors and can take advantage of the economy of scale. In this case, the more units it produces and sells, the lower the production costs per unit – so, for example, its per-unit research and development costs might become much lower than its competitors.

Some of the best-known businesses with such cost advantages are large retail companies like Walmart and Costco, as well as similar grocery businesses in other parts of the world. Due to their size, these companies can purchase products from suppliers at lower costs per unit than their competitors. It is also very likely that they will get better credit facilities from suppliers. At the other end of the value chain, customers pay cash when they buy the products, but the grocery company does not pay the suppliers cash on delivery. This enables the company to operate on small margins while having a large portion of its assets financed 'for free' by the suppliers.

At the end of the day, these large grocery companies sell the products to the customers at lower prices than is possible for their smaller competitors while remaining able to create better profitability and a higher return on capital than other industry players.

12.
The Moat Seen from the Customers' Perspective

It is generally impossible to directly measure how strong a company's moat is. However, there's a chance you'll be able to describe and understand the moat's value if you can figure out what its substance is and why the company's customers need or prefer its products or services. Hopefully, you will also note the company's high return on capital and likely that it has a high 'earnings before interest and taxes' (EBIT) margin on its sales.

Sometimes it remains very difficult to define a company's moat even when the business shows good or high returns on capital. But the more you study the company and keep asking *why*, the more you will learn and the better able you'll be to figure out whether it has a secure moat and, if so, how it is defined and why the business has been able to maintain its strong position.

Something you need to analyze very carefully is when a company experiences an unexpected increase in sales and earnings margins, which can lead to a sudden increase in profits and accordingly high returns on capital. Such situations are often caused by one of two extraordinary events. Either there has been a short-term imbalance between supply and demand – where for whatever reason supply becomes scarce for a limited period and prices immediately rocket – or there has been a sudden dramatic increase in demand from customers.

One of the best examples of this phenomenon happened during the COVID-19 pandemic, when global transportation companies were suddenly in much higher demand and could increase their prices tenfold because the short-term supply of transportation equipment – especially containerships – was inflexible. Revenues exploded, as did earnings and return on capital. However, as soon as the impact of COVID-19 reduced and the global supply chain was restored, the demand for transportation normalized and return on capital did too. These suddenly *great* businesses reverted to their true identities as *mediocre* businesses.

The home-decor industry experienced a similar short-term boost during COVID-19. As consumers were prohibited from traveling, dining out, or attending entertainment venues, millions of households started spending money on updating and fixing their homes, including painting. Paint companies saw sudden sales growth, improved earnings and high returns on capital. But once the lockdowns were over and the need for decorating products diminished, the industry faced a tough period with poor earnings. Everything balanced out, and the industry reverted to what it had always been – a mediocre industry with very few opportunities for any player to create a secure moat around its earnings.

At the other end of the spectrum, there are companies and industries with many protective elements to their moats. Strong moats can withstand the uncertainties of the market. They are often related to certain types of products and consumer habits:

1. Repeat sales of the same product/service, where customers have the habit of buying the same product again and again. Consumers buy many food and personal products on such a recurring basis. Additionally, consumers may subscribe to online services, repeatedly purchasing the same service.

2. Small-item products selling at an insignificant price relative to a customer's overall spending. Here, the purchase is of little concern: consumers sometimes don't even look at the price and simply buy the product without further consideration.

3. Products or services supported by a strong brand or image that generally speaking influences the customer with positive emotions – whether happiness, control or safety.

4. Products or services that have a defined lifespan where their consumption cannot be extended. For example, monthly subscriptions to services like Netflix or software programs, where access is lost after the subscription period unless

> you continue paying the fee. By contrast, we retain durable
> consumer products such as our old sofas and beds. If we
> want to, we make them last another year or two.

5. Products or services that satisfy an unavoidable need – or
    where the consumption of the product is simply necessary.
    For instance, your dog, cat, or any other pet gets hungry
    every day (just like you), so their need for food must
    be met; and pet owners often feed their pets the *same*
    food every day. Pet-food (and other food) companies are
    excellent examples of branded businesses with a protective
    moat.

In practice this means that the fewer options or alternatives the customer has when buying the product or service, the better the business opportunity. Likewise, the more the customer needs or desires your product or service, the better the chances are for building a solid and profitable moat and creating a business with high return on capital.

Conversely, the more players selling the same product within an industry, the less attractive the industry and the individual business become. Additionally, the lower the customers' need for the product and the less important it is who sells it, the fewer chances there are to build a moat business.

In short, a strong moat business is one that has managed to put itself in a very favorable and sustainable position with its customers when compared to its competitors. It is a business that sells a product that the customers genuinely need or desire without having any bargaining power. The best businesses can set the price of their products or services without facing any negative consequences from competitors or customers.

If a company's product enjoys a particularly strong and favorable reputation among consumers, you can consider that the product has secured a 'share of the customers' mind'. The product lives in the consumers' consciousness and has a kind of priority access to their wallet – even if a similar product is available at a lower price.

At the opposite end of this priority spectrum are the unknown or undifferentiated products, where the consumer has no brand preference and simply chooses based on price and availability, caring little whether the purchase is from Company A or Company B, providing the need is met at the lowest possible cost.

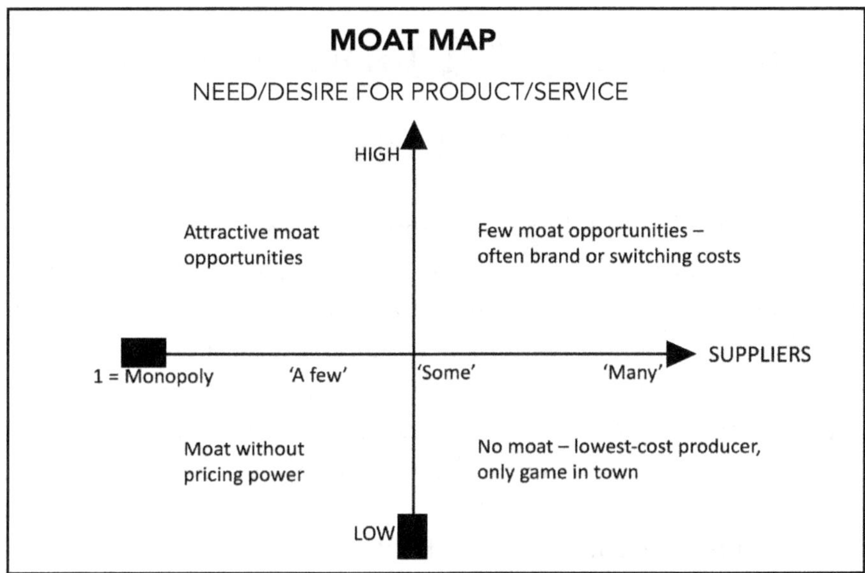

Examine the product or service your company offers. Determine whether it is something customers truly need or strongly desire, or whether it has little real-world consumer relevance. Then assess how many alternative suppliers exist. By looking at these two factors combined, you can form a solid understanding of whether a moat exists – and why.

13.
How to Evaluate Whether the Moat Is Sustainable Ten Years into the Future

When you focus on finding and investing in great businesses with solid moats, you differentiate yourself from the average investor and create a very solid and potent platform for outperforming the stock market over the long term. If you can also analyze the threats and opportunities around your company and its moat, then you will greatly distance yourself from the short-term focus of most investors on the stock market.

It doesn't matter very much what your company's results will look like next quarter. What matters is how much money your company will make ten to twenty years down the road, if it still has a durable moat and is still generating high return on capital. For you, the upcoming quarterly result is useful only to check that your analysis and long-term earnings expectations are in order. Besides that, you can use the company's information to explore and adjust your understanding of its moat.

It can be very difficult to keep this long-term focus until you become an experienced investor with solid self-confidence supported by a convincing performance record. It sometimes becomes hard to keep a cool head when your company releases quarterly results that are less positive than you and the market expected. In such cases, investors and often the financial press react negatively and the share price drops – sometimes much more than it should. But it is nevertheless extremely important that you remain calm and consider the long-term perspectives of the company and, most importantly, remind yourself of how strong its moat is.

Since founding my own unlisted company back in 1996, I have learned time and time again that all companies experience a weak quarter every so often – or even a few weak quarters in a row. It is also my repeated experience that one quarter's performance never defines a company's future. So, why should you even consider selling your great company, just because it has a somewhat weak quarter?

In such instances, we need to think like true owners of a business, which we are! Let's take the famous Danish unlisted company LEGO, which sells its creative LEGO toys all over the world. Would LEGO's owners consider selling the company just because the business showed weak numbers in one quarter? No. Given the company's history and prospects, LEGO's owners would not even come close to dumping the company and selling their shares because of a single poor quarter. So why should you, as an owner of a great company with soft numbers, do that simply because your company's shares are listed on the stock exchange and it is easy to push the 'sell' button?

As an owner and a manager, you are of course very interested in understanding the story behind the numbers, and you need to ask a lot of 'Why?' questions; but you also need to sit tight and focus on the company's moat, profitability and ability to create high return on capital in the long term.

In doing so, as rational investors, we still have the most important question in front of us: *Will the company's moat still exist in ten years – and if so, why?*

LOOKING TEN YEARS AHEAD

The task of peering into the future and answering this question may seem overwhelming. But let's work through the necessary considerations and see if we can find a method with solid reference points to give us a degree of confidence that we're heading in the right direction.

As the saying goes, it's better to be roughly right than precisely wrong. So, applying that here, the goal isn't necessarily to describe *exactly* what the business will look like in ten years, but rather to understand the company's position and earnings potential within a reasonable range. Only then can we assess whether the business is likely to continue generating enough profit over the long term to deliver attractive returns on our investment.

It's helpful to once again recall Charlie Munger's observation: if we invest in a company that generates, say, an 18% annual return on invested capital, and we hold that company for twenty to thirty years, we will end up with an outstanding investment return – even if we initially felt the stock price was high.

What Munger is really saying is that if you can identify a company with a competitive advantage – a strong moat – and the moat is durable over time, you will achieve exceptional returns, even if the valuation at the time of investment seems a little steep.

As we have already looked at the different kinds of moat that are available for a company – *intangible assets, switching costs, network effects* and *cost advantages (including economy of scale)* – our task is to analyze whether the company's moat is durable and can withstand all possibilities over the coming years.

In practice, this means that whenever you get any kind of relevant news from the company, its competitors, or the industry, you must ask yourself whether it indicates that the moat will strengthen or weaken over time or remain unchanged.

Based on the strength and sustainability of the company's moat and the long-term growth available, you will be able to create a picture of how the company's revenue, costs, earnings and return on invested capital will develop. As Warren Buffett has stated, our task is to try to establish the company's figures for the next ten years – just as Value Line and Morningstar present the previous ten-year historic numbers for each listed company.

Your future-earnings picture will not be precise, but it doesn't need to be. Its purpose is as a 'question generator' – so that every time you receive new information about your company and its industry you can ask yourself: What does this piece of information mean? Does it influence the strength of the moat and the future-earnings power positively or negatively? What kind of reaction from management or competitors should I expect over the short and long term?

Nothing lasts forever; the platform the company stands on and the value drivers that influence business and economics will keep changing. Nonetheless, as you become more experienced in thinking long-term about the company's future, you will realize that it's usually only a few factors that determine whether the company can maintain its moat.

THE DURABILITY OF THE MOAT

The durability of some moats is easier to assess than others. For example, technology-based moats can be incredibly strong for some years, only to disappear like dew in the sun because technological developments overtake the company's product and its consumer appeal in a very short space of time. For a classic example of this we can look to the Finnish cellphone company Nokia, which absolutely dominated the market in the late 1990s but which besides its brand name had nothing to protect its sales when Apple introduced the iPhone. After that, Nokia essentially disappeared from the cellphone market in no time at all. One could – and should – reasonably ask whether it's possible that some other technology company might eventually dethrone Apple. While that's certainly not impossible, Apple's moat comprises not just its brand name but also its functionality and, not least, its enormous advantage in today's market, where the smartphone has a far more central role in consumers' daily lives and behaviors than it used to. In Nokia's heyday, people used their cellphones to make calls and send SMS messages. Now, in addition to calls and messages, smartphones are used for everything from payment to calendars, cameras, video replay, scanning, news media and social media. In practice, the smartphone – and Apple's in particular – has such high utility for consumers that its value far exceeds the price of the handset. Many of us, if we were made to choose between owning a car or a smartphone, would wave goodbye to the car.

So, for the investor studying Apple's moat, the question is not just what Apple's earnings per share will be next quarter or in the current fiscal year but whether Apple can maintain its moat and perhaps expand its brand, product usage and customer appeal – and do it better than its competitors over the next many years.

Looking at another industry, one might ask whether the increasing megatrend of eating out in favor of home cooking will continue to develop over the next ten years. There is a high probability that it will, but that's not the same as knowing that a chain like McDonald's will be able to maintain its moat and earnings power – based on its brand and market position – over the long term.

Assessing a company's moat and earning power ten years down the road largely relies on evaluating how the relevant industry's underlying megatrends will evolve. Once that is done, however, it is then necessary to assess the extent to which the company's market position within the industry will change and in what direction. (We will take a deep dive into megatrends when we look at management excellence in Part IV.)

Next, it's prudent to investigate whether there are any factors that could fundamentally alter the relationship between the company and its customers. Customers might be able to increase pricing pressure on the company's and competitors' products in the future, just like the rise of the internet did for so many industries and companies.

It is my experience that, generally, the faster an industry changes overall, the greater the risk that a company's moat will erode within a relatively short period of time. Similarly, the greater the fluctuations in market share from year to year among individual companies within an industry, the less likely it is that companies in that industry can put any decent moats in place. In other words, the slower an industry develops and the more stable the market structure within it, the lower the moat risk.

The only situation where 'speed of change' is a plus is when a company can develop a whole new industry or business or product. Again, think about Apple's iPhone or Facebook.

Change is a constant for every business, one way or the other. As an investor, your job is to understand what level of change is acceptable and how much it will influence the company's earnings. To do that, you must focus on the customers and their preferences and needs.

Often, when we look back in life, we are surprised by how much has changed within just five or ten years. As a business analyst, you need to do a full 180 turn away from this focus and instead look forward to try to identify the nature and consequences of the next five to ten years of change.

It is a simple idea, but not easy to manage. As the Danish philosopher Søren Kierkegaard famously said: 'Life can only be understood backwards; but it must be lived forwards.'

Key takeaways from Part III

- Generally, great businesses have high return on capital.
- When you want to assess the quality of a company, you focus on ROUNTA; when you are more focused on excellent management and the return on the *total* capital invested company, you use ROIC and compare it with ROUNTA.
- Some industries are better to invest in than others.
- If a company shows high ROUNTA and grows earnings at a good speed, it is a great company and able to compound value very quickly.
- Companies with low ROUNTA and low growth are straight-out bad companies.
- Most companies are something in between a bad company and a great company.
- A company can maintain high ROUNTA – only by having a protective moat around its business, keeping the competitors out and the customers in.
- There are four different kinds of moat: *intangible assets, switching costs, network effects* and *cost advantages (including economy of scale)*.
- A company has created a strong moat around its customers if the product occupies a share of the customer's mind.
- Great businesses with a strong moat often sell products where the customer has few other choices or doesn't want to consider buying a competing product.
- Only a great company with a durable and sustainable moat is a truly great company.
- Figure out the one or two most important factors for the moat long term and watch them carefully.

PART IV:

Invest in Excellent Management

14.
Excellent Management Always Stands Out

Owning great companies does not in itself guarantee investment success or that you'll outperform the stock market over the long run. Equally important is the quality of the company's management.

A rational starting point is accepting that not all managers are equally skilled, experienced, or shrewd. In my experience, management quality plays a critical role not only in the company's long-term performance but also in how the market values the business. Excellent management tends to result in consistently higher market valuations, while poor leadership often drags a company's valuation down – even if the underlying business is strong. When you think about it, how can it be otherwise?

Evaluating management performance is inherently more qualitative (non-measurable) than quantitative (measurable). It is relatively straightforward to analyze a company's financials over the past five to ten years and determine whether it has been – and is – a strong business. But assessing management – judging whether they are truly excellent – is far more nuanced. There is also the fact that management changes over time, with new people taking charge, whereas the underlying business remains more or less the same.

The only way to evaluate management effectively is to learn what to look for and then consistently study management's behavior, decisions and communication over time. Through this continuous practice, you will begin to recognize patterns and sharpen your ability to make sound judgements. Your goal is to determine whether your great company is also being led by outstanding management – and, just as importantly, how management does a great job.

Just as a championship horse needs a first-class jockey to win the race, a great company needs excellent leaders to reach its full potential.

With experience, you'll find that great management tends to stand out. They share two defining characteristics: they act rationally, and they think like long-term business owners. Having these two characteristics pretty much automatically makes them shrewd value creators if the company is a great business. But these attributes are not always easy to spot – and your job is to determine whether your company's leadership truly has them by studying their actions, decisions and mindset. If they do, and it is a great business, then you are more than halfway there.

We will first explore the telltale signs that management thinks like a long-term business owner. During the rest of Part III, we will focus on analyzing whether management also act rationally.

15.
How Excellent Management Thinks and Works

The best place to find managers who truly think like business owners is within companies still led by their founders – or where founders remain influential co-owners. These leaders often have a deep emotional and financial stake in the business, along with a long-term perspective that closely aligns with shareholder interests. Besides that, founders already have a proven track record; by studying the company, you are actually studying their ability to create value.

However, don't assume that a manager who owns stocks in the company will necessarily have an owner's mindset. A CEO or even an entire management team and board who own equity in the company won't automatically think like true owners. It's critical to ahnalyze how management became co-owners in the first place.

There is a meaningful difference between a CEO who owns a large stake because he or she founded and built the company from scratch and a CEO who received a substantial number of stocks through a generous compensation package loaded with stock options. Simply being handed options doesn't create an owner's mindset. Ownership in name is not the same as ownership in spirit.

So, how do you tell the difference?

A manager who thinks like a business owner prioritizes the long term. They focus on building a stronger, more resilient and more profitable company – knowing that all owners will benefit from them doing so. Founders often embody this mindset. They see themselves as being in the same boat as every other shareholder and treat fellow owners as partners.

Excellent managers with an ownership mentality also believe in clear, consistent communication. They keep shareholders informed about the company's progress, challenges and future direction – not just during good times, but especially during adversity.

Two areas where a manager's mindset is revealed most clearly are operational efficiency and risk management. Nearly all managers will claim to care about these priorities, but in practice not all follow through.

QUALITY OF OPERATIONAL MANAGEMENT

To evaluate the quality of a management team you must study and observe how the CEO and CFO approach operational issues – and how transparently they communicate with shareholders when something goes wrong.

Poor managers rarely communicate about a lack of operational efficiency. They often fail to recognize warning signs early, delay action and – perhaps worst of all – wait too long to inform shareholders about the problems. When management suddenly delivers a negative surprise without prior signal or strategy, it's often the case that the problem has been festering behind the scenes for some time.

If you're caught off guard by bad news such as lower sales than expected, disappointing earnings, or an unexplained deterioration in business fundamentals, you should immediately begin questioning the quality of leadership – especially if the update comes without a thoughtful analysis or recovery plan.

In situations like these, you need to ask yourself three key questions:

1. Is the negative surprise a result of management failing to understand what caused the operational issues?
2. Did management see this problem coming but chose to ignore it or delay disclosure? If so, does this reflect a lack of respect for shareholders – yourself included?
3. Based on management's reaction to the issues, do you still have confidence in their long-term ability to lead the company and create value?

In my experience, how you answer these three questions should determine whether you remain a shareholder or move on. If you identify a management problem, the best time to deal with it is immediately. If the board fails to act, then you must act by exiting your investment.

Giving subpar leadership a second chance and letting the operational challenges run further can be a costly mistake.

On the other hand, excellent management teams keep you well informed. They don't just report about the operational issues – they anticipate them early on, and communicate and share thoughtful plans to mitigate damage. When any issues (not only operational problems) arise, excellent managers are quick to provide a clear action plan and maintain your trust through transparency.

EFFICIENCY

Every management team wants to grow their company. Revenue growth is celebrated endlessly, as the annual rankings of your nation's 100, 500, or 1,000 largest companies by sales testify. But rarely, if ever, do we see public rankings based on operational efficiency, profits or ROIC – even though these are some of the most important drivers of long-term value.

This is where the difference between great and mediocre leadership becomes clear.

While all managers chase growth, only the best also focus on the operational levers that determine how much profit the company actually generates. Poor management often pursues top-line growth at the expense of margins and returns, sacrificing long-term value creation.

Outstanding managers, by contrast, focus on the full picture. They work to improve both sales and profitability. They don't just seek to sell more – they aim to sell smarter and more efficiently. They invest in product quality, customer satisfaction, cost controls, production efficiency and everything else that affects operational earnings and the company's long-term bottom line.

Over time, excellent management spends more energy on optimizing earnings than it does on simply increasing revenue. They are fully aware that aggressive sales growth can come at a high cost — if not immediately, then later, when unsustainable practices start to drag down performance.

These leaders never lose sight of what really matters: value creation. Ultimately, a company's true value is defined by all the earnings and free cash flow it can deliver to its owners — now and in the future. Nothing more, nothing less. Excellent management always keeps sight of this fact.

WIDENING THE MOAT

The best managers are laser focused on improving every part of the business that strengthens the company's competitive moat — its ability to fend off competitors and grow the customer base.

One of the most effective ways to do this is by continuously improving the company's products and services. That might mean enhancing functionality, improving design, increasing user-friendliness, or reducing environmental impact. These innovations and product improvements don't just please the customer — they also reinforce the company's market position and give the marketing team valuable tools to attract new demand.

Great managers understand that product quality and innovation are not just tactical advantages but strategic imperatives. Every improvement, no matter how small, contributes to the long-term durability of the moat and the business's capacity to prosper.

FOCUS ON COSTS

Outstanding managers — especially founders — are relentless in their efforts to minimize production costs wherever possible. Cost efficiency isn't just about protecting the bottom line — it's about gaining strategic flexibility. Lower costs boost profitability and allow the company to stay competitive by maintaining or lowering prices without compromising quality.

When reading annual reports and quarterly statements, or listening to management presentations, pay close attention to how costs are addressed.

Is cost control discussed clearly and consistently? Are there specific initiatives aimed at improving efficiency?

Little or no mention of costs is a red flag. A lack of focus on expenses usually signals some degree of operational sloppiness.

Before you start digging into the costs in detail, look at how the earnings as part of sales – the EBIT margin (see Appendix) – has developed over the last five years. A stable or rising EBIT margin is a sign of increased profitability or that sales are growing faster than costs in general. But if the EBIT margin shows a downward trend you need to watch out, as that means costs are rising faster than sales and profitability is weakening.

Cost-related efforts typically span several core areas, including:

- Input materials and supply-chain management
- Research and development costs
- Production processes and equipment efficiency
- Per-unit production costs
- Marketing and customer acquisition
- Sales operations and support
- Distribution, shipping and logistics
- General and administrative overheads
- Inventory levels and working capital
- Organizational structure and staffing

Of course, any executive will tell you they're focused on controlling costs. But action speaks louder than words and unfortunately sometimes you experience both no talk and no action even though everybody can see the cost issues growing. When cost discipline is ignored and management don't communicate on the issue, you should start asking the hard questions – or consider parting ways.

BUILDING A CORPORATE CULTURE

Whether they founded the company or joined later, truly great leaders understand that long-term success depends on the strength of the team behind them. One of the clearest indicators of a company's health is its corporate culture and how employees feel about their work, the mission and the leadership.

As an outside investor, you won't have direct access to this internal atmosphere. You can't interview employees or observe day-to-day operations. However, there are important signals you *can* monitor – especially management turnover and organizational announcements. Any changes at the executive level are typically disclosed to the public. Over time, you'll learn to read these announcements not just for what they say, but for what they reveal between the lines.

I've found it's essential to pay close attention to every announcement regarding organizational or management changes. These updates can indicate whether a company is strengthening its leadership – or whether deeper issues are bubbling beneath the surface.

Let me provide a few concrete examples from my own investment work over the past fifteen years:

- **A MedTech company** had for many years languished in mediocrity, despite its underlying business having the potential to become a great enterprise. A new majority shareholder took over and announced via a stock-exchange release that a dynamic new CEO would be appointed, with a mandate to revitalize the business, eliminate unnecessary costs and reinvest the savings into forward-looking and value-creating activities. In the preceding ten years, the company's valuation remained largely stagnant. Following the announcement of the CEO change, the stock has delivered an average annual return of 18%, in addition to the dividends paid to shareholders.
- **A communications software company** had declared its ambition to build a global business through acquisitions of competitors around the world. Midway through a financial year, the company unexpectedly announced that its CFO had decided to step down – without citing a new job

opportunity as the reason. Shortly thereafter, the company disclosed that earnings from the acquired companies were falling short of expectations and that it would be writing down the value of those acquisitions by several billion US dollars. In other words, a significant portion of shareholder value was lost thanks to the company and board's overly aggressive pursuit of global expansion at inflated acquisition prices.

- **The board of a company without a dominant shareholder** announced that, for the third time in as many years, the CEO had chosen to resign after only ten months in the role. The company had fundamentally stronger business potential than its long-term earnings had suggested, but the board had clearly failed to rise to the challenge and seemed primarily focused on collecting sizeable – and excessive – board fees. Without a strong anchor shareholder, it is virtually impossible to drive meaningful change, which would have to start with replacing the board itself.

- **A publicly listed company is led by the third generation of the founding family.** Over time, the family has lost its drive and ambition, resulting in years of mediocre performance. The share price has remained virtually flat – by mid-2025, it was at the same level as in 2004. That's twenty years with no return to shareholders beyond modest dividends. There have been multiple CEO appointments and new external board chairs over the years, but each new leader has eventually been worn down by the limitations imposed on strategic development or potential sales to a larger global player. In mid-2025, the company announced once again that much of the board, including the chair, would step down after just two or three years in their roles. This final example proves the rule by exception: here, unfortunately, the problem lies with the company's majority shareholder, who resists progressive change because the family is financially secure and regards the company as a symbol of legacy and public image rather than a business in need of transformation.

So, always pay attention to announcements about management changes and make sure you know who the person calling the shots truly is, and whether they think like a real business owner and excellent manager.

16.
Management and the Focus on Risks

Throughout my career, I've consistently observed a common trait among business leaders: an overwhelming focus on growth and opportunity, often at the expense of addressing risk. This tendency isn't surprising – ambition and optimism are almost prerequisites for rising to the top of any organization. Without a bias towards progress, few leaders would have the drive to push through the obstacles that leadership demands.

But while vision and optimism fuel progress, they can leave a company vulnerable if they are not balanced with a sober, strategic awareness of risk. One of the most important responsibilities of the CEO – and by extension of investors and co-owners – is to identify, monitor and prepare for both visible and latent risks that threaten the business and the economic moat that protects it. The CEO must recognize and respect the fact that he or she is the overall risk manager. This job cannot be outsourced or distributed to lower-level managers.

Most business risks don't emerge suddenly. They accumulate gradually, often out of sight, before surfacing as significant disruptions in the form of declining demand, operational inefficiencies, or financial strain. A risk may not be immediately visible but that doesn't mean it isn't of growing significance. In fact, often the most dangerous risks are those that go unnoticed until they've reached a potentially existential scale.

It's true that some business risks can be mitigated through insurance – against accidents, fires and other unexpected events. But these are typically *event-specific* risks. They are external, episodic and manageable through actuarial assessment and financial coverage. However, the greatest threats to a business's long-term value rarely fall into this category.

The most dangerous risks are non-insurable. They are structural, gradual and deeply embedded in the dynamics of the company's industry or the broader economy. These are the risks that erode a company's competitive advantage and, over time, its earnings power. They are the changes in the landscape that render business models obsolete, consumer behaviors unpredictable, or regulatory environments unfavorable.

These risks don't usually appear on a balance sheet; and yet they can determine whether a business thrives over the next decade or fades into irrelevance.

It is beyond the scope of this book to outline every risk across every industry. But whether you are a CEO or an investor, the discipline of continuously evaluating these long-term structural risks is essential. Many of them are rooted in large-scale global forces – what we often refer to as megatrends – and others arise from unique industry-specific conditions.

While no company can insure itself against the macro consequences of, say, climate change, technological disruption, demographic shifts, or geopolitical realignment, it *can* prepare. And preparation often makes the difference between resilience and decline.

Importantly, shifts in long-term earning power don't always play out slowly. Sometimes, seemingly small developments in the present become inflection points that dramatically reshape a company's future – and much faster than anticipated.

Over the years, I've found it immensely useful to maintain a general list of megatrends, to track both the opportunities and risks embedded within them. This list is not exhaustive and evolves over time. A version compiled twenty years ago would look very different than the one I maintain today; and I'm certain that the list will look different again ten years from now, as new forces emerge and existing ones fade into irrelevance.

One thing is clear: the more stable and mature the industry, and the fewer disruptive megatrends it faces, the lower the long-term risk of structural decline. Conversely, industries undergoing dramatic transformation – or heavily exposed to multiple megatrends – carry far greater strategic risk. In these cases, management's ability to monitor, assess and adapt becomes absolutely critical.

Yet, many business leaders still focus disproportionately on the *positive* aspects of megatrends. They look for tailwinds, new markets, or technologies that promise growth. This optimism is understandable but incomplete.

Truly excellent management balances ambition with prudence. They pursue opportunity with vigor, but they also remain acutely aware of the risks that can cause lasting harm to a company's earnings power and in turn its long-term value.

The best leaders view risk not as a distraction, but as a central part of their strategic responsibility. And the best investors pay close attention to how well those leaders fulfil that responsibility – and especially how they communicate about it.

17.
Management and Megatrends

The following is a distilled version of the broader list of megatrends I maintain as part of my own ongoing investment work. As discussed, I revise and update this list regularly and I'm often surprised by how much it evolves in just a few short years. What's clear is this: while no one can predict the direction of the global economy with precision, you *can* develop a well-informed view of how key trends are likely to impact specific industries or individual businesses. And the better your understanding of these underlying forces, the greater your ability to assess the future of the company and the quality of its management.

When analyzing an industry or a particular business, it's critical to develop a clear and balanced view of both *positive* and *negative* megatrends. Some trends act as powerful tailwinds, accelerating growth and profitability. Others present long-term headwinds, gradually eroding margins, relevance, or demand.

Once you've identified the megatrends relevant to a business, take a close look at how management engages with them. Does the leadership team acknowledge these trends, address their implications and outline a strategy for adaptation or exploitation? Or do they ignore or downplay them? Remember: the way management communicates about both opportunities and threats offers crucial insight into their strategic maturity – and their ability to create lasting value. Excellent management communicates directly and straightforwardly about both tailwinds and headwinds.

This list is not exhaustive, but it captures many of the fundamental shifts reshaping markets and industries today. But remember that the impact from global, regional and even local megatrends can differ quite substantially depending where you are situated in the world.

GLOBAL MEGATRENDS (LATE 2025)

- **Deglobalization**
  - A growing focus on supply-chain resilience and security has begun to outweigh the drive for ultra-low production costs, leading to significant restructuring of global manufacturing footprints
- **Shifting trade dynamics**
  - Changing trade agreements and tariffs create geopolitical tensions that reshape the flow of goods and capital between regions
- **Energy transition**
  - Growth in renewable energy and the demand for rare-earth materials, alongside associated geopolitical risks
  - Structural shifts in the demand for fossil fuels
  - Increased climate volatility, changes in population centres, evolving consumer preferences, and the rise in environmental disasters
  - Heightened attention to environmental impact – anti-diesel sentiment, pressure to reduce CO^2 emissions and the push for lower water and energy consumption
  - Electrification of transport, including the widespread adoption of electric vehicles
- **Inflationary trends**
  - Structural inflation driven by tariffs, deglobalization, transformations in labor markets, commodities, capital costs and technological disruption
- **Public debt and fiscal pressures**
  - The long-term implications of rising government debt and the sustainability of current fiscal models
- **Technological revolution**
  - Pervasive innovation across virtually every industry
  - Artificial intelligence creates accelerated productivity and displaces traditional workflows and jobs

- Eliminating costly middle layers in the supply chain
- Automation and robotics transforming production and service delivery
- A massive shift from offline to online across commerce, education, media and social engagement
- Mobile or remote working reshaping talent attraction, retention and commercial real-estate needs
- Digital transparency via search engines placing downward pressure on pricing and profit margins
- Mobile-first lifestyles with increased smartphone use requiring new business models and customer-engagement strategies
- The transition from print to digital
- Big data enabling hyper-personalization and predictive analytics
- Autonomous transport and the coming reality of self-driving vehicles

CONSUMER MEGATRENDS (LATE 2025)

- **Aging populations**
  - People are living longer, placing increasing demands on healthcare systems and creating large-scale shifts in consumption patterns
- **Digital consumption**
  - As spending on electronics and digital services rises, disposable income for other categories is often reduced
- **E-commerce and home delivery**
  - The proliferation of online shopping continues to challenge traditional retail models, increasing demand for efficient package delivery and last-mile logistics
- **Wellness and lifestyle**
  - Growing interest in health, fitness and preventative care is reshaping the food, beverage and healthcare industries

- **Urban living**
  - A movement of people from countryside to cities in many countries
- **Individualism and solo living**
  - More people living alone (often in cities), influencing home design, consumption habits and how products are marketed
- **Reprioritization of work and career**
  - Cultural shift away from career-centric lifestyles towards more flexible, experience-focused living
- **Changes in eating habits**
  - Declining interest in cooking at home – broad implications for food producers, grocery retailers and the restaurant industry
- **Stay-sober movement**
  - A trend towards alcohol-free drinking and living is reshaping the beverage industry and influencing social behavior
- **Travel and leisure evolution**
  - Vacation patterns, destination preferences and travel spending habits continue to change, often rapidly
- **Do-It-Yourself versus outsourcing**
  - Mixed trends in do-it-yourself behavior, with some consumers outsourcing more of their daily life while others embrace self-sufficiency in areas like home improvement or gardening

Global megatrends will vary in influence depending on whether your company operates globally, regionally, or locally. Similarly, consumer megatrends can differ significantly across regions and even within local markets. The key is to recognize these powerful tailwinds or headwinds and analyze how management deals with them, as they can have a material impact on the company's future. For this reason, the megatrends overview should be updated at least twice a year – or more often if necessary.

This list is not meant to be definitive and is not static. But it should serve as a prompt for deep thinking. I encourage you make your own list and consider how these powerful forces interact with the companies and industries you're evaluating. The more clearly you can see the structural winds behind a business – or the storms on its horizon – the more confidently you can assess the work and quality of a company's management and its long-term potential.

HOW TO IMPLEMENT THE RISK WORK AND MANAGEMENT EVALUATION IN YOUR THINKING

Most industries are influenced by more than one megatrend at any given time. Some of these trends have sweeping implications for society, reshaping economic systems, consumer behavior and industrial structures. Others may appear minor on the global stage, yet have a profound and often transformative impact within a specific sector or business.

Given this complexity, the most rational approach for both management and investors is to think in terms of *scenarios*, *consequences* and *probabilities*.

Rather than attempting to predict a single outcome, you should develop a structured range of potential future scenarios:

- **A worst-case scenario**, outlining the most adverse plausible impact on revenue and earnings from mostly headwinds
- **A base-case (or middle) scenario,** reflecting moderate and likely conditions from both headwinds and tailwinds
- **A best-case scenario,** envisioning favorable developments and tailwinds

Each of these scenarios should be linked to specific megatrend developments and their likely effects on the business. By assigning probability estimates to these outcomes – and that is your job – it becomes possible, at least in broad terms, to gauge the expected trajectory of revenues and profitability.

Let's consider a small example. After thorough analysis of the company's financials and management, the megatrends and your expectations for future development, your probability picture looks like this:

- **Worst-case scenario (20% chance):** revenue will grow only around 2% annually and earnings will stay flat
- **Base-case scenario (70% chance)**: revenue will grow about 6% annually and earnings will also grow about 6%
- **Best-case scenario (10% chance):** revenue will grow strongly, around 10% annually for a number of years, and earnings will grow even more – about 15% annually – due to economy of scale

Based on these three scenarios, you can calculate the most likely result by multiplying each scenario by the probability it will happen and then adding together the results from all three scenarios. Using the example above, we can see the statistical results are as follows:

revenue growth: (20% x 2%) + (70% x 6%) + (10% x 10%) = (0.4% + 4.2% + 1%) = 5.6%

earnings growth: (20% x 0%) + (70% x 6%) + (10% x 15%) = (0% + 4.2% + 1.5%) = 5.7%

Our expected revenue growth and earnings growth are almost the same – and, as we can see, very close to the base-case scenario.

Let's now compare the calculations of a more optimistic investor with those of a more conservative investor and see how the results of our scenario-based thinking change. Both the optimistic investor and the pessimistic investor agree with the financial development in each scenario, but put different probabilities on the three scenarios. The more optimistic investor sees a 50% chance for the best-case scenario, a 40% chance for the base-case scenario and only a 10% on the worst-case scenario.

Based on these probabilities, the optimistic investor gets the following results:

revenue growth: (10% x 2%) + (40% x 6%) + (50% x 10%) = 7.6%

earnings growth: (10% x 0%) + (40% x 6%) + (50% x 15%) = 9.9%

The more conservative investor assumes there's a 50% chance that the worst-case scenario will happen, a 40% chance for the base-case scenario and only a 10% chance for the best-case scenario. On this basis, the conservative investor gets the following results:

revenue growth: (50% x 2%) + (40% x 6%) + (10% x 10%) = 4.4%

earnings growth: (50% x 0%) + (40% x 6%) + (10% x 15%) = 3.9%

My recommendation is to consistently work with probabilities, paying particular attention to the worst-case scenario. Your objective is to grow your wealth at a healthy pace, but each time the worst-case scenario becomes reality you risk a *permanent loss of capital.*

In other words, it is always – and I do mean *always* – a sound strategy for the average investor to avoid investments where the worst-case outcome could reasonably result in the company failing to survive. If the company doesn't survive, neither does your investment.

As Warren Buffett famously put it: 'Rule number one is never to lose money. Rule number two is never forgetting rule number one.'

As the business environment evolves and new data emerges, the scenarios and probabilities should be revisited and adjusted accordingly. Changes in technology, regulation, geopolitics, or consumer behavior may shift probabilities or even render one scenario obsolete. The ability to update these forecasts thoughtfully and with discipline is crucial for investors and a hallmark of forward-thinking, agile management.

While public disclosures of such assessments may be limited in scope, the best managers often provide investors with high-level insight into their strategic thinking about long-term risks and opportunities and an idea of their strategic responses.

As an investor, you can mirror this discipline in your own analysis. Identify the two or three *most important positive drivers* likely to shape the company's long-term success. Just as importantly, isolate the two or three *most critical risk factors* – those that could materially impair revenue or profitability if they come to pass.

This exercise in scenario thinking not only sharpens your understanding of a company's true potential and the quality of its management, but also trains you to think probabilistically – a fundamental skill for any serious investor navigating an uncertain future.

18.
Check Your Management Team Against Competitors

One of the most reliable ways to evaluate the leadership is by measuring management's performance relative to its competitors over time.

You should begin by comparing the company's trends in sales growth, operating margins and return on capital with those of its direct competitors and within the broader industry. If the company consistently outperforms on these metrics – achieving superior revenue growth, wider margins and stronger returns on capital – this is a strong signal that the management team is not just competent but potentially excellent.

However, if the company lags behind its peers in growth or margins or both, deeper analysis is required. In some rare instances, below-average margins may still be acceptable or even positive, but only if the company is intentionally pricing its products below those of its competitors to gain market share and is still maintaining a high return on capital. Otherwise, such underperformance likely signals strategic or managerial weaknesses.

The most relevant financial metrics will vary by industry. In capital-intensive sectors, for example, *return on capital* is paramount. In consumer-facing industries, *gross margins* and *brand preference* may offer deeper insight.

Tailor your focus to industry-specific dynamics and use these metrics as your compass to assess whether management is leading the pack or losing ground.

In the Appendix, I will evaluate and discuss all the relevant financial figures and how to use them when you invest. In the meantime, here are several useful key figures you can apply to compare the performance of your company with competitors over a number of years – and not just the last quarter or year:

- Revenue growth
- Gross margin
- Operating margin
- Growth in earnings per share
  - Based on reported earnings + amortization of intangible assets
  - Free cash flow
- Debt/equity
- Return on tangible assets
- ROUNTA
- ROIC
- Return on equity (ROE)

By tracking your company's performance on these parameters over a period of three to five years, and comparing it with the performance of two or three of its closest competitors, you gain a powerful tool for assessing both the company's strengths and its management's effectiveness. This also provides an excellent basis for asking yourself – and the management team – a series of important 'Why?' questions.

It must be emphasized that different key metrics may provide the best basis for comparison depending on the industry. Furthermore, it is worth keeping in mind that comparing the key metrics alone is insufficient. The crucial thing to ask yourself is why there is a difference between two companies' key figures. In other words, comparing your company's numbers with those of its competitors is very useful for achieving a deeper understanding of the industry and your business – this work helps to expand and deepen your circle of competence.

Likewise, studying your company's financial performance and how it compares with competitors is important but insufficient on its own. It is also vital to study and follow what happens inside your company and what management decides to do. Over the years, I have learned that, as an investor, you must pay extra attention whenever the board and management of the company receive shareholders' permission at the annual meeting to make big changes or management simply announces major strategic changes or a somewhat revised focus. When they are first made, such decisions will not immediately show up in financial performance. But they could, over the years, lead to dramatic negative changes in the company's earnings power and valuation. It is your job as an owner to keep an eye on management and how they carry out strategic development and capital allocation.

One of the best ways of comparing your company with competitors is to study the competitor CEOs and how they work strategically and operationally. In fact, the competitor CEOs are probably your best source of knowledge about your own company and your own management team. Start by reading the CEO letter in your competitors' annual report or quarterly updates and take it from there – you will learn a lot.

19.

Are Owners of the Company and Management in the Same Boat?

To understand what drives management, you must understand the structure of their remuneration and assess whether management's compensation is aligned with your interests as an owner. If management's incentives are *not* aligned with your goals, then you and management are not truly in the same boat. Excellent management teams recognize the importance of aligning their compensation with the interests of the owners. In fact, such management often chooses to invest personally in the company, reinforcing the mindset of thinking like an owner.

THE SALARY PACKAGE

Most often, the salary package consists of a fixed salary, a pension scheme and a bonus scheme. The total compensation may be high or more modest; regardless, the most important factor is whether the package is structured to reflect the owners' interests. As an owner, your goal is for management to perform at a high level and for the company's real value to grow accordingly. Note the emphasis on both 'performance' and 'real' value. In many companies, the bonus scheme – which can constitute a very large part of total compensation – is not actually linked to management's performance or to the development of the company's intrinsic value. Instead, it is often tied solely to the company's stock price.

A typical example is a salary package that includes a bonus scheme based on options. The board may decide that management – possibly including both executives and board members – will receive free options, granted without any connection to the company's financial performance or earnings growth. These schemes usually lack any reference to how the company performs relative to its industry or how much capital has been invested to generate sales and earnings over time.

Instead, the options are granted 'free of charge' and after a vesting period of three to five years can be exercised at the then-current market price of the company's shares. In other words, management pays nothing for the options, and they are not awarded based on performance relative to industry peers or competitors. If, at the time of exercise, the share price is significantly higher than the company's real value, management reaps a substantial and yet often unjustified profit.

These types of option schemes are essentially like a coin toss – but with a major advantage skewed in management's favor. If the coin lands on 'heads', management wins big, regardless of their actual performance during the vesting period. If the coin lands on 'tails' and the company's share price is low when the options are exercised, management loses nothing – because they didn't pay for the options in the first place. Heads, they win big; tails, they lose nothing.

It is almost standard practice for listed companies to include some form of stock options in executive compensation packages. However, very few of these schemes are structured to reward management based solely on performance relative to earnings development in their specific industry.

My advice is to exercise great caution as an investor when you observe that the board has issued stock options representing 3–5% – and in some cases up to 10% – of the company's share capital to management.

As a general principle, I believe that ownership in a company should be acquired through real, out-of-pocket investment, not granted as a reward. Yet year after year, we continue to see numerous examples of multimillion or even billion-dollar windfalls as management teams exercise stock options of various kinds.

The worst cases involve a large number of free stock options combined with ongoing share buyback programs. These buybacks often occur at share prices that far exceed the company's intrinsic value. This ensures that the value of management's options rises significantly, even if the company is not actually creating long-term value. In such scenarios, management profits at the expense of other co-owners, effectively transferring value away from shareholders. It is therefore essential to analyze whether management and you, as an owner, truly share the same incentives and are in the same boat.

20.
Management and Rational Capital Allocation

For the stock investor, the two greatest risks that can damage an investment outcome are paying an excessively high price when you invest in the company (which we will discuss how to avoid later), or when management makes irrational decisions about the allocation of the company's earnings and other capital resources. In other words, the ability to use capital in the most value-creating way is one of the cornerstones of excellent management and very important if you aim to outperform the stock market over the long term.

Let us begin by reviewing how management get access to capital resources and how that capital can be utilized. We can then examine how to rationally allocate capital in various situations.

Fundamentally, the company has four capital resources to finance its business development:

- Cash flow (earnings) from operating activities
- Capital from creditors – the capital made available to the company in the form of unpaid invoices and other outstanding liabilities
- Equity (owner's capital within the company)
- Debt (capital provided by banks and other lenders)

Management's understanding of how crucial it is to allocate capital rationally and carry out that allocation accordingly has significant consequences for the company's long-term value creation. In my experience, not all managers in listed companies understand the importance of rational capital allocation.

Management can allocate the company's earnings and capital resources in five ways:

- Investments in the company's operational system. That is, all larger investments that are not wholly financed through ongoing operations. These might include investments in buildings, machinery and equipment, for example, or the establishment of new subsidiaries and product lines. In general, these internal investments serve two purposes. First, to maintain existing operational systems; and second, to expand the platform and position the company for growth in revenue and earnings in the coming years.

- Acquisition of other companies and/or assets. This includes all external investments, including the acquisition of competitors and other companies, product rights and other forms of existing assets, that management undertake to enhance and improve the company's market position and future earning potential.

- Repayment of debt or storing capital. This is a fairly common form of capital allocation. It is not immediately critical for the company's long-term development. However, if management maintains a very large, non-income-generating cash reserve over many years, and continues to accumulate more capital, this will likely be inconducive to long-term value creation. Conversely, a less competent management might be tempted to undertake very large, debt-financed acquisitions that increase the company's financial risk in a dramatic way in some years, making debt repayment more or less essential for the company's survival.

- Payment of dividends to the owners. This is also a fairly common form of capital allocation, though it is not always appropriate. One of the best ways to establish whether management can be described as excellent is to examine their decision-making about dividends and how those decisions are carried out.

- Buyback of the company's own shares. This can be
  an incredibly value-enhancing way to allocate capital,
  providing the shares are repurchased at an attractive price.

Let's take a closer look at these five ways of allocating capital, as they are essential to the company's long-term profit potential and increase in earnings per share.

INVESTMENTS IN THE COMPANY'S OPERATIONAL SYSTEM

When assessing whether management makes rational capital-allocation decisions according to the five options outlined above, it is essential to focus on both the specific allocation decision and the wider business and economic contexts in which the company operates as well as its prospects.

Overall, it is crucial that management first and foremost ensures that operating investments are made as necessary to maintain the company's competitiveness and its ability to capitalize on future opportunities for growth in sales *and* earnings.

It can be quite difficult for outsiders to assess how large these investments should be and in what areas they should be made. It is therefore vital that management explain both the investments and the underlying rationale to co-owners and investors.

A rational investor, regardless of other factors, holds a strong position when evaluating management's operating investments. All else being equal, and if the company generally achieves a high return on invested capital, making further operational investments is quite attractive providing the returns on them remain consistent with previous investments. Conversely, if the overall return on invested capital is low, making additional investments is often not very attractive – although it may be necessary to keep the company running and prevent further deterioration in the business.

In short, the higher the return on invested capital, the more attractive it is for the company's owners – and for overall value creation – that management can invest more capital in the business, thereby driving further growth in sales and earnings.

ACQUISITIONS OF OTHER COMPANIES AND/OR ASSETS

For many business leaders, few things generate more adrenaline than the opportunity to acquire another company – whether it's a direct competitor, a smaller 'add-on' or even a company operating in a completely unrelated field. Yet acquisitions are one of the most common ways company owners lose substantial amounts of money. These losses typically stem from either overpaying for the acquired business or overlooking significant hidden problems within the target company – issues that were either missed or, worse, ignored in the heat of deal-making excitement.

As an investor and co-owner, you must evaluate whether management is making a rational capital-allocation decision when pursuing an acquisition. To do this effectively, you need to focus on the following two key criteria.

Business logic

In virtually every corporate acquisition, the acquiring company's management presents the transaction as logical and value-enhancing. Press releases routinely describe the deal as strategically sound and beneficial to shareholders.

But history tells a different story. A large percentage of acquisitions ultimately fail to create lasting value for shareholders. In fact, many end up being poor capital-allocation decisions. As such, it's critical for investors to assess whether the acquisition truly makes business sense. Smaller acquisitions that align closely with the company's existing operations and deliver tangible strategic benefits are usually rational decisions. By contrast, the larger the deal and the less aligned the target company is with the acquirer's core business, the greater the risk involved.

Purchase price

Assessing the business rationale is only half the job. Equally important is determining whether the price paid for the acquisition is justified – as Benjamin Graham famously stated, 'Price is what you pay; value is what you get.'

The same principle that applies when you evaluate a stock also applies when management evaluates an acquisition. Paying too much for a company is one of the most common – and most damaging – mistakes a management team can make.

At the time of the deal, no management team ever admits that the price is excessive. On the contrary, the cost is often justified by projections of accelerated growth and expanded earnings. These justifications are typically supported by anticipated 'synergies' expected from integrating the acquired business. As a rational business investor, it is your responsibility to scrutinize those projections and assess whether the investment can generate an attractive return – and whether the combined entity can sustain high returns on invested capital over time.

Each acquisition is different. Management's approach to capital allocation will vary in quality and discipline over time. But in my experience, executives tend to be overly optimistic when assessing strategic value and often overpay – especially when the economic environment is strong and optimism is widespread.

I've witnessed many situations where, with board approval, a management team embarked on an aggressive acquisition campaign as part of their endeavor to become a large player in their given industry. These strategies often involve multiple high-priced deals. Initially, everything appears promising, and the share price may rise on the news of strong growth. However, this optimism often proves short-lived. The acquired companies underperform, synergies fall short, and goodwill impairments follow. Shareholder value erodes and the stock price plummets.

It's like a party: fun while it lasts – but the hangover can be painful and expensive.

Keep in mind that the highest acquisition prices are typically paid when market sentiment is euphoric and driven by greed. This environment is often characterized by inflated business valuations and a wave of careless investment decisions across the corporate landscape. As a business investor, this is precisely when you must proceed with increased caution.

The most rational business acquisitions – in terms of both strategic logic and price – tend to occur after periods of economic or industry downturns, when expectations are more grounded and valuations more reasonable. These are also times when the broader stock market is valued more fairly, offering you some of the most attractive opportunities for long-term, rewarding investments.

REPAYMENT OF DEBT
OR STORING CAPITAL

Management decisions to repay debt are typically responses to past capital-allocation choices. There is nothing inherently right or wrong about repaying debt. In general, the less debt a company carries, the lower its financial risk.

A rational investor can readily conclude that, all else being equal, a debt-free company with a strong moat in a stable industry is a lower-risk enterprise. However, being debt free *and* holding a large idle cash reserve might indicate poor capital-allocation discipline. Excess cash that isn't deployed towards value-creating opportunities means that shareholder capital is earning low returns. In such cases, owners effectively miss out on potential gains that could have been achieved through better use of the capital.

PAYMENT OF DIVIDENDS AND
SHARE BUYBACKS

Dividends should be paid after all value-enhancing capital-allocation opportunities have been considered and executed. Only once management has determined that no further attractive investments can be made does it make sense to return excess capital to shareholders via dividends.

A rigid dividend policy – for example, one that commits to distributing 50% of annual after-tax profit – is almost never a sign of sound capital allocation and excellent management. Dividends should never be treated as an automatic entitlement. Instead, they should reflect a deliberate and disciplined decision that no better alternatives exist for the reinvestment of retained earnings.

Even when no further investments are available, paying dividends may not always be the most rational use of capital – especially if the company's stock is trading below its intrinsic value. In such cases, a share-buyback program can offer significantly greater value to shareholders than spending the same amount of money paying dividends.

For instance, buying back stock at 75% of the intrinsic value has two powerful benefits. First, management is investing in a company it knows intimately – one it understands better than any external acquisition target. The investment risk is minimal, and the discount to intrinsic value provides a built-in margin of safety.

Second, buybacks reduce the number of outstanding shares. This increases each remaining shareholder's ownership stake and proportionate share of future earnings. Consequently, earnings per share – and likely the stock price – will rise, assuming the overall company value remains stable.

On the other hand, if the company's stock is trading at or above intrinsic value, buybacks can be harmful. Repurchasing shares at inflated prices means the company is overpaying, which benefits selling shareholders at the expense of those who remain. In such cases, distributing excess capital via dividends is the more rational choice.

RATIONAL CAPITAL ALLOCATION
IN GENERAL

We must conclude that rational capital allocation requires management to adjust its financial decisions based on the company's current circumstances and business opportunities – including its stock price relative to its intrinsic value. There is no one-size-fits-all capital-allocation strategy that applies universally.

Furthermore, a company that adheres to a rigid dividend policy – such as distributing 50% of annual profits as dividends – is not demonstrating excellent management in capital allocation. Such a fixed policy suggests that management is not exercising the judgement necessary to allocate capital in a thoughtful and value-maximizing manner.

It should also be clear to you – and ideally to all managers in listed companies – that the difference between rational and irrational capital allocation can lead to vast disparities in long-term value creation. Exceptional management understands this difference.

21.
Using ROIC to Evaluate Management Excellence

You'll remember that ROUNTA – return on unlevered net tangible assets – is the best metric for assessing the quality of a business. As we've previously discussed, ROUNTA reflects a company's ability to generate returns on the capital invested in its operational assets. However, ROUNTA is not the most appropriate metric for evaluating how well management allocates capital. For that purpose, ROIC – return on invested capital – is more relevant. You'll recall that while the two are similar, ROIC includes intangible assets (such as goodwill), whereas ROUNTA excludes them.

ROUNTA = ROIC – intangible asset

To my knowledge, no company has ever reported negative intangible assets in its financial statements. We can therefore conclude that ROIC will always be less than or equal to ROUNTA.

It's not uncommon to see a company with a ROUNTA of, say, 35% – a great business – yet with a ROIC of only 10%. This often occurs when management has made several acquisitions over the years and paid purchase prices that include significant goodwill.

Even if the acquired businesses are great in isolation, with ROUNTA figures above 25%, if management pays well above the value of the operational assets, a large portion of the purchase price must be recorded as goodwill or other intangibles. Regardless of the quality of the acquired business, management must be evaluated based on the return on the full investment amount, including goodwill.

In short: ROUNTA helps assess the quality of the business, while ROIC is essential for evaluating management's capital-allocation effectiveness.

Let's begin with some basic conclusions and work our way towards more 'revealing' situations where a rational investor might start to question whether management fully understands the consequences of poor – or even value-destructive – capital allocation.

HIGH ROUNTA AND HIGH ROIC

Naturally, if a company grows purely organically and does not engage in acquisitions, there will typically be very few intangible assets, and the ROIC will be roughly equal to the ROUNTA. However, as stated, ROIC can never exceed ROUNTA. In other words, when both ROUNTA and ROIC are high (for example, ROUNTA > 20–25% and ROIC > 15%), this indicates that the company is historically a great business and that management has allocated capital reasonably well.

However, it is worth noting one important exception. In the case of truly exceptional businesses, ROUNTA can sometimes be negative, simply because the company is so efficient that it doesn't require any equity or debt. For example, software companies that receive prepaid subscription fees from customers may be able to base their operations solely on those incoming payments.

If such a company also acquires similar businesses and most of the acquisition price is goodwill, ROUNTA often becomes negative, since goodwill is excluded from the ROUNTA calculation. However, goodwill *is* included in ROIC, and ROIC is almost never negative – it only happens when the company has an extraordinarily large cash position.

HIGH ROUNTA AND LOW ROIC

It is crucial to understand that a discrepancy between a high or even negative ROUNTA and a relatively low ROIC (for example, just 10% or lower) will be closely tied to management's capital-allocation decisions.

As an investor, your first step should be to analyze how ROIC and ROUNTA have evolved over the past five to seven years. Where ROUNTA has remained consistently high but ROIC has declined significantly, this often suggests that management has made some very expensive acquisitions. While the acquired businesses may indeed be great businesses, management may have overpaid, thereby deploying a large amount of capital at unattractive returns.

Let's illustrate this with a simple example. Management decides to acquire a business with US$20 million in operating assets and annual profits of US$10 million – representing a ROUNTA of 10/20 = 50%. That's an attractive return and suggests a high-quality business. However, management is unable to buy the company for US$20 million and ends up paying US$250 million. The acquired business continues to earn US$10 million annually; but now, from the acquirer's perspective, this equates to a ROIC of 10/250 = 4%.

As an investor, you must conclude that management has deployed a substantial portion of the company's capital at a relatively poor return. It is unlikely that the return on this investment will ever be attractive unless there is a clear plan to significantly increase earnings by organic growth or integrating the acquired business with existing operations.

In such situations, management often make optimistic statements about the acquisition and the expected future growth. My advice to investors is to stick to the facts. Ask yourself: *If I demand a minimum ROIC of 15%, how much profit must this US$250 million acquisition generate – and how long am I willing to wait for it to materialize?* The answer is US$250 million × 15% = US$37.5 million – a significant jump from the current US$10 million.

Assuming a high annual growth rate of 10%, it would take approximately fourteen years for earnings to reach US$37.5 million. That's a long time to wait for an adequate return on the capital invested.

LOOK FOR ROIC AT 15% OR HIGHER

If a company follows a strategy of organic growth combined with regular acquisitions – like Warren Buffett's Berkshire Hathaway or other 'serial acquirers' – I recommend that you, as an investor, closely examine what management says about expected returns on invested capital. Look for indications that management demands a return of at least 15% on acquisitions. Many serial acquirers explicitly set this as a goal – stating, for example, that any acquired company should 'pay for itself within five years', which corresponds to a 15% annual return.

Of course, there may be cases where a company's ROIC is temporarily low due to earnings challenges. If historical data shows that both ROUNTA and ROIC were previously high, and the current decline appears to be temporary, rather than structural, the business could represent an attractive investment opportunity. Often, when earnings decline, the company's market value drops as well – sometimes even more than is justified by the earnings decline. So do make sure that the business is fundamentally great before you invest.

With that in mind, it's also good to consider one other potential situation. If management make multiple acquisitions at high prices (even at low ROIC), this can initially drive strong increases in reported earnings and the stock price. This happens because many investors focus solely on earnings growth, which acquisitions naturally boost. However, few investors consider how much capital is required to achieve that growth.

LOOK AT GROWTH IN EARNINGS COMPARED TO GROWTH IN INVESTED CAPITAL

You should always compare earnings growth with growth in invested capital. If invested capital grows much faster than earnings, you can be almost certain that when earnings growth eventually slows or reverses – regardless of the reason – the company's market value will react swiftly and sharply. It's not uncommon to see the stock price of such companies drop by 20–40%, or even more.

Just as high interest rates act as a form of gravity on asset prices in general, low return on invested capital acts as gravity on a company's long-term value creation.

Let's remember Charlie Munger's wise words: a business that earns 6% on capital over time will not produce better than a 6% return for investors. A business that earns 18% will, over time, produce outstanding results.

Key takeaways from Part IV

- Excellent management always stands out from the crowd.
- All managers are not equally skilled, experienced or shrewd.
- Excellent managers think like business owners.
- Excellent managers focus hard on operational efficiency.
- The excellent manager thinks daily about widening and deepening the moat.
- Excellent managers build and maintain a supportive corporate culture.
- Excellent managers focus as much on risk as on opportunities.
- Understand and evaluate how much time your management team spend on megatrends and how they will potentially influence the future of the company.
- Megatrends are both positive and negative and excellent managers spend a lot of time working out how to benefit from tailwinds and mitigate the consequences of headwinds.
- Excellent managers and boards of directors understand they should be compensated and incentivized in ways that align them with the company owners.
- Excellent management understands the enormous value of rational capital allocation.
- There is no one-size-fits-all capital-allocation strategy.
- It is neither value creation nor a sign of excellence when management overpay when acquiring a company.
- Paying dividends can be a sign of bad capital allocation and lack of excellent management if the share price of the company is below the real value of the business.
- A rigid dividend policy is almost always a sign of bad capital allocation and lack of excellent management.
- Use ROIC compared with ROUNTA to assess how well management has invested all the capital in the company.

PART V:
Using Warren Buffett's Hurdle Rate for Your Investment Decisions

22.
The Correct Value of a Business Is Always a Judgement – Not a Fact!

When we're thinking about how to correctly value a business, let's start with some basic truths. No mathematical investment model can guarantee you'll determine the exact right value of a company. Actually, there is no 'correct value' of a company. The so-called intrinsic value is not a single number – so we should never fixate on this. The value of a business is influenced by countless moving parts, and you would need to be right about all of them – from now until the company ceases to exist – to calculate its value correctly. You would need to accurately predict the evolution of interest rates over time, the company's annual cash flow and how management will act and allocate capital. You would also need to be entirely confident in your own ability to get all this right.

This is a classic 'known versus unknown' situation. So, it's vital that you, as an investor, constantly ask yourself: *Do I know that I know; or do I know that I don't know; or do I not know that I don't know?*

Later, we'll evaluate how to analyze your knowledge, define your circle of competence and create your investor profile. For now, let's concentrate on the fact that as a rational investor you can dramatically differentiate yourself from the market average by focusing your investments on areas where you know what you know. This means avoiding speculative bets where you know that you *don't* know, but behave like you do – because that is what everybody else is doing.

To repeat the simple truth: it is impossible to know everything about a company's future – from now until judgement day – including earnings, growth, interest rates and how management will allocate the capital that belongs to shareholders. This is beyond even Warren Buffett.

Nevertheless, this 'I know it all' scenario is the foundation for the theoretically correct model for valuing a business: the **discounted cash flow (DCF)** model. DCF is also the most used model in the global financial sector. This is a mind-blowing fact that should give you pause to consider your market advantage and the opportunity you have to do something different.

But to use your advantage takes guts. You must think and act totally differently from nearly everybody else – you must think and act like Warren Buffett does.

To help you, remember that Buffett's track record over the last seventy-plus years speaks for itself. When I discovered this opportunity to distance my thinking and my investment approach from the average investor, I knew it was a no-brainer – especially when I really understood how rational Buffett's thinking is and how simple it would be to implement in my own investment work.

But let's start by looking at the DCF model and gaining some understanding of why it is inherently impractical yet so widely used.

23.

The DCF Model: Theoretically Correct – but Hopeless in Practice

Let's play along and assume we're able to foresee the future perfectly – accurately forecasting every variable involved in valuing a business. That being the case, the value of a company could theoretically be calculated by discounting all future free cash flows that the business will generate and returning it to you as an owner – that amount is the true value of a business.

This is the premise behind the discounted cash flow model, commonly referred to as the DCF model or simply the DCF in financial circles.

I'll now present the DCF model, but don't let it make you nervous – this is *not* the formula we're going to base our investment decisions on. The general DCF formula is:

$$DCF = \sum (FCF_t / (1 + r)^t) + (TV / (1 + r)^n)$$

Where:
- FCF_t = free cash flow in year t
- r = discount rate
- n = final year of forecast period

TV = terminal value

In short, the DCF formula requires you to estimate the company's free cash flow for each year over a chosen projection period (typically five to seven years, though the exact duration is up to you). These free cash flows are then discounted back to their present value using a discount rate, because future cash flows are worth less than cash received today. Cash flows beyond the projection period are aggregated into a terminal value (TV), which is also discounted back to the present. Adding these discounted cash flows together gives the theoretically correct value of the company – supposing that all the assumptions underlying the calculations are accurate, which of course they never are!

Normally the person using the DCF will forecast each year's cash flow for several years and then use the TV to calculate the value of cash flows beyond the forecast period. The TV often represents more than 50% of the total valuation derived by DCF, making it a critical component of the model. So, let's look at the TV:

$$TV = FCF_{n+1} / (r - g)$$

Where:

- FCF_{n+1} = free cash flow in the first year after the forecast period
- r = discount rate
- g = perpetual growth rate

The terminal value (TV) is the most disruptive factor in applying the DCF model, because you can arrive at just about any TV you want by slightly adjusting the assumptions – assumptions that are virtually impossible to establish as accurate or not!

Without spending too much time over-analyzing TV, let me just illustrate that if we (for example) set FCF_{n+1} to 500, we can very easily justify a TV anywhere between 6,250 and 50,000 purely by making very small incremental changes to 'r' and 'g'.

As TV often represents 50% or more of the valuation of the company, it is easy to understand why it's critical to approach DCF results with a healthy degree of skepticism and judgement. It is also why Warren Buffett has never done a DCF in his very long and very successful investment career.

Yet still the DCF model remains widely used throughout the financial industry. Nearly every professional investor, analyst and financial institution relies on some version of it when valuing a business.

This is partly why the stock market and the price of individual stocks are so volatile. Changing just two numbers in the DCF model means you can conclude that the value of the company is 50% or 75% higher or lower!

As Columbia Business School's former Professor Bruce Greenwald so aptly put it: 'When you put garbage into a model, you can be sure what you'll get out the other end – yes, you guessed it: garbage!'

So why is the DCF model so widely used?

In short, because it's theoretically correct and continues to be taught at business schools around the world – including at Copenhagen Business School, where I studied finance many years ago. The DCF is deeply embedded in financial education and its use is considered standard practice. Moreover, no one gets blamed for relying on it because everyone else uses it too. This is a remarkable reality. As a rational investor, you must pause and consider what this means – and, more importantly, what opportunities it creates for you.

In practice, professionals often supplement DCF valuations with other models. These include models based on recent transactions in similar industries and the classic 'multiples' approach, where you estimate a company's earnings – or **free cash flow (FCF)** – for the next twelve months and apply a valuation multiple. This multiples approach leads to statements like: 'The company should be trading at fourteen times earnings,' or 'This business is fairly valued at sixteen times FCF.'

Once again, as a rational investor, you should pause and ask: *Why are those the 'right' multiples?*

Which brings us back to the original point: all company valuations are based on the variables you choose. That means every valuation is ultimately a judgement – not a fact.

Nevertheless, many analysts and professionals consider the DCF model and multiples approach to be the 'safe' choices. People often don't want to stray too far from the crowd. Yet straying from the crowd is precisely what Warren Buffett has done for decades. Let's take a closer look…

24.
Warren Buffett's Investment Hurdle Rate

What Warren Buffett does to prepare for an investment is remarkably simple. He applies the principle of thinking like a business owner and combines it with a solid margin of safety. He also consistently uses a straightforward *investment hurdle rate* to guide all his investment decisions. A hurdle rate is the minimum return that an investment must achieve to be deemed acceptable. In other words – and this is an important aspect of your demand for returns – your hurdle rate equals the absolute lowest return you will accept; and it must be sufficiently high that you get attractive results and your capital grows at a good clip.

In other words, when Buffett invests, he isn't focused on the stock price or how it might develop in the future. He focuses on the company's earnings and expected growth in earnings over the coming years and decides whether they are sufficient to deliver his required rate of return. That's how a business owner thinks when deciding where to allocate capital – and I strongly encourage you to adopt the same mindset.

Buffett asks himself: 'When I look at this company, its earnings and the expected growth in earnings in the coming years, what price am I willing to pay based on the return on my money I demand?'

You can flip this question around, asking yourself: 'If I buy this company at current price, will its earnings and growth in earnings give me the annual returns on my money that I require – does it pass the hurdle rate?'

The answer should be a simple 'Yes' or 'No.'

At no point does Buffett spend a second thinking about how the stock price will develop after he buys the stock.

Buffett has explained his approach using a bond analogy. When you buy a bond, the certificate tells you exactly how much interest you'll receive each year (your coupon rate) and when you'll be repaid the principal amount. In other words, as a bond investor, you know your future returns at the time you invest.

Buffett likens a stock certificate to a bond without the numbers printed on the coupons and with no expiration date. Your job, as an investor, is to estimate what the future 'coupon payments' – that is, the company's earnings – will be. Once you've got that estimation, you compare it with the price you must pay for the stock and then decide whether the returns meet your hurdle rate.

Here's perhaps the most important insight I've gained in my entire investment career:

Most investors cheer when stock prices rise, because they measure their success based on how much the stock price has increased since they bought in. Buffett, as we know, focuses on the company's earnings and whether they meet his required return (his hurdle rate).

For Buffett, this means that falling stock prices are actually very good news. Lower prices make it easier to find businesses with earnings that meet or exceed your hurdle rate. The cheaper the stock, the more attractive the investment becomes.

If you're still working and saving for retirement – meaning that you are a net investor in the stock market of the future – you too should cheer for falling stock prices. They allow you to invest your future income at higher expected returns, which will ultimately benefit your retirement savings. When markets are high, the returns on new investments are lower – and that can hurt your future financial security.

Understanding the contrast between these two mindsets, and choosing Buffett's approach and methodology, will provide you with your greatest opportunity to outperform the stock market over the long term.

Time and again, Buffett has told shareholders – and anyone else willing to listen – that successful investing is about thinking like a business owner and keeping things simple. It's not about building elaborate DCF models or creating sprawling Excel spreadsheets filled with hundreds of financial metrics and variables.

In fact, both Buffett's late business partner Charlie Munger and Alice Schroeder, author of the definitive 2008 Buffett biography *The Snowball*[6], have said they've never seen Buffett use a DCF model. Schroeder, who had unrestricted access to Buffett's files while writing the book, stated that when it comes to investing, 'Buffett is a very simple guy. He doesn't do any kind of discounted cash flow or any models.'

There is an obvious conclusion to draw from this: if the most successful investor in history doesn't rely on complex financial models, then nor should you. That's why this book has devoted significant attention to understanding Buffett's core investment principles, and what defines a great company – run by excellent management – the foundational qualities behind every one of Buffett's investments.

In countless shareholder letters and annual meetings, Buffett has made clear that his focus isn't on how a company is performing *right now*. Instead, he analyzes each business from a long-term perspective, asking how much money it will likely make ten to twenty years into the future. While most investors focus on the short-term stock-price movements, Buffett thinks like a long-term business owner and spends his time considering what could go right or wrong over the long haul.

Don't underestimate the importance of Buffett's long-term focus and his unique starting point. This perspective on investing is the key reason for his extraordinary success.

BUFFETT'S INVESTMENT HURDLE RATE

At Berkshire Hathaway's 2003 annual meeting, Buffett explained that he would invest in a company only if he was confident that its pre-tax profits offered him a 10% real return on his investment. The word *real* is

---

6 Alice Schroeder, The Snowball: Warren Buffett and the Business of Life (Bantam Books, 2008).

important here because it refers to returns that increase at least as fast as general inflation is increasing prices in the wider world. In other words, if inflation is 3% per year and prices are therefore increasing by 3% annually, your company's earnings must also increase by at least 3% per year if you start out with a 10% return before tax.

So, Buffett looks at a company's pre-tax profits and how the earnings are expected to grow over time, to make sure that earnings are expected to grow at least as fast as inflation. When he is confident that the earnings can grow as fast as or faster than inflation, Buffett looks at the stock price and asks himself whether he can get at least 10% real return before tax on his investment. Yes or no?

Buffett doesn't focus on the share-price performance after making an investment. He knows that over the long term the value of the company follows earnings – so, if his judgement about earnings growth is correct, he knows the valuation of the company and the stock price will mirror that growth.

As should be obvious, Buffett's mindset and methodology are fundamentally different than those of most investors on the stock market.

Buffett's thinking is also theoretically sound, since an investor's long-term return is generated by the company's earnings and the growth rate of those earnings. Everything else being equal, as a company's profits grow year by year the value of the company increases accordingly.

25.
How to Use Buffett's Hurdle Rate in Your Investment Decisions

Buffett uses pre-tax profit rather than after-tax earnings in his own investment calculations, reflecting his unique position as the owner of many businesses consolidated under the parent company Berkshire Hathaway. For Buffett, using an after-tax hurdle rate doesn't make sense because Berkshire pays taxes at the group level.

However, most individual investors own shares in companies, not entire businesses – so for them it's more appropriate to use after-tax profit when applying a hurdle rate and calculating potential returns.

Of course, the 'raw' after-tax earnings reported in a company's income statement often require some adjustments to reflect the business's true earning power. Those adjustments and how to make them are explored in detail in the Appendix. For now, we'll use basic numbers to keep things as simple as possible.

BUFFETT'S PRE-TAX HURDLE RATE CONVERTED INTO AN AFTER-TAX HURDLE RATE

Converting Buffett's 10% pre-tax hurdle rate into an equivalent after-tax hurdle rate is straightforward. If you work under a 22% corporate tax rate, you adjust the 10% pre-tax rate accordingly:

after-tax hurdle rate = 10% × (1 − 0.22) = 7.8%

If the corporate tax rate is 25%, this becomes:

after-tax hurdle rate = 10% × (1 – 0.25) = 7.5%

APPLYING THE AFTER-TAX HURDLE RATE

Using the after-tax hurdle rate makes it quite simple for you to make a clear 'yes or no' investment decision.

Let's assume the relevant corporate tax rate is 22%, and you've identified a great company with outstanding management. You're confident the business can grow its earnings by 5% per year for the foreseeable future, matching or exceeding expected inflation.

If the company earns US$10 million after tax, the maximum price you'd be willing to pay for the entire company (based on a 7.8% after-tax hurdle rate) would be:

US$10 million / 0.078 ≈ US$128 million

If the company has 5 million shares outstanding, this total price translates as:

US$128 million / 5 million shares = US$25.60 per share

Here, we've set aside the discussion of how much free cash – cash that belongs to the owners and that management could choose to distribute – the company has on its balance sheet. However, for simplicity's sake, if we say that the company had US$10 free cash per share standing in the bank, and that you bought the entire business for US$25.60 per share, you could go to the bank and immediately get back US$10 per share – making the buy 'a steal' at US$15.60 per share.

Let's double-check the math to confirm that this price at US$25.60 per share yields the expected 7.8% return:

- After-tax earnings: US$10 million
- Shares outstanding: 5 million
- Earnings per share (EPS): US$10 million / 5 million = US$2
- If you pay US$25.60 per share, your return is: US$2 / US$25.60 = 7.8%

As you can see, this simple framework gives you a rational, objective basis for evaluating whether a company's earnings justify the return you demand – your hurdle rate.

THE IMPLIED PRICE/EARNINGS (P/E) RATIO

Using the 7.8% after-tax hurdle rate, we can calculate the equivalent **price/earnings (P/E) ratio**, a common measure of how much you must pay for US$1 of earnings. The P/E ratio is essentially the opposite of the return yield of 7.8%.

We calculated the return rate of 7.8% as 2/25.6, so we calculate the P/E ratio as 25.6/2 ≈ 12.8 or ≈ 13. In other words, we are willing to pay approximately 13 times the after-tax earnings per share – and if we do that and the company's growth mirrors or outperforms the inflation rate, we will get real return of at least 7.8% on our money. (Remember that your after-tax hurdle rate is influenced by the actual tax rate.)

Likewise, when Buffett demands a 10% pre-tax return, it is equivalent to a pre-tax P/E ratio of 1/10% = 10.

This simple relationship between your hurdle rate and the P/E makes it easy to determine the price you're willing to pay for your company or its stock.

WHY WARREN BUFFETT USES A 10% PRE-TAX HURDLE RATE

As a rational investor, you might ask two obvious questions:

1. How did Buffett decide on a 10% pre-tax hurdle rate?
2. Does he use this 10% rate regardless of how quickly the company can grow earnings over the coming years?

According to Buffett at the Berkshire Hathaway 2003 annual meeting, the 10% real pre-tax hurdle rate is entirely arbitrary and unscientific. It is also not influenced by prevailing interest rates.

He has referenced this 10% pre-tax hurdle rate on multiple occasions. In his 2014 annual letter, for example, he spent more than three pages describing how he applied it when purchasing a farm in Nebraska and a commercial property in New York. In both cases, he estimated pre-tax earnings to be roughly 10% of the purchase price, with the expectation that those earnings would grow at least in line with inflation.

Although Buffett says the rate is arbitrary and has never disclosed how he arrived at the 10% figure, a logical origin can be traced back to Benjamin Graham's *The Intelligent Investor*[7], which Buffett has often called the most important investment book he's ever read.

In this book, Graham introduces the concept of a hurdle rate. He advises investors to seek a minimum excess return of 5% per year over the risk-free rate (typically the yield on ten-year US Treasury Bonds). So, if the risk-free rate is 5% and you earn 10% on a stock investment, you achieve a 5% annual excess return – equivalent to a 50% cumulative excess return over ten years, providing a strong margin of safety.

Buffett does not explicitly cite Graham when discussing his hurdle rate, but he has frequently indicated that he expects the US economy to grow at about 5% nominally. Historically, the risk-free rate tends to align with nominal GDP growth – again, around 5%. Therefore, Buffett's 10% hurdle rate closely mirrors Graham's model: when investing in stocks, investors should aim to earn the risk-free rate plus an additional 5% as a margin of safety. If the risk-free rate is about 5% historically then you should aim for at least 10%. But Buffett has also emphasized that he does not dip below the 10% hurdle rate, even when the risk-free rate drops below 5% or even approaches zero, as we saw during the COVID period.

THE HURDLE RATE COMPARED TO THE STOCK MARKET IN GENERAL

For the sake of thoroughness, let's examine whether Buffett's expected returns provide a reasonable margin of safety compared to the general return requirements of the stock market.

7Graham, 1949.

As we've just calculated, Buffett's 10% pre-tax hurdle rate translates into a 7.8% after-tax return, assuming a 22% corporate tax rate. Historically, the S&P 500 has traded at around 16–17 times after-tax earnings. If you pay 16.5 times the earnings, your expected starting return, as we've learned, is:

$$1 / 16.5 \approx 6\%$$

Now, if we compare the market's average return rate of 6% with Buffett's 7.8% hurdle rate, we see that Buffett requires a higher return than the market standard. The extra return is calculated as:

$$7.8\% / 6\% = 1.3, \text{ or } 30\% \text{ more than the market return}$$

This 30% excess return is effectively Buffett's margin of safety.

BUFFETT'S HURDLE RATE IN ACTION

It's possible to 'hurdle-test' some of Buffett's well-known investments via the stock market.

When we study Buffett's investments, it becomes evident that they have often been based on his 10% pre-tax hurdle rate and the assumption of approximately 5% annual earnings growth. This applies to both the acquisition of entire companies and the purchase of shares in listed businesses.

For example, in 2011 Buffett and Berkshire Hathaway paid US$9 billion to acquire the company Lubrizol, which had just over US$1 billion in pre-tax earnings. This equated to a starting yield of around 11% (US$1 billion / US$9 billion). At the time, Lubrizol was considered a slow-growth company, so we can assume a 3–4% growth rate, which was sufficient to cover expected inflation of about 2–3% and meet Buffett's 10% real return target before tax.

- Lubrizol, 2011:
- Earnings before tax ≈ US$1 billion pre-tax

- Expected growth rate in earnings ≈ 3–4%, or at least as high as the expected inflation of 2–3%
- Purchase price = US$9 billion => starting investment return of 1 billion/9 billion ≈ 11%

Also in 2011, Buffett invested over US$10 billion in IBM stocks. It's publicly known that he paid about US$170 per share. According to SEC filings from that time, IBM earned approximately US$17–18 per share before tax – which aligns closely with Buffett's 10% pre-tax hurdle rate.

IBM was also viewed as a slow-growth company, but had announced a large share-buyback program. This meant that earnings per share (EPS) could be expected to grow faster than inflation, even with modest total earnings growth. On this basis, it's fair to conclude that Buffett saw the investment as meeting his hurdle rate: a 10% pre-tax starting yield, with future EPS growth supported by buybacks.

- IBM, 2011:
- Earnings before tax ≈ US$17-18 per share
- Expected EPS growth rate = at least as high as or higher than inflation
- Purchase price = US$170 per share => starting investment return of US$17–18 per share / 170 per share ≈ 10%

Reviewing examples from Buffett's own writings and discussions and from his known investments on the stock market, it's quite clear that he applies the same hurdle rate for normal-growth companies, regardless of market conditions or interest-rate levels.

So why shouldn't we do the same – and in doing so, fundamentally separate ourselves from the broader stock-market mindset?

26.

Applying the Hurdle Rate to High-Growth Companies

Now let's address our second question about Buffett's hurdle rate: Does Buffett use this 10% hurdle rate regardless of how quickly the company can grow earnings over the coming years?

It should be obvious that a company experiencing high year-over-year earnings growth (say, > 10%) that you are certain will continue for several years offers much greater value and potential returns than a company growing more modestly (say, 5% per year).

A company earning US$5 per share before tax and growing earnings at 5% annually will double its earnings to US$10 in about fifteen years. By contrast, a company starting with the same earnings but growing at 15% annually will double its earnings in less than five years.

Clearly, if both companies are priced equally, the faster-growing business is the more attractive investment, offering much higher long-term returns to the owners.

The first company, growing at 5%, is a classic 10% pre-tax hurdle-rate investment. According to Buffett's framework, he would not pay more than around 10 times US$5 in earnings – or about US$50 per share.

However, it's highly unlikely that Buffett – or indeed you or I – will find a company whose earnings are set to grow at 15% annually for many years trading at just 10 times pre-tax earnings. I must highlight a key point here: it is inherently risky to invest in a company at a high valuation based on the expectation that it will sustain rapid growth for many years.

While it isn't irrational to anticipate strong growth, history is full of cases where lofty projections proved unsustainable and resulted in significant investor losses.

In practice, very few companies – especially large, mature ones – can maintain > 10% annual growth for many years. Even smaller companies with lots of potential rarely sustain 15% annual growth over a long period.

At Berkshire Hathaway's 2004 annual meeting, Buffett confirmed this cautionary view, saying: 'There's a real danger in projecting out high growth rates. And I will very seldom – virtually never – get up into high digits. You can lose a lot of money doing that.'

So, how does Buffett deal with rapid-growth companies?

To answer this, we can look to Alice Schroeder's description of Buffett's approach based on her review of his old investment files. According to Schroeder: 'He just wants a 15% Day-1 return, and then it grows from there.'[8]

If you're wondering how this 15% Day-1 return connects with the 10% hurdle rate, they're actually two sides of the same coin. When you start with a 10% pre-tax return and expect the company to grow earnings at 5% annually, your Day-1 return effectively becomes: 10% (earnings yield) + 5% (growth rate) = 15%.

According to Schroeder, when Buffett invests in fast-growing companies, he simply twists the concept a bit. In those cases, he wants to earn a 15% pre-tax return on his money when the company has doubled its earnings. Let's break this down further. A 15% return on pre-tax earnings when the company has doubled is equivalent to a 7.5% return on today's earnings. In other words, Buffett may be willing to reduce his pre-tax hurdle rate from 10% to around 7.5% pre-tax if he's confident the company will grow fast and double its earnings within a few years. If that happens, his return doubles as well – growing from 7.5% to 15% pre-tax over that period.

THE IMPLIED P/E RATIO FOR HIGH-GROWTH COMPANIES

If the starting point is a 7.5% pre-tax return (and the tax rate is 22%), the after-tax equivalent is 7.5% x (1–22%) = 5.85%. The implied P/E ratio

---

8 Alice Schroeder, author of The Snowball, speaking at the Darden MBA (McIntyre) Value Investing Conference, 2008.

of a 5.85% after-tax return is 1/5.85% = 17.1 (or, in round numbers, 17).

Likewise, when Buffett demands a 7.5% pre-tax return, it is equivalent to a pre-tax P/E ratio of 1/7.5% = 13.33.

The conclusion:

- **For normal-growth companies** Buffett is willing to pay 10 times earnings before tax. This is equal to 13 times after-tax earnings (22% tax rate), which you can use for your investments.
- **For sustainable high-growth companies** Buffett is willing to pay about 13–13.5 times earnings before tax. This is equal to 17 times after-tax earnings (22% tax rate), which you can use for your investments.

The sharp investor will make an interesting observation.

When Buffett invests in normal-growth companies (with around 5% growth), he demands a 7.8% after-tax return (22% tax rate) on his money while the market in general is offering something like 6%, as we discussed. In other words, Buffett gets his margin of safety from an expected higher return than the market delivers on average.

When Buffett invests in high-growth companies, he demands a return of about 5.85% (22% tax rate), or about the same as the market offers in general at around 6%. When investing in high-growth companies, Buffett is willing to pay an average market price, but he demands a much higher growth rate in earnings than the market offers, so the higher growth becomes the margin of safety.

THE HURDLE RATE IN ACTION FOR HIGH-GROWTH COMPANIES

Due to Berkshire Hathaway's immense size and its need to focus on large-cap investments, Buffett rarely finds high-growth opportunities where he can apply a growth-adjusted hurdle rate.

However, this high-growth hurdle rate was likely used in August 2015, when Berkshire announced its acquisition of Precision Castparts

Corp. (PCP). Before the acquisition, SEC filings showed that PCP was earning approximately US$17.4 per share before tax, and the company was growing rapidly – primarily through acquisitions.

Applying the high-growth framework, we would require a 15% pre-tax return on future earnings, assuming those earnings double. If earnings per share grow quickly from US$17.4, doubling to US$34.8, then Buffett would be willing to pay up to: US$34.8 / 15% = US$232 per share. This valuation closely aligns with Buffett's actual acquisition price of US$235 per share.

Here is a summary of the full hurdle-rate framework:

BUFFETT'S HURDLE RATE	Earnings before tax	Earnings after tax (22%)
Normal growth ≈ 5%	10%	7.80%
High growth > 10%	7.50%	5.85%
P/E normal growth	10	12.82 ≈ 13
P/E high growth	13.33	17.1 ≈ 17
THE STOCK MARKET (AVERAGE)	Earnings before tax	Earnings after tax (22%)
Normal growth ≈ 5%	7.80%	6%
High growth > 10%	≈ 2.5–5%	≈ 2–4%
P/E normal growth	12.5	16–17
P/E high growth	≈ 20–40	≈ 25–50
MARGIN OF SAFETY		
Normal growth ≈ 5%	≈ 30% higher return	≈ 30% higher return
High growth > 10%	Much more growth	Much more growth

The key insight from this overview is simple. When Buffett invests in companies with normal growth, he requires a higher return on his investment – measured by the company's pre-tax earnings – than the market average, which he achieves by paying less than the average market price; this is where his margin of safety lies. When Buffett invests in companies at the average market price, he requires significantly higher growth in future earnings than the market average; this is where his margin of safety comes from.

Now that we have established a solid foundation for our investment hurdle rate for both normal- and high-growth companies, let's summarize what we've covered so far:

- The three basic investment principles that form a rational and fundamental platform for our investments
- How to identify and limit our investments to great companies
- How to ensure that our great company is run by excellent management
- Our investment hurdle rate for investing in great companies with both normal and double-digit growth rates
- The margin of safety provided by our hurdle rate – through the extra return compared with the market when investing in normal-growth companies, or through outperforming market growth when investing in high-growth companies

27.

Investing Based on the Future Valuation of the Company

In many areas of life, it is good to consider things from different perspectives before making a commitment. Even when your decision-making is informed by fundamental principles and guidelines and your conclusions follow careful analysis, taking a pause to consider the opposite perspective can be greatly beneficial. The same holds true for the business investor.

One of Charlie Munger's non-negotiable principles was that analysis of any situation or problem should involve starting at the endpoint and working backwards – 'Invert! Always invert!' was his much-cited motto.

While both Warren Buffett and Munger have for decades preached that successful investment requires keeping it simple, that does not mean the processes involved are unsophisticated. Both men are known for thinking deeply and rigorously about every aspect of owning great businesses, including the evaluation of management, understanding the markets in which the company operates, assessing its moat and anticipating how value creation might develop over time.

Let's start with the explanation of inverted thinking that Warren Buffett gave during a 2022 interview with the renowned American journalist Charlie Rose. During the interview, Buffett stated that:

> **'You need the right orientation! […] Ninety per cent of the people – I am pulling the figure out of the air – that buy stocks don't think of them the right way. They think about something that they hope goes up the next day or next week. And they think about the market and hope it goes up – and if goes down they feel worse – I feel better […] I think about what the**

> **company is going to be worth ten or twenty years from now! And I hope it [the stock] goes down when I buy it – because then I will buy more.'[9]**

If you can estimate what your company will be worth at some point in the future, and you know the company's price today, you can, in a straightforward way, calculate the return on your investment. Your return can be calculated as the difference between the company's value in x years and its current price, plus the dividends you receive during that period. In financial terms, this is expressed simply as:

$$\text{return = capital gains + dividends}$$

If you calculate the company's future value – say, five or ten years from now – and compare it with the company's current market value, you can estimate the average annual capital gains you can expect. Adding the return from dividends (dividend / market price) to that gives you the total return.

If your required return is 15% annually, and your calculations show that your average annual return from capital gains plus dividend yield amounts to 15% or more – and if the company and its management meet your standards – then you are, in principle, ready to invest.

HOW BENJAMIN GRAHAM ESTIMATED A COMPANY'S VALUE

In the original first edition of *The Intelligent Investor*, Graham's explanation was consistent with Buffett's:

> **'The aggressive investor should obtain the best available estimates of what a number of stocks are <u>worth</u> [Graham's emphasis] apart from their market price. He will then make his choices from among those**

9 Prosperity Partner, 'Warren Buffett Charlie Rose Full Interview', 26 December 2022 <https://www.youtube.com/watch?v=9UyMLPVCAVY&t=751s> [accessed 24 November 2025].

which are selling at the largest discounts from their indicated values. These values will be based chiefly upon the expected average future earning power, capitalized at a rate which reflects the quality of the issue in view.'[10]

In other words, Benjamin Graham's recommendation was that to determine a company's value, the investor should estimate its future earnings and capitalize (that is, multiply) those earnings with a capitalization factor.

On this basis, we can analyze Buffett's statement: 'I think about what the company is going to be worth ten or twenty years from now.' Buffett devotes his energy to analyzing and assessing a company's fundamentals and management to form an estimate of what the business can be expected to earn ten to twenty years into the future. That projected-earnings figure is then multiplied by a capitalization factor to arrive at the company's estimated value in ten to twenty years. This value can then be compared with the company's current market price, making it straightforward to decide whether a business is attractive to own. This process also makes clear whether Buffett will likely achieve his target of 15% annual return over time.

This way of thinking is a direct consequence of Charlie Munger's principle: 'Invert – always invert!' We begin with the end goal and work backwards to see if the desired return can be achieved when we reach that point. It is simultaneously simple and sophisticated.

It is important not to overlook the return an owner receives in the form of dividends. The stock market gives so much attention to share prices and price movements that dividends are often neglected or forgotten, but they can represent a significant portion of returns. For example, if a company pays a dividend equivalent to 3% of its share price, that alone accounts for one fifth of the required 15% annual return. In other words, the share price would only need to rise by 12% annually for the investor to achieve the full 15% yearly return.

---

10 Graham, 1949.

THE CAPITALIZATION FACTOR

If you know the relevant factors and can reasonably project the average rate at which company earnings will grow, it is not especially difficult to estimate future earnings. For example, if a company's earnings grow by an average of 7% annually over ten years, its earnings will roughly double. Thus, if a company earns US$10 million today and grows at 7% per year, its earnings in ten years will be about US$20 million.

But which capitalization factor did Graham recommend that investors apply – and should we use the same factor for all companies regardless of their characteristics?

This is where the inspiration Buffett took from Graham becomes particularly evident. I will briefly outline Graham's method of determining the capitalization factor, and you will quickly see the connection.

In *The Intelligent Investor*, Graham explains that the key lies in the following 'quality factors' that determine how high the capitalization factor should be.

The company's general long-term prospects

A company's long-term outlook naturally depends on its ability to protect earnings through a moat and the extent to which the company and its industry benefit from tailwinds or face headwinds in the form of megatrends. All else being equal, the greater the business and the higher the expected long-term growth rate, the higher the capitalization factor.

Management

According to Graham:

> **'It is fair to assume that an outstanding successful company has unusually good management. This will have shown itself already in the past record; it will show up again in the estimates [of earnings] in the next**

five years, and once more in the previously discussed factor of long-term prospects. The tendency to count it still another time as a separate bullish consideration can easily lead to expensive overvaluation.'[11]

In other words, excellent management holds significant value, but this value should be accounted for only once – this can be in the current earnings capacity, the future earnings potential, or in the capitalization factor, but not in all three.

Buffett's focus on 'investing in great businesses – run by excellent management' is fully aligned with the qualities Graham outlines here.

Financial strength and capital structure

Graham states succinctly that, all else being equal, a company with plenty of cash and no debt is clearly a better investment than a company burdened with significant debt and financial obligations. Essentially, the stronger the financial position, the higher the capitalization factor.

Dividend record and current dividend rate

In 1949, when Graham wrote *The Intelligent Investor*, investors had yet to become sophisticated in their approach to what's now called capital allocation. At that time, it was common to evaluate companies primarily on their ability to pay dividends to shareholders each year. While this approach is not wrong per se, it is neither fully comprehensive nor entirely accurate.

Updating Graham's perspective for today's landscape requires consideration of both a company's ability to generate free cash flow and management's ability to rationally allocate earnings and other capital. If two companies have the same earnings and expected growth, the company that can grow without the need for substantial capital (and that can therefore return a significant portion of profits to shareholders as dividends) will be worth more than the company forced to reinvest a large portion of earnings to finance growth.

---

11 Graham, 1949.

* * *

The next step is to establish the relevant capitalization factor. According to *The Intelligent Investor*, the best companies – based on the above criteria – should be capitalized with a factor of 20. In other words, estimated earnings are multiplied by 20 to arrive at the company's future value. This corresponds to an earnings yield of 5% (1/20) and roughly matches the risk-free rate.

For companies with slightly less attractive (or average) characteristics, a capitalization factor of 15 to 16 – which equals the historical market average – may be used, while less appealing companies might justify a factor of only 10 to 12. Some companies may be of such poor quality that they are not worth investing in at all.

One of the greatest advantages of this approach to company valuation is that it incorporates both projected future earnings and the company's fundamental qualities – whether management or financial strength. This brings a new dimension to Buffett's classic pre-tax investment hurdle rate of 10% real return (inflation adjusted), which initially does not consider qualitative evaluations. As Graham rightly emphasized repeatedly: 'Price is what you pay – value is what you get!'

A PRACTICAL METHOD FOR APPLYING FUTURE VALUATION

Let's try to combine Buffett's focus on a company's future worth – and associated risks – with Graham's considerations of future earnings power and the capitalization factor. In this way, we can build a rationale that works within established frameworks and provides a solid foundation for investment.

In recent years, the risk-free rate has generally been in the range of 4–5%. It has also been higher and lower at times, but we can assume economic growth of roughly 2–2.5% on average, with inflation contributing a similar amount, for a total of around 4–5%. Using this as a minimum yield leads to a capitalization factor of approximately 20–25 (1/0.05

– 1/0.04). Historically, the market has averaged a capitalization factor of 16–17. Naturally, lower-quality companies should offer a significantly higher return to compensate for the increased uncertainty and risk. It is therefore entirely rational to apply a capitalization factor of, for example, 10 –12 for such companies – perhaps even lower, depending on their situation. However, it is important to remember that we are fundamentally seeking 'great businesses – run by excellent management'; according to Charlie Munger, it is often preferable to invest in such companies even if they initially appear expensive.

Tempting as it is, it is also reasonable to avoid the assumption that a company's earnings will grow at very high rates for many consecutive years in the future. Most companies grow at 4–6% per year; some may grow at around 8%; but very few sustain growth above 10% per year over a long period. Short-term growth can exceed 10%, but assuming high growth rates when estimating a company's future value can be quite risky. In other words, when projecting future earnings, it is most appropriate to use growth rates of no more than 10% per year.

Regarding the time horizon, it is not essential to apply a specific number of years or to follow Buffett in valuing a company ten to twenty years into the future. Given the enormous capital he manages and his permanent ownership of many businesses, Buffett looks very far ahead because he cannot 'move around in the market' like the average investor. As he has explained, his preferred holding period is 'forever'. This is natural for him but not for the typical investor. For the average investor, it's about thinking long-term while also taking advantage of the significant discrepancies that occasionally arise between a company's market price and its intrinsic value. In other words, think long-term but also exploit the shorter-term opportunities that Mr. Market provides.

Empirical studies have shown that, in most cases, the market corrects itself and individual companies trend back towards fair value within three to five years. Put differently, if you base your valuation on what the company will be worth in five years, there is a high probability that the market value will eventually align with the company's true value within that period.

Here is the practical valuation, aligned with the thinking of Buffett, Graham and Charlie Munger.

future value year five = (estimated earnings year five – *maximum annual growth 10%)* **× (capitalization factor** – *maximum 25)*.

Let us use a practical example for a company with an expected annual growth rate of 8%, where we set the capitalization factor at 20. Let's also assume that the current earnings are US$10 million with 10 million outstanding shares – giving earnings per share of US$1. These earnings grow at 8% per year over the next five years, resulting in earnings in year five of US$1.47 per share. (To calculate this, multiply the current earnings per share, US$1, by 1.08 five times: $1 \times 1.08 \times 1.08 \times 1.08 \times 1.08 \times 1.08 = 1.47$.)

Applying the expected capitalization factor of 20, the future value of the company per share is $1.47 \times 20 =$ US$29.4.

We can then ask ourselves: *What price am I willing to pay if I require a 15% annual return and the value per share in five years is US$29.4?*

Ignoring any potential dividends, the answer is roughly half the price: = US$14.7 per share. This is due to the simple fact that a compounded 15% annual return approximately doubles the value over five years ($14.7 \times 1.15 \times 1.15 \times 1.15 \times 1.15 \times 1.15 \approx 29.4$).

As an individual investor, you must also include the company's dividend payments as part of the return calculations, as discussed above. The larger the annual dividend relative to the company's present market value, the smaller the required annual increase in market value to achieve your target return – whether that target is set at 15% per year or another rate.

We have now further developed Buffett's investment hurdle rate based on his own statements, combined with Graham's recommendations in *The Intelligent Investor*, while prioritizing ownership of great businesses, run by excellent management, for the long term.

In our example, we maintain our hurdle rate at 15% Day-1 return based on future valuation. The complete formula for calculating our return is:

earnings year five × capitalization factor = business value year five

(business value year five / present market price) ^ (1/5) – 1 = annual expected capital gain in %

When you then add the expected annual dividend as a percentage of the current market value (dividend yield), you arrive at the total expected return:

annual return = expected capital gain in % + expected dividend yield in %

EXAMPLE CALCULATIONS OF ANNUAL RETURN BASED ON FUTURE VALUATION

Now let's illustrate the method with three different examples, each contributing in its own way to a broader understanding of the flexibility and robustness of calculating annual returns based on future valuation.

Company 1

Current earnings per share (EPS): US$1
Expected annual earnings growth: 10%
Capitalization factor: 25
Dividends: None
Present share price: US$22

EPS year five = US$1 × (1 + 10%) ^ 5 = US$1.61
Business value year five = 25 × US$1.61 = US$40.25
Annual expected capital gain (%) = (40.25 / 22) ^ (1/5) − 1 = 12.84%

As the company is not expected to pay any dividends, our expected annual return over the next five years is 12.84%, which is below our hurdle rate of 15%.

If we had set a hurdle rate of 8% to 10%, which roughly aligns with the historical average annual market return, we would have adjusted our buy threshold accordingly. Remember, the hurdle rate you choose is your decision – but always ensure a solid margin of safety.

Working with the numbers, you can see that Company 1 will deliver a 15% return if you can buy the shares at US$20 compared to the current share price of US$22 – a decline of only 10% is required.

I mention this as a teaser for deeper thinking. As Charlie Munger often notes, it can sometimes be worth paying up for a great company. If you have found a fantastic, long-lasting compounder that will continue to deliver for the next five, ten, or twenty years, the difference between paying US$22 or US$20 per share may not be critical. As Warren Buffett said, you need the right orientation!

Company 2

Current earnings per share (EPS): US$1
Expected annual earnings growth: 5%
Capitalization factor: 16
Dividend: US$0.50
Present share price: US$13

EPS year five = US$1 × (1 + 5%) ^ 5 = US$1.28
Business value year five = 16 × US$1.28 = US$20.48
Annual expected capital gain (%) = (20.48 / 13) ^ (1/5) – 1 = 9.52%
Expected dividend yield = US$0.50 / 13 = 3.85%
Annual total return = 9.52% + 3.85% = 13.37%

Company 2 pays a respectable dividend, but it is insufficient to achieve our target 15% annual return. However, compared with the historical average annual market return of approximately 8–10%, the investment provides an acceptable margin of safety. Most investors would seriously consider an investment offering an annual expected return above 13% in an average-quality company with a capitalization factor of around 16.

Company 3

Current earnings per share (EPS): US$1
Expected annual earnings growth: 8%
Capitalization factor: 20
Dividend: US$0.25
Present share price: US$15

EPS year five = US$1 × (1 + 8%) ^ 5 = US$1.47
Business value year five = 20 × US$1.47 = US$29.4
Annual expected capital gain (%) = (29.4 / 15) ^ (1/5) – 1 = 14.41%
Expected dividend yield = US$0.25 / 15 = 1.67%
Annual total return = 14.41% + 1.67% = 16.08%

With an expected annual return of 16%, it is likely time to push the buy button. The investment is projected to deliver a strong return and offers a solid margin of safety compared to market returns of roughly 8–10%.

An important consideration is that you must decide your hurdle rate independently; 15% is simply a realistic, conservative example that I use myself. It is also likely that actual returns over a five-year period may exceed 15% from time to time. When this occurs – and you have already invested at a level that reflected a 15% expected return – it is up to you to take advantage of further declines in the share price, allowing you to invest with an even higher expected return. As Buffett emphasizes, he feels great when the share price drops after he has invested because it gives him an opportunity to buy more at even better returns.

RISK CONSIDERATIONS WHEN USING FUTURE VALUATION

Let us begin by evaluating the maximum price, relative to current earnings, that we could pay for a company based on this investment approach and the parameters we have established.

This situation arises when a company is expected to grow 10% per year, distributes all its earnings as dividends and is assigned a capitalization factor of 25. The current share price that would result in an expected return of 15% is approximately US$24.06 ≈ 24.

Here are the calculations:

EPS year five = US$1 × (1 + 10%) ^ 5 = US$1.61
Business value year five = 25 × US$1.61 = US$40.25
Annual expected capital gain (%) = (40.25 / 24.06) ^ (1/5) − 1
= 10.85%
Expected dividend yield = US$1 / 24.06 = 4.15%
Annual total return = 10.85% + 4.15% = 15.00%

In other words, our 15% hurdle rate, combined with a maximum assumed growth rate of 10% over five years and a maximum capitalization factor of 25, ensures that we cannot pay more than US$24 per dollar of earnings for a company that is expected to grow 10% annually and that is also able to distribute all earnings to shareholders via dividends or share buybacks. Warren Buffett has referred to such businesses as 'double rifle' companies, where owners benefit from both free growth and dividends. According to Buffett, these companies are the most valuable to own and true compounders.

Our goal is also to avoid an investment framework that leads us to invest in numerous highly priced growth companies. Instead, our aim is to make conservative investments in great businesses for the long run.

I have intentionally not addressed the issue of taxation on dividends and capital gains above, as these vary widely between countries. Investors should, of course, adjust for local tax considerations.

To reiterate:

> **The most important factor is not whether you pay 3–5% more or less for a great business run by excellent management; it's that you do not invest in companies where the underlying valuation assumes extremely high growth over many years or where the applied capitalization factor is unrealistic.**

Over the years, I have seen even well-regarded financial institutions use calculations based on an annual growth rate of 25% over a ten-year period. I have likewise seen purchase recommendations for companies at a capitalization factor of 100. Keep your feet on the ground!

We'll end this chapter with a repetition of Warren Buffett's most famous quote: 'Rule number one is not to lose your money; rule number two is not to forget rule number one!'

Now, let's turn to the important question of when it is appropriate to sell your company.

28.
When to Sell Your Company

When it comes to selling your company, it's important to think carefully about your reasons for doing so. If you're thinking like a business owner, you will be aware that it's almost always a mistake to sell a great business! You should also bear in mind that you don't make money buying or selling stocks; you make money while you own the company.

That doesn't mean you should never sell your shares in a company. But it is not rational to sell simply because the stock price has gone up or down significantly. As a rational, long-term investor, you sell your stocks when the original reasons for buying them no longer apply.

There are four rational reasons to sell your shares in a great company:

- *The company's moat is diminishing* – as the moat is the source of the company's enduring advantage, its disappearance leads to declining returns on invested capital.
- *Growth has stalled* – within either the company or the broader industry, making it difficult for earnings to keep pace with inflation over time.
- *Management is underperforming* – they're no longer allocating capital rationally or their operational focus and discipline is declining.
- *The valuation no longer justifies ownership* – future earnings, even years ahead, can't deliver the required returns that match general market returns.

All four reasons relate to the company's fundamentals and outlook. As an investor, it's your job to monitor these areas with the same focus you applied to your initial investment. That means watching the strength of the moat and the return on capital, evaluating whether earnings growth can continue at a sufficient pace, and assessing whether management remains focused and rational.

When the company's valuation becomes particularly high, consider whether long-term earnings potential still supports the price. If not, it may be time to sell.

An additional rational reason for selling is that you've found a more attractive investment opportunity. In that case, it makes sense to sell shares in the least attractive company in your portfolio and reallocate the capital.

However, before you switch investments, ask yourself whether it would be more rational to reinvest the capital into one of the companies you already own. Your real opportunity cost is the expected return of your best current investment. Why invest in the eleventh- or twelfth-best investment with a 10% or even 15% expected return on your money if your best investment earns 25% and you still have room to invest more?

Finally, remember that you likely have a deep understanding of the company you already own – far deeper than your understanding of a new prospect. Investors often overestimate how well they know a new business, only to later discover that they missed something important.

This risk is hard to quantify, which is why it's essential to ensure a wide margin of safety when considering any new investment.

Key takeaways from Part V

- All company valuations are based on the variables you choose. That means every valuation is ultimately a judgement – not a fact.
- The DCF model is the theoretically correct way to value a business but is hopeless in practice.
- Everybody in the financial sector uses the DCF – and that gives you a great opportunity to do something different.
- If you use Warren Buffett's investment hurdle rate you'll think like a business owner.

- When you invest and evaluate the results, you must look at the business and its earnings – not the stock price.
- If you apply Buffett's hurdle rate, you demand a 10% pre-tax return on your money and a growth rate of about 5% when you invest in normal-growth companies.
- When you invest in high-growth companies, you should demand a 15% pre-tax return on your money when the company has doubled in sales and earnings.
- If you use the future valuation method, you estimate the future value of the company by estimating its future earnings and multiplying them by a reasonable capitalizations factor. When comparing the future value of the company with its present value, you can estimate your annual capital gains; together with the dividend yield, the expected capital gains give you the expected annual returns.
- Annual return = expected capital gain (%) + dividend yield (%).
- If you are still working or saving money, you should cheer for lower stock prices – they will support a higher return on your money over the long run.
- Thinking like a business owner, you know that you don't make your money buying and selling your stocks – you make your money while owning your company.
- It is almost always a mistake to sell a great company.
- You sell your company only when the reasons you bought it no longer exist.
- Your real opportunity cost is the expected return of your best current investment.
- It makes no sense to invest in the eleventh- or twelfth-best investment with a 10% or even 15% expected return on your money if your best investment earns 25% and you still have room to invest more.

PART VI:
Understanding Yourself is the Most Important Factor

29.
Investment is a Test of Character

As you gain experience as an investor, you'll discover that reading reports, analyzing financials and calculating your hurdle rate are not the most challenging or decisive factors for success. In time, your ability to assess whether a company is a truly great business – and whether it is led by outstanding management – will become the most critical skill for sound decision-making. Regardless of whether you're analyzing an interesting company to invest in, making the investment itself, being an owner of the company, or eventually deciding to sell, the crucial thing to acknowledge is that *you* are the only constant factor in this process.

Understanding yourself as a decision-maker and what makes up your 'investment DNA' is without a doubt the most important factor.

The only way to remove yourself from the equation is to hand over your investments to a money manager – and even that would be an investment decision made by…you.

Investing is, therefore, first and foremost about temperament, with you as the lead actor. So, to make the most of this insight, you must analyze yourself and how you make decisions. Without self-awareness, I dare say that your chances of achieving long-term investment success are extremely minimal.

EXAMPLES OF INAPPROPRIATE INVESTMENT TEMPERAMENT

It is easy to make mistakes in your investment work when you let emotions rule your decisions and actions instead of thinking rationally. The most common and widespread sign of an inappropriate investment temperament is when a person checks the price of his or her stocks several times a day. This behavior triggers the feeling of whether you have 'won or lost' today. The rational investor, who thinks like a long-term co-owner of a company, does not look at stock prices several times a day. This investor focuses on news from the company, which they study and analyze to see whether the investment case has changed – whether the company's long-term earnings power has improved or deteriorated.

Another common temperamental mistake is selling 'winners' instead of selling stocks in a company that has been a loser for you. In investment parlance, you 'cut your flowers and water your weeds'. Often this behavior is driven by the feeling that liquidating an investment means you've once again either 'won or lost' – and the desire to appear as a winner, especially to yourself, is very human.

Most people learn that there's usually a very good reason why a company and its stock has become more valuable. In the vast majority of cases it is because things are going well: the business and its earnings are growing, and management is doing a good job. Correspondingly, there's usually a good reason why a company has become less valuable over the years. Generally, it is because things are not going well for the business and management is struggling to perform. The rational investor recognizes this and realizes that it is most likely best to sell the poor performer and keep the value-creating business.

The desire to appear successful to others can fuel another bad behavior that blurs our rationale. Telling the outside world about our investment successes while neglecting to mention the investments that have done less well, or where we've suffered a big loss, presents a positively distorted picture of our performance and accomplishments.

The rational thinker is comfortable with the fact that as investors we make mistakes, and is unafraid to talk about them. This investor also knows that short-term investment results are basically irrelevant. It's the long-term results, and how we conduct our investment work, that are worth discussing and reflecting on.

Another widespread and inappropriate behavior is spontaneous and impulsive investment decision-making in response to the strong feelings caused by some piece of information. The two emotions that typically drive irrational split-second decisions are the fear of 'losing' or the hope of 'winning'. These emotions generate huge volatility when they strike many active investors in the market at once. The stock market either soars because most participants hope and believe that big gains are coming – or, conversely, virtually everyone panics and sells off in a frenzy, driven by fear of losing everything. This phenomenon of whipsaw volatility can also take place at industry or company level.

In these situations, the rational investor acts in the opposite way and becomes, as Warren Buffett so rightly put it, 'greedy when everyone else is fearful and fearful when everyone else is greedy'.

So how do you analyze yourself as an investor and figure out whether you have the right temperament – or what it takes to develop it?

This analysis should be as structured and rational as your investment analysis of businesses and management. The challenge is that you will be unable to carry out this self-analysis until you have made several investments – both buying and selling. However, the biggest hurdle will likely not be your lack of experience but your ability to remain honest with yourself.

To help you with this undertaking as best I can, I will now go through my own self-analysis instead of describing the process of 'understanding yourself' in generic terms.

30.

Analyzing Yourself and Your Investment Decisions

Before you begin analyzing your investment decisions and yourself as an investor, you should spend time thinking about and reviewing the biggest decisions you've made in your life more generally and how you arrived at them.

Why start here?

Because your investment decisions and your investment work will always be heavily influenced by who you are as a person and the way you function and act in general.

Think about it. It is rare that a spontaneous and impulsive person who lives a fast-paced private life with little structure or discipline will be a calm and well-considered stock investor – someone who considers all the probabilities before making and executing decisions. Conversely, a very anxious person who is constantly worried that something will go wrong, and who easily gets sick to the stomach from fear of making poor decisions, will likely find it hard to remain calm and take advantage of opportunities when the stock market takes a big dive for one reason or another.

THE BIGGEST GENERAL DECISIONS

To give you an idea of how reflecting on your major life decisions can reveal important insights about yourself and your temperament, here is a non-exhaustive list of my own most significant business-related decisions. Each of them offers some understanding of my personality as a private person and as an investor. You should look for similar 'defining decisions and personal priorities' in your own life.

166

- I drew up a 'life plan' when I was thirteen, while on a skiing vacation with my parents in Norway. It was, of course, naive, but it included a goal that has guided much of my life – and particularly my investment work. Even back then, about fifty years ago, I knew I wanted to become a lifelong learner and continue to educate myself throughout my life. I later realized that you cannot become a successful long-term stock investor if you are unwilling to keep learning. Being a long-term investor is no different from being a business owner – you cannot remain successful unless you constantly learn about your industry and your business, and understand your position and competitive strength relative to the expected future. The world, your industry and your business are always changing. The only constant in the business world is change, so you must stay curious and keep learning.

- I made my first investment aged thirteen, when my father helped me buy 12% bonds with the money I received as a confirmation gift – about US$200. At fourteen, I started a job delivering newspapers at 3.30 a.m. each day and worked an entire summer holiday at a warehouse to save US$1,000, which I used to buy one kilo of silver – a 'hot investment' in the mid-1970s. (Unfortunately, I was cheated and defrauded, and after seven years of litigation I recovered only US$140 of my money.) At the time, I didn't realize the pattern in my behavior, but I've since come to see that I decided early on to work hard and save money, even if it meant postponing consumption until later in life.

- I've always been quite good at math and had a strong ability to remember numbers and other factual information. This led me to pursue a financial education and a master's degree in finance from Copenhagen Business School. But as soon as I graduated, I accepted a job as a financial journalist at Denmark's leading newspaper, Berlingske. At the time, I couldn't imagine a better learning environment – I was able to call CEOs of all the major Danish companies, asking questions

and gaining a lot of knowledge and insights from management
in big companies. Later, I became the paper's business editor,
which gave me access to international corporations and their
CEOs as well. While my salary wasn't particularly high, I received
a world-class education in high-level business. In other words, I
chose learning over earning.

- At thirty-five, I started my own business, PROSPECT, which I ran
  for fifteen years. PROSPECT was a consultancy firm, advising
  boards and management in listed companies and private-
  equity groups about financial and strategic communication.
  My work in PROSPECT laid the foundations for me to think like
  a business owner and understand management thinking and
  high-level business issues – the 'owner approach' and business
  understanding I have applied to investing since becoming a
  full-time investor in 2009.

- I've lived my entire life in the same city – a quiet suburb 25
  kilometers north of Copenhagen, Denmark. I've never had
  expensive hobbies and have always lived in an ordinary home.
  In terms of my personality as an investor, this clearly reflects that
  I think long-term and have little desire to move around or 'show
  off'. I'm most comfortable co-owning the same businesses for
  many years, and I usually make just one or two investments
  a year. Often, it's simply adding to an existing position in a
  company I already co-own. Some years, I make no changes to
  my portfolio at all.

Analyzing these key decisions helped me build a deeper understanding of
my investor profile and of how I function as an investor generally. I do think
long-term, and I'm quite patient – sometimes too patient. I also strongly
identify with the business-owner mindset. I enjoy learning about new
companies and understanding how they operate. My journalistic background
means I naturally gather information and use it to build a narrative: the
investment case. I'm more of a saver than a spender. I don't chase flashy
investments like silver – been there, done that, learned my lesson.

When you reflect on yourself in the same way, the conclusions you
draw about yourself will almost certainly differ from mine – and so will

your investor profile. You might feel that you'll never become a seasoned, patient and shrewd investor. But let me emphasize that no one starts out fully formed, not even successful investors. It takes time to build the experience and insight needed to understand how you function as an investor.

However, I can offer a significant point of encouragement. Unlike many other disciplines, investing is built on the accumulation of knowledge. In other words, what you learn today, or this year, can be applied for the rest of your investment career.

Let me give you a few examples. Once you've learned to think long term and to avoid being swayed by short-term fluctuations on the stock market, that lesson sticks. The same investment philosophy you adopt today will still apply ten, twenty, or even thirty years from now.

Likewise, when you learn how to read the signals in a management team's thinking and begin to understand what different situations tend to reveal beneath the surface, that insight will remain relevant five, ten, or twenty years down the line. The leadership team you'll be evaluating in a decade will almost certainly be working in a completely different industry, but human psychology and behavior don't change.

Your task is to accumulate knowledge and experience – as quickly as possible.

ANALYZING YOUR INVESTMENT WORK

So far, so good – but my general analysis doesn't say much about how I've actually made my investment decisions. So:

- How did I conduct my investment research?
- How did I make and carry out my investment decisions?
- Once invested in a company, how did I behave as a co-owner?
- How did I ultimately decide to sell my shares and stop being a co-owner of the company?

To build the full picture about my temperament, I had to go through all my investments one by one, from start to finish.

The amount of data you'll have to analyze your investments and identify your character traits will depend on how many years you've been working as an investor. The good news is that after no more than five to ten investments and the first three to five decisions to sell, you'll begin to see patterns in how you operate and start to understand yourself better.

If you're at the other end of the spectrum and have many years of investment experience, you might believe that you already have it under control and know yourself well. And you probably do, to some extent. But even as a very experienced investor, this kind of analysis will deepen your knowledge and insight about yourself.

I can guarantee that you will continue to make mistakes. So, remember to use those situations as opportunities to learn more about yourself and figure out how you can improve.

HOW DO YOU CONDUCT YOUR INVESTMENT RESEARCH?

The first element of the analysis is in fact the most personal. How people find potentially interesting companies to invest in, how they begin researching them and how they continue monitoring a specific company will vary greatly from individual to individual. Here are several research methods I've used over the years:

- You can use various online stock-screener tools to scan the market and identify companies that, based on key figures, pass initial filters and appear interesting. Once you've narrowed the list, you can start taking a closer look at each of the companies that made it through your filters and lie within your circle of competence.

- Using resources like Value Line or Morningstar, you can review companies one by one and see which ones catch your attention. Every year, I go through Morningstar's factsheet of all Nordic-listed companies on the OMX NASDAQ, which includes companies from Denmark, Finland, Norway and Sweden – and each year, I find something of interest.

- You probably read business news and some industry magazines. When a company is described in a way that you find interesting, you can dig deeper by reading its annual report and other relevant materials.

- You can identify generally attractive businesses and begin subscribing to their reports and announcements, which are then delivered to your inbox for review. Over time, I've focused my investment universe and research on around seventy 'great businesses' listed on the Nordic stock exchanges and I subscribe to their announcements. I also read the press release every time a company goes public (IPO) in the Nordics. If an IPO company seems to have an appealing business model, I start following it and it becomes part of my investment universe.

- You can also read research and equity reports from various analysts. There's nothing inherently wrong with this, but be aware that investment based on an analyst's report means relying on someone else's assessments. Also, equity analysts work for brokerage firms whose goal is to encourage trading – buying or selling – so the firm can earn commissions. In short, you're not in the same boat as the analyst.

- One of the simplest and most effective research methods is also free – and fun. Just look around you. Observe what people are buying and how your friends and family and young people spend their time and money. When you spot a popular product or emerging trend, look into the companies behind it – this could uncover an interesting investment opportunity.

- Lastly, you can take part in forums where likeminded investors meet to present and discuss specific investment cases. You can then conduct your own in-depth analysis based on the ideas and feedback shared.

The best way to conduct structured and consistent research is to make reading part of your daily routine. Most private investors have jobs outside their investment activities and need to do their reading in the evenings or at weekends. Regardless of when it fits into your schedule, it's crucial to incorporate reading into your routine.

Being an investor is largely about spending time gathering information and slowly building knowledge about specific industries or companies.

Professional investors or money managers can find it easier to allocate time for research, but daily distractions and the urge to constantly follow the market can limit effectiveness. Don't forget that spending too much time tracking market movements can be largely unproductive. At the end of the day, you haven't really accomplished anything.

Of course, it makes sense to pay attention to Mr. Market when volatility is high and stock prices swing wildly. These moments can present excellent opportunities to buy when the market is deeply depressed or to sell when prices are unreasonably high. But stock prices remain within reasonable bounds 90% of the time and tracking the market hour by hour – or even day by day – is a waste of time.

In my own research, I am always looking for great businesses that might be of interest. As I mentioned, I closely follow seventy companies and keep an eye on roughly twice that number. Those seventy companies are all high-quality businesses, but most of them are currently priced so high that the expected returns have no chance of meeting my hurdle rate. However, prices may eventually fall, and the companies might become attractive investment opportunities.

All the companies I follow are, in one way or another, either excellent businesses or part of important industries that are worth monitoring – whether that's thanks to exposure to significant megatrends or because they serve as good indicators of broader market movements. Some are competitors of businesses I already own and are important to follow.

The goal of your research and reading is not to discover a new attractive investment every week or every month. The purpose of a structured and continuous research process is twofold: first, to build the fundamental knowledge required to recognize a good opportunity when it appears and then be able to act with a prepared mind; and second, to steadily expand your circle of competence and develop a clear picture of which industries and companies you genuinely understand.

What matters is not how large your circle of competence is, but how deep your knowledge goes – and that you are fully aware of where the boundaries lie. You can succeed as an investor only if you remain disciplined and make your investments within this circle.

HOW DO YOU MAKE YOUR INVESTMENTS?

For some people, making an investment can be quite exciting – it's like the beginning of a new relationship. But remember, the relationship must be formed between you and the company, not between you and the stock price. When you make an investment decision, you chose to become an owner of the business and should begin to see yourself as part of the company's present and future.

The decision to invest should not revolve around paying some cash to get the stocks and then simply watching the stock price to see if it turns out to be a successful investment. The investment decision makes sense only when your reasoning is sound: when you are laying out money today to buy a part of a business because your analysis has convinced you that the company's future earnings power will enable it to return significantly more money to you over time. Simultaneously, you expect the increase in earnings to drive up the value of the company and thus increase the stock price over time. If your analysis is correct and the company's management allocates capital rationally, your investment will become successful.

The best way to stay grounded in these fundamental truths when making investment decisions is to always remind yourself that stock prices can go anywhere in the short term – but the stock's direction and destination are largely determined by earnings per share in the long term.

It is far more important to focus on estimating a company's future earnings power than to fixate on the exact purchase price. If you have conducted your analysis rationally and are reasonably accurate in your projections for earnings five to ten years ahead, and providing your estimated returns align with your hurdle rate, it won't matter much whether you pay 2% more or less for the stock.

Let's look at an example. After a thorough analysis of the company's fundamentals, you conclude that it's a great business run by excellent management. You determine that the current earnings of about US$8 million before tax reflect the company's normal earnings power. You conservatively estimate that the company will grow earnings by 8% per year for the next decade – a solid growth rate over that time span and considerably higher than the expected inflation rate.

According to your hurdle rate of 10% real return before tax, you are willing to buy the company at US$80 million.

Fast forward ten years and you were right. The company has grown earnings at 8% per year and now makes US$17.3 million before tax – more than double the initial figure. That means your return on the original investment has risen from 10% to 21.6% (17.3 / 80); and, as we know, *stocks follow earnings per share*, so it is very likely that the value of your investment has appreciated accordingly. On top of that, you've probably received a substantial amount in dividends – or perhaps management reinvested the earnings wisely to your benefit and that of your fellow shareholders.

Of course, you don't get the appreciation of the value of your stocks in your hand, just like you don't get the increase value of your house or apartment paid out as 'money in hand'. But if you decide to capitalize part of your returns besides the dividends you get paid, you can simply sell some of your stocks.

Now, does it really matter if you paid exactly US$80 million for the company or 2% more – US$81.6 million? Not really. At US$81.6 million, your return on your original investment would be 21.2% after ten years, and dividends and capital allocation would have been the same.

Providing you pay close to the sum implied by your hurdle rate, you're on relatively safe ground – *if* your business analysis is correct. Problems arise when your analysis is flawed and you end up paying a much higher price than you should have done.

Let's say you misjudged the company's earnings power and growth rate. Instead of US$8 million pre-tax, the company's normalized earnings are only US$6 million pre-tax. And instead of 8% annual growth over the next ten years, earnings grow by just 4%.

After ten years, the company's pre-tax earnings are only US$8.9 million – barely more than the (incorrect) number you used to make your original decision. That being the case, your return will still hover around 10% – but it's well below expectations, and the dividends you receive will also be much lower than anticipated.

In hindsight, you shouldn't have paid anywhere near US$80 million. In fact, you probably shouldn't have bought the company at all. A 4% annual growth rate barely keeps pace with inflation – assuming inflation remains below 4% during the decade.

The conclusion should be clear: it is far more important to get your analysis of the company and its future earnings power right than to worry about paying 2% more or less. The key question when making and carrying out an investment is: are you investing in a great business with strong earnings growth, or in a mediocre one with limited prospects?

Here are some of the most common reasons investors make random or irrational investment decisions:

- *Emotional bias toward a megatrend or industry.* An investor believes an emerging trend will create enormous value and invests on hope – without using a conservative hurdle rate or assessing whether industry growth will translate into strong earnings growth.
- *Fear of missing out (FOMO).* An investor sees a stock price rising rapidly and jumps in without using the hurdle rate or analyzing the fundamentals of the business and its future earnings.
- *Overreaction to falling prices.* An investor notices that a stock has dropped dramatically and assumes it must now be a bargain, as present earnings compared with the present share price meet the hurdle rate. But the investor invests without thoroughly examining the company's prospects, forgetting that a stock that has already been reduced by half from US$100 to US$50 can still fall another 50% to US$25 if the prospects are mediocre.
- *Personal identification with the product.* An investor loves a company's product and feels good about it, so they decide to buy the stock without using the hurdle rate and regardless of the company's actual financials and prospects.

As a stock investor, you must analyze your past investments and honestly assess what motivated each one. Go through your buying and selling decisions. Once you've done that, you'll quickly begin to see whether your investments were based on emotion or on solid analysis of the company's future earnings potential – assessed with consideration of your core investment principles and hurdle rate.

That said, it would be naive to assume that any investor can always be entirely unemotional and purely rational. But you can get close – and that is the ongoing challenge and goal for every serious stock investor: stay rational and be patient – very patient!

HOW DO YOU ACT AS A BUSINESS OWNER?

You would need to be a fairly large co-owner of a company to be able to call the chairman, CEO, or CFO and ask for a meeting to discuss the company's general situation and financial performance, or to put to them even more detailed questions about management's operational decisions and capital allocation. But all investors have access to and can read the company's reports and announcements, and can follow various investor presentations online. You may also be able to participate in the company's general meeting.

Furthermore, the vast majority of listed companies have an investor-relations department that all investors can contact and ask questions. So why not do that, if your objective is to learn as much as possible about your company? In my experience, most private investors tend to refrain from contacting the company and asking questions – which is something I have always found regrettable and inappropriate, from an investor's point of view.

You must always bear in mind that as a stockholder you are one of the owners of the company. The board and management work for you – you are the boss! Therefore, you absolutely have the right to contact the company and ask any questions you may have. To me, it seems natural that you have a responsibility to yourself as co-owner and that being proactive is part of taking your ownership seriously, ensuring that you're in the best possible position to assess the company's development.

There are no first-class shareholders and second-class shareholders. The only difference between two shareholders is the number of shares they own and their relative voting power. But voting power does not give the large shareholder any special rights when it comes to information and the right to ask questions.

WHY DO YOU DECIDE TO SELL YOUR STOCKS?

At some point, the time will come when you decide to sell your stocks. The decision to sell is central to long-term investment performance and is much more complex than the decision to buy.

This is because of the simple fact that people won't usually have co-owned the companies they are buying stocks in and have no prior financial relationship with them – unless they are buying more shares in a company they already own, or, more rarely, deciding to reinvest in a company they previously owned but sold.

Hopefully, by the time you sell your shares in a company, you will have shared a long history together. You will have built up a great deal of knowledge about the business and the industry, and you'll understand how management thinks. In other words, you'll be about to say goodbye to something you know well and have spent a lot of time on. The company you're selling has, we hope, delivered an increased value of your stocks over the years and maybe also some dividends that have contributed to your growing wealth – or perhaps it has underperformed and even caused you losses. No matter how the business has performed, it is very easy to be influenced by emotions when considering a sale. But remember, the stock doesn't know who you are and that you are the owner of it. The stock has no emotions about who owns it – so why should you let your decisions be guided by emotions?

Your task is to review all your sales decisions and explain to yourself why you sold. On this basis, you will slowly build an image of yourself as a seller. The most important aspect of your sales analysis is to uncover the extent to which your decisions to sell have been made solely on a rational basis – and how often you've allowed emotions to influence the outcome.

31.

The Characteristics of Your Most Successful Investments and Biggest Failures

Once you have analyzed all your investment decisions, you should have a very clear picture of how you conduct research, how and why you invest, what you do while holding a company, and how and why you eventually decide to sell. You will realize that you have carried out an extremely important analysis of yourself, your temperament as an investor and your overall investment approach. Now, it's time to take this analysis to the next level.

Being as honest as you can with yourself, you need to look at both your most successful investments and those that became your biggest failures and identify the defining characteristics of your winners and losers.

Start by putting all your investments into one of three groups. Group 1 consists of your best investments – those that have delivered the best performance and perhaps followed the trajectory you anticipated for them. Group 2 includes your failures – those that have delivered the worst performance or where the business development turned out completely differently than you expected it to. In other words, this group should focus on investments where you misunderstood something fundamental about the company and its future. Make sure this group includes all your loss-making investments. Finally, Group 3 contains all the investments that can be considered average.

It may be difficult at first to determine what actually made an investment one of the best or worst of your career. To inspire you, let me share my analysis of the core characteristics of my own most successful investments and biggest investment mistakes. Later in the book, I'll provide a more thorough analysis of these successful investments and big mistakes in the hope that you can copy the best and avoid repeating the worst. For now, here is a general overview.

CHARACTERISTICS OF MY MOST SUCCESSFUL INVESTMENTS

My best investments have typically been characterized by the following:

- Investments in great businesses (defined by having a high return on capital) that were run by founders. The companies also had a long runway of growth ahead at the time I made the stock purchase. Several of my best investments have been in companies that were so-called true compounders – where the biggest challenge I faced was simply remaining calm and allowing them to prosper and increase their earning power over the years.

- Investments in great companies that for one reason or another had run into temporary business problems that negatively affected their earnings power and suppressed the stock price. When you understand the business of such companies and can determine that the problems are operational – not systemic – and therefore solvable, you have the opportunity to make truly outstanding investments. A few of my very best investments fall into this category.

- Investments in 'serial acquirers' with rational capital allocation and a large long-term compounding effect. In fact, Berkshire Hathaway, led by Warren Buffett, is the world's largest and most successful serial acquirer. A serial acquirer is defined by how management allocates the company's earnings and other financial resources. Earnings and resources are used to acquire new businesses instead of being paid out to shareholders. If this capital allocation and investing in acquisitions is done rationally, it creates a compounding machine – which is always a highly attractive investment. We have quite a few serial acquirers in the Nordic countries, and a couple of them have been among my best investments.

CHARACTERISTICS OF MY BIGGEST FAILURES

The most significant mistakes I've made throughout my entire investing career involved choosing for one reason or another *not* to invest when I should have done.

There are many reasons you might refrain from investing despite all the signs that you are looking at an attractive and rational opportunity. Here are some of the misguided rationalizations that I now believe caused me to make my own mistakes in this respect:

- Concern that I might have missed something in my analysis of the company's business model
- Being overly focused on the company's current short-term situation
- Underestimating the company's future growth potential and its ability to generate high returns on invested capital
- Believing the stock price was just a bit too expensive

The worst investments I did make have typically been characterized by the following:

- Investments in companies where management began to make irrational decisions about capital allocation. This irrational behavior was driven either by their desire to build a business empire through overly expensive acquisitions, or by their wish to invest the company's capital in new and supposedly promising business areas that, for several years, consumed a large portion of the company's earnings power and ultimately never became profitable. Overpaying for acquisitions or investing in ventures that never succeed is a waste of the company's financial resources – and in these cases, my money.
- Investments in companies where neither management nor I realized that the competitive strength – the moat around

- the company's earnings power – was deteriorating rapidly and permanently. As we have discussed, stock prices follow earnings per share; and in these cases, earnings declined and return on capital fell over time along with the stock price – and my investment.
- Investments in companies where I initially overestimated the company's normalized earnings and future growth rate, resulting in buying at an over-valuation. When you overestimate normalized current earnings, you use up your margin of safety the moment you make the investment. If you then later discover that you also overestimated the growth rate in sales and earnings, you suffer a double blow. I got creamed – and deservedly so – because I had failed to do my analysis properly and my reasoning was flawed.
- Investments in companies where I underestimated the long-term earnings growth and thus sold my stocks far too early, missing out on substantial gains. Selling such compounders are by far the most expensive selling mistakes I've made.

I hope this gives you some inspiration to examine the characteristics of your own most successful investments and biggest losers. I'm sure you'll also conclude that some of the biggest mistakes you have made as a stock investor stem from investments you never made despite your business analysis being correct and the company being inside your circle of competence. Your reasoning went wrong, and you did not make the move. Likewise, some of your best decisions may have involved exiting investments you should never have entered in the first place. Figuring these things out – and everything in between – is what investing is all about.

32.

Describing Your Circle of Competence and Your Investor Profile

Every person has their own experience, knowledge and insights – and a unique circle of competence when it comes to investing.

Some investors are knowledgeable about certain industries and businesses, others are experts in real estate and still others have more experience with fixed-income investments such as treasuries, corporate bonds and other instruments where the returns are known at the time of investment.

No one has a circle of competence that includes all industries and businesses. In fact, most investors have a much smaller circle of competence than they think – unless they've done the analysis. But the size of the circle is not the issue. With your circle of competence, the most important thing is not how large it is but rather that you know where its boundaries lie – what is inside and what is outside. There is enormous value in knowing where the edge of your circle is: this makes it far easier to say no to most investment ideas. That not only improves your long-term investment performance but also saves time and makes your investment process far more efficient.

This 'extra time' should be spent studying what lies inside your circle. The deeper your understanding, the better your performance – so you must continuously work on deepening your knowledge within your circle of competence.

When it comes to investing in stocks, you can start by listing the industries you know nothing about. These are industries or businesses where you simply cannot build up the necessary knowledge to realistically assess how the company's earnings might develop over the next ten years. These industries clearly fall outside your circle of competence.

Next, list the industries where you do have some experience or insight and explain why you believe you have that insight. Then ask yourself honestly: *'Do I truly have the knowledge required to assess how this industry or business will evolve over the next ten years?'* If the answer is yes, then that industry belongs inside your circle of competence.

DEFINING THE CIRCLE OF COMPETENCE

To illustrate how to think about defining your own circle of competence, let me share my own thinking and analysis of the circle that defines me and my investment work.

I have been a business owner since 1996. For almost thirty years, I've owned and worked with businesses and management teams across various industries.

I made my only fixed-income investment in 1974, when I bought a few bonds for US$200. Although the real-estate market is interesting – and perhaps easier to understand than some industries and businesses – it would be wrong to include real estate in my circle of competence, as I've never invested in any property other than the house I live in.

So, my first step in defining my own circle of competence is to acknowledge that certain industries and businesses are within it, while fixed-income and real-estate investments are outside.

Is that a problem for me?

Not at all. I'm comfortable having all my investments in stocks. I know that, over the long term, the stock market is a better generator of wealth than the bond market or the real-estate market. I am a business owner and I'm patient. I don't mind the volatility or the price fluctuations that come with stock investments.

Here are the industries I consider to be within my circle of competence, and why:

- **The insurance industry.** I worked for three years as the investor-relations director for one of the largest insurance companies in the Nordic region. I understand the business model very well.

- **The retail industry.** My family on both my mother and father's sides have been business owners in the retail sector for generations. While I was growing up, my mother ran a children's clothing store for twenty-five years. Over time, I have come to understand the different business models within the retail industry very well.

- **Media companies.** My work as a business editor and financial journalist at one of Denmark's leading newspapers provided me with valuable knowledge of the media industry and the factors that drive earnings in this sector. It has been a very fast-moving industry over the last thirty years due to digitalization and changing consumer habits, but I understand *some* business models in the media industry and specifically those based on subscription or advertising.

- **Professional business services and IT software supporting operational business functions.** I founded and managed a professional consulting company for fifteen years, during which we acquired several business services and used many different IT software systems in our operations. I understand the business model and especially the supply–demand dynamics.

- **Simple industries and companies that sell easy-to-understand consumer products to repeat customers.** Through my consulting business, I worked closely with clients – board members and management teams – who educated me about their company strategies and operations. If the industry is simple and the repeat-selling products are too, I can research and build sufficient knowledge to understand the consumer demand and the company's value drivers.

- **Founder-led companies.** As the founder and manager of my own company, I have deep insight into how entrepreneurs think and how they typically run their businesses.

It is also easy to list several industries in which I have absolutely no expertise or advantage over other investors. Though this list is not exhaustive, the following industries clearly fall outside my circle of competence: biotech and research-based companies; engineering and construction companies; contract manufacturers in general; banks; exploration and mining companies; online gambling and gaming companies.

It's important to remember that your circle of competence is not static – it's dynamic. As you read and study, you can expand and deepen your insights and perhaps push the boundaries of your circle a little further outwards. But industries inside your circle may also change so dramatically that they no longer function as they did before and your knowledge relates to the past, not the future. If that happens, you must acknowledge that you're no longer competent in the field. Consequently, your circle of competence may shrink.

INVESTOR PROFILE

Based on your analysis of your business career, temperament, investment research and track record, along with your defined circle of competence, you should now have a relatively clear picture of your investor profile.

This will help you identify the types of investments that will give you the highest probability of success. If you find great businesses – run by excellent management, operating within your circle of competence and aligned with your investor profile – then there is a strong likelihood that you'll be making sound, rational investments, assuming you can purchase the stock at a price that meets your required return based on your hurdle rate.

As you gain more experience, you will also become increasingly skilled at recognizing the types of companies and investments you should avoid.

To help you craft your own investor profile, you're welcome to draw inspiration from mine – which is based on my personality, temperament, business experience, investment track record and circle of competence.

My investor profile:

> **I am a long-term co-owner of great businesses – run by excellent, owner-oriented management with a strong focus on operational efficiency and rational capital allocation.**
>
> **I prefer founder-led companies with a long runway for growth or serial acquirers, provided they meet the characteristics above.**
>
> **I do not invest in fixed income or real estate. I avoid investments that do not generate ongoing income, such as gold, cryptocurrency, or art. I also stay away from startups and companies going public through IPOs.**
>
> **I am aware of my tendency to overestimate normalized current earnings and future growth when investing, so I deliberately try to make very conservative assessments.**
>
> **I always invest with Warren Buffett's investment hurdle rate in mind, targeting a 15% Day-1 return. The hurdle rate and the 15% Day-1 return ensure that I invest with an adequate margin of safety, protecting me against my analytical errors and wrong decisions.**
>
> **My investment focus is on industries within my circle of competence: insurance; retail; professional services; IT software; simple industries with repeat sales; and media companies.**
>
> **I am a very patient investor and make very few investments each year – and I am completely fine with that.**

One way to test yourself and your investor profile is to ask whether it would matter to you if the stock market were closed for a year or two, from which point you could invest only in private, non-listed companies. A true business investor identifies their areas of insight and expertise, focuses on companies within those domains and pays less attention to whether a company is publicly traded or how frequently its shares are bought and sold.

If you prepare your investor profile in a similar way, I believe you'll arrive at the same conclusion I did: 100% of my performance has come from investments made within my circle of competence and aligned with my investor profile, while the combined result of all other investments has been largely irrelevant.

I believe that your chances of outperforming the stock market over the long term depend on you choosing investments that match your investor profile and fall within your circle of competence.

That said, it's impossible to completely avoid making mistakes, even with years of experience behind you – that's part of the game. However, if you invest rationally and truly understand yourself as an investor, you'll have a much better chance of making fewer – and less costly – errors over time.

Key takeaways from Part VI

- Investment is first and foremost about temperament.
- To understand yourself as an investor you must understand yourself as a person.
  - Analyze the biggest decisions you have made in your life generally
  - How did you conduct your investment research?
  - How did you make your investment decisions?
  - How did you act as an owner of your company?
  - Why did you decide to sell?
- Identify the characteristics of your most successful investments and biggest failures.
- Make a thorough analysis of what you really know and what is inside and outside your circle of competence.
- When you are in doubt about whether a company or a scenario is inside or outside the circle, you can be sure that it is outside.
- When you are done with the analysis and have described your circle of competence, write your own crisp and concise investor profile.
- Make sure that all your future investments are within great companies, run by excellent management, and are aligned with your circle of competence and your investor profile.

PART VII:
Lessons from My Biggest Successes and Failures

33.

How to Measure Your Performance – Successes and Failures

When evaluating whether your investments have been successful overall, it's important to compare your long-term performance to one or two relevant stock indices.

A stock index can be defined in many different ways and can represent a variety of well-defined company classifications. In the United States, the three most widely recognized stock indices are the S&P 500, the Dow Jones Industrial Average, and the Nasdaq Composite.

The S&P 500 is a free-float market capitalization weighted index consisting of 500 of the largest publicly traded companies in the United States.

The Dow Jones Industrial Average is a price-weighted index of 30 of the largest and most influential publicly traded industrial companies in the United States.

The Nasdaq Composite is a free-float market capitalization weighted index that includes all listed companies (several thousand) on the Nasdaq exchange. Because the Nasdaq exchange contains a very high concentration of technology companies, the index is broadly viewed as a technology-leaning benchmark.

Beyond these, there are numerous stock indices that cover specific industries, sectors, regions, and individual countries. There are also indices designed to represent large-cap, mid-cap, and small-cap segments of the stock universe.

The key is to compare the performance of your portfolio with one or more **relevant** benchmarks. If you primarily own smaller or mid-sized companies, then the appropriate benchmark should reflect that size segment. If you invest exclusively in the US, or Asia, or Europe, then your selected benchmark should also correspond to that region.

When you compare your performance with the index, you need to include all costs related to your investments and investment work, such as transaction fees, custodial charges and any other relevant expenses. Likewise, you should subtract any relevant fees from holding the index certificate to ensure a fair, apples-to-apples comparison.

It's not uncommon for an investor's performance to match the index before costs; but after fees, many investors struggle to keep pace with the market. In some years, an investor may very well outperform the market and feel like the 'king of the castle'. However, as we have seen, you shouldn't place too much emphasis on short-term performance – meaning anything under three years. If you've outperformed the index over a period of five years, or even better, ten to fifteen years, you can reasonably conclude that you've created value through your investment decisions. Even then, there will inevitably be years when you underperform – possibly even two or three in a row.

It's not that difficult to compare your overall performance to an index. The real challenge lies in selecting the most relevant index for the comparison. Sometimes it can be helpful to compare your performance against two or three indices. What matters most is choosing indices that represent the markets you invest in and that include, as accurately as possible, the companies you own.

Still, rational investing comparison requires more than just comparing your returns to the market. For each investment, you should also review your original analysis and investment case. What did you expect from the company and its financial development, and have those expectations matched the actual results? Did you correctly understand the company's business model and moat? Did you more or less accurately forecast its financial development? Did you properly assess the management team's operational capabilities and capital allocation? And did you in the end invest at a reasonable price?

In other words, you must track both your performance relative to the index and the quality of your work as a business analyst.

With that in mind, let me walk you through seven of my actual investment cases – four cases that I consider successful and three where my analysis and the outcome of my work were very poor. These seven cases cover only six companies, as one company represents both one of my best investment cases and my most costly blunder.

I have used the book's structure and the normal investment structure in my review of the selected cases to best illustrate the progression of the investment. Likewise, at the end of each case, I have briefly described the lessons I learned. I hope these lessons will help you to avoid making the same mistakes and provide a foundation for you to repeat my successes.

After careful consideration, I find it fair to all parties to withhold the name of one of the companies that were behind my mistakes. The name of this company (and it's management) is irrelevant to understanding my misanalysis and poor decisions. Conversely, I have no problem mentioning the names of the companies included in my successes. This is partly because all but one of the companies have subsequently performed excellently and partly because the management has created significant value for the owners – which is, of course, what it's all about.

34.

Case 1: The No-Brainer

Introduction

When you invest in a great business, run by excellent management, with a solid moat and long-term growth prospects, you can hardly avoid making a good investment if the purchase price is reasonable. At the time of investment, you know there is a high probability that you're looking at one of those rare opportunities in your investment career. You must back up the truck and load up big time. It's a no-brainer.

Business description

Generic Sweden AB is a software-as-a-service (SaaS) company that operates in messaging services across all business sectors. The company provides its corporate customers with a platform for digital communication services that can be integrated into a company's internal or external communication flows. These services are delivered through a communication-platform-as-a- service (CPaaS) model. The platform is designed to meet the highest standards of security and reliability.

Generic Sweden's customers span all industries, with a strong presence in alarms and security, healthcare and e-health, as well as e-commerce and logistics. The company was founded in 1993 and is based in Stockholm, Sweden.

The revenue model follows the classic SaaS structure – annual fees combined with variable income based on usage. The growth strategy is also traditional: 'land and expand' – or grow alongside your customers. Historically, the company's market focus has been Swedish corporations, many of which have international growth ambitions.

Research

As part of my continuous research work, every year I go through the Morningstar factsheet for each company listed on the Nordic stock exchange, OMX Nasdaq. In the summer of 2019, I came across Generic Sweden and noticed that the company had changed its business model from selling individual IT solutions supported by consultancy services to a standard SaaS solution. In addition, Generic Sweden had divested its consulting business to make the business model a pure play.

Until then, I had not been interested in Generic Sweden, as I knew very well that you never get optimal results when you have two different business models operating within the same company – in Generic Sweden's case, individual software systems and a consulting business.

Inside my circle of competence?

During my fifteen years as a business owner of a consulting company, I gained insight into the professional business service industry and not least into software systems that are integrated into companies' operational business systems. I understand the business model and the value drivers. Besides that, we used SaaS products in my consulting business, and I know how 'sticky' the product/service is. We also had quite a few listed software companies as clients from which I had learned a lot.

Great business?

When Generic Sweden sold off its consulting business in 2018 and announced that it would focus on its self-developed standard SaaS business, it was immediately clear that this would create a great company with a strong moat. When you're able to get your product – in this case, Generic Sweden's software – deeply embedded into a client's operating system, you're offering a very sticky product. The client simply cannot function without it, and the annual cost of the service becomes almost irrelevant – it just needs to work.

Even if the client starts to consider the cost, they typically abandon their concerns the moment they realize the enormous effort that would be required to switch to a competing service and the operational risks involved. Generic Sweden's customers remain loyal as long as the software delivers what it's supposed to, which is operational efficiency.

Generic Sweden was also positioned to achieve a high return on invested capital, as the company didn't require much capital to finance operations and growth. And growth was practically a given. One of the strongest global megatrends, in 2019 and even more so today, is that all companies must digitize and make their value chains – especially the dialogue with the customers – as efficient as possible.

Excellent management?

First of all, I noted that the company's CEO and several board members were significant co-owners. In addition, I did my research to learn about the companies the management team had previously worked for. Through my dialogue with management, I also became convinced that they would allocate capital and future earnings in a rational way.

In a very asset-light business like Generic Sweden, earnings are typically paid out as dividends, since the company's growth doesn't require much capital. I saw no indication that the board would begin spending capital on ill-advised acquisitions to build an empire.

In short, I concluded that as a co-owner I would be in the same boat as the management and the board.

Hurdle rate and valuation?

I valued Generic Sweden the same way I pretty much always value a company when I find it very likely that there will be a double-digit growth rate for the coming years.

I used Warren Buffett's hurdle rate for fast-growth companies, according to Alice Schroeder's description: 'I want a 15% return [before tax] on double of the present earnings.'

As I was not buying the whole company and was a 'normal investor', I translated the numbers to after tax with a 22% tax rate: 15% before tax = 11.7% after tax. So, I wanted an 11.7% return on the double of Generic Sweden's present earnings after tax, or net profit.

It was then quite easy to calculate the hurdle rate and the indicated price. If Generic Sweden had to give me an after-tax return of 11.7% on the double of present size, I would demand half that return: = 11.7/2 = 5.85% of the company here and now or a P/E of no more than 17.

In the summer of 2019, Generic Sweden had earnings after tax of about SEK 0.53 per share and according to my hurdle rate of 5.85% I was willing to pay a price of no more than 0.53/5.85% = 0.53/0.0585 = SEK 9.06. I ended up buying about 5% of the company at an average price of about SEK 8.5, equivalent to a P/E ratio of about 16.

Generic Sweden AB	2019
Metric	Growth/Percentage
Revenue	16%
Earnings	36%
Earnings per share (EPS)	SEK 0.53
ROIC (average)	NEGATIVE
ROUNTA (average)	NEGATIVE
Purchase price	SEK 8.5
P/E ratio at purchase	≈16

When I invested in Generic Sweden in 2019, the company had no debt and a net cash position of nearly SEK 3 per share. In other words, I effectively purchased the company at a 'net price' of SEK 5.5, or a post-tax P/E of 10.

As shown by Generic Sweden's metrics at the time of acquisition in 2019, the company's ROIC and ROUNTA were both negative. The explanation is straightforward. At that time, the company's cash balance exceeded its equity, and it had no debt. Generic Sweden was – and remains – a company that, in principle, does not require external capital, given its highly 'asset-light' business model.

As a result, growth is essentially self-funded, and virtually all profits can be returned to shareholders or reinvested in other value-creating opportunities. In recent years, Generic Sweden has distributed a substantial portion of its earnings as dividends; and as of the end of 2025, the company's ROIC is about 235% and the ROUNTA about 519%. Both metrics indicate an exceptionally high return on capital.

Working as a co-owner

Since my investment in the summer of 2019, I have been in regular dialogue with the CEO, Jonas Jegerborn (Jonas joined the company in 2018 as CEO and ended his turn at the helm in early 2025 after seven fantastic years). I have also from time to time had contact with the other large shareholders of the company. My focus has been on improving my understanding of the business and the value drivers; of these, keeping sales growth at > 10% per year and maintaining earnings margins are the most important for the long-term compounding of value.

In addition, I have studied and closely followed the development of two of Generic Sweden's biggest competitors, both of whom have pursued a very aggressive growth strategy with lots of acquisitions of smaller players all over the world – which is the opposite of Generic Sweden's focus on organic growth.

How did the investment work out?

From 2018 to 2024, Generic Sweden increased sales with about 200%, or about 20% per year on average. In the meantime, earnings after tax – or net profit – has gone up even more as margins have increased. Earnings have increased 320%, or about 27% per year.

As we have seen, stocks follow earnings per share over the long term – and the share price of Generic Sweden has certainly delivered proof of this. The share price has increased from about SEK 8.5 per share to about SEK 50, or 34% on average per year, as the market has revaluated Generic Sweden as a better business than it was prior to 2019.

In addition, management has paid out dividends of over SEK 7 over the six years and my investment has more or less been paid back. Generic Sweden is truly a 'double rifle' – free growth and the opportunity to pay out the year's profit as a dividend at the same time.

At the time of writing this book, Generic Sweden still makes up a share of my portfolio. Not many companies have such a strong business model and are able to compound like Generic Sweden. It is easy to be a co-owner of a great company – run by excellent management.

Lessons from the investment case

- When you have invested in a truly great business, with a strong moat and high return on capital, time is your friend.
- If this company is also run by excellent management, you don't have to fear that bad capital allocation will spoil the party.

- Over the long run, stocks follow earnings per share.
- Your most important job – your *only* job – is to simply watch the company compound value.
- It is almost always a bad idea to sell a truly great company – run by excellent management.

35.

Case 2: Watch Out when Management Changes Strategy and Capital Allocation

Introduction

Often, one of the most successful investment decisions you can make is to say, 'NO! I don't want to be part of this new strategic direction.' When management changes the growth strategy and capital allocation, it can be wise to say goodbye – even if the company is growing nicely and shows solid returns on invested capital, suggesting the moat is still intact.

Business description

In 2014, I invested in the Swedish company Byggmax AB. In the 2013 annual report (and in earlier reports), which I used in making my investment decision, Byggmax presented itself as 'a company focused on selling high-quality standard building materials at the lowest possible price.' The report also stated: 'We aim to do this in as simple and accessible a manner as possible in all our 105 stores across the Nordic region. We will therefore remain true to our pricing model, meaning: no campaigns, no sales, and no discounts. At Byggmax, the same low price applies to every customer.' Byggmax's goal was simply to become 'the world's best DIY retailer'.

Research

In June 2010, Byggmax was listed on the OMX Nasdaq stock exchange, and I began following the company because I liked its low-cost business model and focus on organic growth. However, I was in no hurry to become a co-owner. IPOs often occur when the sellers believe it's a good time to divest part of their ownership. I prefer to pick my own buying time and ensure I know at least as much about the company as the seller does – something that is rarely true in an IPO. So, I observed Byggmax for a few years and gradually became more comfortable with the business model and management's growth strategy.

Inside my circle of competence?

Business models in retail are often simple and easy to understand. On top of that, there was my family's involvement in retail for generations. I grew up watching my mother run her children's clothing store and during those years learned about financial statements, inventory, supplier payment terms and key performance indicators.

Great business?

Most of the time, retail is about buying a product at one price and selling it at a higher price without altering the product. You sell what you buy. Sometimes, you add a little value by advising customers – but that's it. Retail is about price, and the industry is typically very competitive. The players with a real moat are often low-cost leaders too. Consumers like to save money!

Byggmax showed stable and sustainable growth. Its financial performance and prospects were convincing. From 2008 to 2013, sales grew by more than 11% per year, and operating earnings grew slightly faster. I was aware that the DIY industry could be volatile and was still feeling the effects of the 2008–09 financial crisis and the dip in housing prices. Still, the 2013 annual report showed that Byggmax's earnings provided a solid return on capital.

In 2014, Byggmax was a low-cost player with a moat confirmed by a high return on capital.

Excellent management?

Before the IPO in 2010, Byggmax was owned by the Nordic private-equity fund Altor, which remained the largest shareholder until 2013. The chairman and the CEO had been in place for years, and I was confident in their focus on organic growth and return on capital. Based on that, I saw no need to contact the company before investing.

In 2015, the chairman resigned at the annual general meeting and passed the role to another board member. At that point, I reached out to the company to discuss the benefits of share buybacks over dividends. This led to a conversation with the new chairman, who made it clear that buybacks were not part of the board's agenda.

Hurdle rate and valuation?

Expecting Byggmax to continue growing earnings at a double-digit rate, I used Warren Buffett's hurdle rate for fast-growing companies: 'I want a 15% return before tax on the double of earnings.' As outlined in the Generic Sweden case, a 15% pre-tax return translates to an 11.7% after-tax return (assuming a 22% tax rate). Therefore, I wanted an 11.7% return on double Byggmax's current after-tax earnings.

Looking at the 2013 net profit, Byggmax earned SEK 3.03 per share. Doubling that gives SEK 6.06. To achieve an 11.7% return, I was willing to pay no more than 6.06 / 0.117 = SEK 51.8 per share. I invested at about SEK 48.

Byggmax AB	2013
Metric	Growth/Percentage
Revenue	≈10%
Earnings	>10%
Earnings per share (EPS)	SEK 3.03
ROIC (average)	7%
ROUNTA (average)	27%
Purchase price	SEK 48
P/E ratio at purchase	≈16

In nearly every company, revenue and earnings fluctuate from year to year. Unlike in PowerPoint presentations, in business nothing moves in a straight line. At Byggmax, I estimated that the average future growth in revenue and earnings would be approximately 10%, composed of 4–5% from general market growth, 2–3% from gains in market share and 2–3% from the opening of new stores.

Before investing, I also calculated the hurdle price using Buffett's rate for lower-growth companies – around 5–7%, still above inflation. As we've seen, Buffett requires a 10% pre-tax return, or 7.8% after-tax. Based on this, I knew I should not pay more than 3.03 / 0.078 = SEK 39 per share.

However, I believed Byggmax had a long runway for growth across the

Nordic region. In other words, I was confident that paying SEK 48 was entirely reasonable. And, I thought, even if the price was slightly on the high side, both time and Byggmax's high ROUNTA would work in my favor.

As reflected in Byggmax's 2013 metrics, the company's ROIC was approximately 7%, primarily due to a substantial goodwill balance representing nearly 50% of total assets. This goodwill was inherent from the time of the company's IPO and was not the result of a series of costly acquisitions in prior years. This aligned well with management's focus at the time on organic growth.

ROUNTA – which by definition excludes goodwill – stood at 27%, reflecting a highly attractive level of profitability and underscoring that Byggmax in 2013 was a strong company.

Working as a co-owner

After making an investment in the spring of 2014, I initiated a dialogue with the chairman in 2015. I stated my belief that utilizing the company's profits for share buybacks would generate greater shareholder value than distributing tax-burdened dividends.

A few months later, Byggmax made its first acquisition and signaled that more takeovers would follow. In other words, the new chairman and board indicated there would be a fundamental shift in the organic growth strategy and capital allocation. I didn't like this and decided to sell my shares.

How did the investment work out?

When I sold my shares in 2015, after being a co-owner for about sixteen months, I made a small profit. Byggmax didn't become one of my major winners, but it was still a successful investment from a quality perspective. My analysis of the business model and financials was correct, and I bought at a price that met my hurdle rate.

More importantly, I made the right decision not to join the company on its 'acquisition journey' under the new board and management team.

Over the past ten years, Byggmax has made several more acquisitions. But, as of today – roughly a decade after I sold – the share price is about the same as it was in 2015. Shareholders have received about SEK 17 in dividends during that time, resulting in a total return of around 35%, or about 3% per year.

Lessons from the investment case

- When management changes the company's growth strategy and capital allocation, you need to stay alert.
- If a low-cost producer in a highly competitive industry starts pursuing an acquisition-driven strategy, management will likely begin investing shareholder capital outside the moat; this leads to lower returns on capital and diminishes the company's strength.
- Even if you invested for the right reasons and your original analysis was solid, you must be willing to change your perspective when the facts change.

36.

Case 3: Buying Commodities and Selling Brands – a Winning Formula!

Introduction

It's always fascinating to study companies that buy raw materials at global-market prices and ultimately sell branded products to consumers. These companies enjoy a significant advantage over many competitors: they control the entire value chain from start to finish, with virtually no suppliers pressuring their margins. The key to success is to ensure that the brand is carefully managed and demand is sustained. Such businesses often have a strong moat and deliver high returns on capital – but they're not always run by great management.

It may be difficult to imagine that there are companies that purchase a simple commodity on the global market at a fully competitive price and then manage to sell a product in which that raw material has been adapted and refined – ultimately fetching a price many times higher than the original cost and resulting in something entirely different in the eyes of the consumer. Yet, there are countless businesses that begin with the procurement of raw material and end up selling exclusive brands derived from that same material. Most spirits brands are based on very inexpensive raw ingredients that are ultimately sold at premium prices. While a portion of the retail price is due to taxes and duties, the net sales price still far exceeds the cost of production – and the strength of the brand ensures continued demand. Vodka, gin, tequila, rum, whiskey and a wide variety of liqueurs are all examples of such transformations from commodity to branded products.

Diageo (UK) is the world's largest spirits producer, with brands such as Johnnie Walker (whiskey), Smirnoff (vodka), Tanqueray (gin), Don Julio (tequila) and Baileys. The French company Pernod Ricard markets

205

brands like Absolut (vodka), Jameson (whiskey), Chivas Regal (whiskey), Beefeater (gin), Havana Club (rum) and Malibu. There are several other global spirits companies with major brands where the production cost of the alcohol is only a few dollars – or even less for some products.

Similarly, many companies and brands in the cosmetics and fragrance industry operate with relatively low production costs while commanding retail prices that are exponentially higher. The largest cosmetics and fragrance companies in the world include L'Oréal Group (France) and Estée Lauder Companies (USA).

Further down the luxury scale but still immensely powerful are global consumer-goods giants that operate across personal care, cosmetics and food. Examples include Procter & Gamble, Kraft Heinz and Nestlé. Maybe the most famous brand based on a simple commodity is Coca-Cola.

Again, the business model relies on low raw-material costs and the ability to sell the finished product as a trusted brand with strong profit margins and loyal customers who purchase the product repeatedly.

When strong businesses like these experiences temporary issues, there may be a rare opportunity for a life-changing investment.

Business description

Pandora is the world's largest jewelry brand and owns its entire value chain, from sourcing recycled silver, gold and other materials to operating thousands of concept stores around the globe. The company focuses on designing, crafting and marketing affordable luxury jewelry made with high-quality materials. Each piece has meaning and is meant to inspire self-expression and allow people to tell their stories.

Pandora products are sold in over 100 countries through 6,800 points of sale, including more than 2,700 concept stores. The company is headquartered in Copenhagen, Denmark.

Research

Pandora was listed on the OMX Nasdaq in late 2010 at DKK 210 per share. As I always do, I paid attention to all IPOs in the Nordic region and Pandora immediately struck me as a company to follow closely – in terms of both performance and management decisions.

Inside my circle of competence?

Pandora's business model is relatively straightforward for anyone familiar with the retail industry. What sets Pandora apart from a typical retailer is that it is both a manufacturer and a retailer. The company controls every aspect of the value chain – from buying raw materials to the production, distribution and sale of jewelry directly to consumers through its own stores and online.

Great business?

The jewelry market, particularly in the affordable segment where Pandora operates, is still largely unbranded. This gives Pandora a competitive edge, and the company continues to gain market share – a sign of its growing moat.

If management can maintain and strengthen the Pandora brand, the company can continue to generate very high returns on capital. In 2024, Pandora reported a gross margin of about 80% and an EBIT margin of around 25%. The ROUNTA – the metric telling us how great the business is – was a whopping 54%. The ROIC was also high at approximately 27%. Thanks to the great business model and strong margins, the owners were also able to look at a return on equity (ROE) of about 80%.

Simply put, Pandora is a money machine.

Excellent management?

In retail – especially in branded retail – management plays a crucial role. If leadership fails to maintain the brand's appeal, the business can deteriorate rapidly. Consumers remain loyal only as long as the product continues to evoke feelings of joy and desirability.

Pandora offered a great case study in management just after its IPO in 2010. Due to poor strategic decisions, the company began selling products outside its core affordable segment, damaging the brand. It also became apparent that management had engaged in 'channel stuffing' to boost short-term results for the IPO.

Just nine months after listing, Pandora issued a dramatic profit warning: expected growth for 2011 was slashed from high double digits to nearly zero. The CEO was dismissed and the chairman stepped in to lead a strategic review aimed at restoring the brand. It was clear that a seasoned CEO needed to be brought in to complete the turnaround.

The situation became a major business scandal in Denmark and made headlines worldwide. Yet beneath the scandal and profit warning it was possible to see that if the brand were properly managed, the business still had significant growth potential.

The chairman did a commendable job stabilizing the company, and the new CEO executed well. In my view, Pandora was on its way back.

Hurdle rate and valuation?

I didn't evaluate Pandora at the time of the IPO, as I generally avoid investing in newly listed companies. The IPO price was DKK 210 per share.

Nine months later, following the profit warning, the share price dropped below DKK 40. On the day of the warning, in July 2011, shares fell by around 65%, valuing the entire company at just 20% of its original IPO price.

It was time to dig deeper and analyze Pandora's normalized earnings. I estimated net profit at around DKK 16 per share, while the stock traded around DKK 50. This implied a P/E of just over 3 or a 33% after-tax return on investment from day one.

Using Buffett's hurdle rate for normal growth – a pre-tax return of 10% or 7.8% after tax (at a 22% rate) – I arrived at a potential purchase price of about DKK 115 per share, more than double what I had to pay. I felt there was sufficient margin of safety and proceeded to make one of the largest investments in my portfolio.

Pandora A/S	2011
Metric	Growth/Percentage
Revenue	≈5%
Earnings	≈5%
Earnings per share (EPS)	DKK 16
ROIC (average)	≈34%
ROUNTA (average)	≈178%
Purchase price	DKK 50
P/E ratio at purchase	≈3.2

When a company has been valued based on extremely high growth expectations from investors, and it turns out that growth is much lower – or even temporarily absent – the market reaction is often severe, and stock declines of 50–70% are not uncommon. If your analysis shows that the company is still a great business, this is precisely the time to be 'greedy when others are fearful'

In 2011 Pandora was a highly profitable earnings engine—a status it continues to maintain. In 2024, Pandora reported a ROIC of 32% and a robust ROUNTA of 39%.

How did the investment work out?

 I sold almost all of my Pandora shares in 2017 at about DKK 600 per share, making it a very successful investment.

While the company has experienced ups and downs—most recently due to sharply rising gold and silver prices—it remains a strong business with high returns on capital.

Since 2011, Pandora's sales have increased by nearly 500%. Earnings per share have grown from DKK 16 to around DKK 60 in 2025, exceeding the DKK 50 per share I paid in 2011. In addition, since 2012, shareholders have received a total of DKK 140 per share in dividends.

Lessons from the investment case

- Companies that buy commodities and sell branded products are often exceptional businesses.
- If you can identify when a business problem is temporary rather than systemic, you may have a unique opportunity to make an outstanding investment.
- In such moments, you must be greedy when others are fearful.

37.

Case 4: First a Very Successful Investment – and Then My Biggest Blunder

Introduction

As should by now be very clear, when you find a great business run by excellent management, and you understand the business model, you have a very good chance of making a successful investment – especially if you can buy the company's stock at an attractive price. Often, the biggest risk of failure isn't found in the company itself but in your own ability to maintain a long-term perspective when the company hits a rough patch. All companies eventually face challenges and how you analyze and respond to those challenges can make a huge difference.

The successful Norwegian insurance company Protector has always been a great business with outstanding leadership. I bought shares at a very attractive price and then Protector ran into problems. I had bought shares for all the right reasons – and I sold them for all the wrong ones. This investment became my biggest and most expensive mistake.

Business description

Founded in 2004, Protector Insurance is a Norwegian company listed on the Oslo Stock Exchange (OSE). It distributes its insurance products through selected brokers and operates under a highly competitive, low-cost business model. As a low-cost provider serving commercial and public sectors, Protector stands out as a challenger in the traditionally conservative insurance industry.

Starting in Norway, Protector gradually expanded to Sweden, Denmark, Finland, the UK and France – with plans for continued growth.

Research

As part of my ongoing search for great businesses, I spent time in 2010 researching companies listed on the OSE. I came across Protector and was immediately intrigued by its understandable business model. I decided to take a deep dive.

Inside my circle of competence?

I understand how insurance companies operate. From 1989 to 1992, I worked as investor-relations director at Baltica, the leading Danish insurance company at the time.

Great business?

Insurance is a price-driven and highly conservative industry. The biggest challenge for an insurer is pricing risk accurately. Unlike most industries, insurance companies receive customer payments upfront and provide the service — risk protection — over time.

If an insurer collects more in premiums than it pays out in claims and administrative costs, it turns a profit. This is reflected in the 'combined ratio' (claims + admin costs / premiums), which should stay below 100. In addition, insurers can invest the premiums — known as 'float' — until claims are paid. Float is essentially a free loan from customers, provided the combined ratio remains below 100.

However, if the combined ratio exceeds 100, the insurer must use investment income from the float to cover losses.

Most customers — whether individuals or businesses — don't want to use their insurance. If they do have to use it, it means that damage or an accident has occurred. Insurance is a low-interest product and that means that price becomes the key differentiator. Thanks to its low-cost model, Protector can offer very competitive pricing while still maintaining a combined ratio below 100. In other words, Protector has a moat, is profitable and has consistently gained market share.

Excellent management?

In 2010, Protector's CEO was Sverre Bjerkeli, one of the company's founders and a major shareholder. Founders often bring direct communication and strong ambition – qualities I appreciate as a former business founder myself.

Sverre and his team – including those managing the float – were doing an excellent job. One thing I noticed early on was his transparency. In earnings presentations, he tackled tough questions head-on and explained how the company planned to address challenges. That's a hallmark of exceptional leadership.

Hurdle rate and valuation?

Valuing insurance companies differs from valuing traditional businesses due to the nature of their revenue and cost structures.

Since claims can take a long time to materialize, assessing true profitability requires looking at multi-year trends. A common valuation method is to estimate a normalized combined ratio and investment return to project earnings. This allows you to derive a valuation range.

Capital allocation also plays a crucial role. If management deploys profits wisely – such as by buying back undervalued shares rather than paying dividends – the business's value increases.

Another approach, used by Warren Buffett, focuses on equity and float. If the combined ratio is below 100 and the company is growing, float becomes a free permanent loan. In this case, the company's value is essentially its equity plus float, with future growth in both driving long-term value.

Back in 2010, using both valuation approaches, I concluded that Protector was significantly undervalued. It had a strong moat, excellent leadership with skin in the game, and a solid margin of safety. I purchased a large position at NOK 11 per share.

Working as a co-owner

After investing, I visited the company and attended investor presentations in Oslo. I had excellent communication with CEO Sverre Bjerkeli, who was responsive to my questions and even welcomed feedback on how the company could improve. Management truly treated investors as partners.

How did the investment work out?

Since 2010, Protector has been incredibly successful. Between 2010 and November 2025, the stock price increased 46-fold – a '46-bagger' – yielding an average return of over 28% annually for fifteen straight years, not including dividends.

However, in 2019, I made my biggest investment mistake: I sold my shares at NOK 60. That still represented a solid return – 21% annually for nine years – but I missed out on much more.

From 2019 to November 2025, the stock rose from NOK 60 to NOK 460, backed by strong profits.

This could have been a life-changing investment. I ended up with a 6-bagger that could have been 46-bagger. That was an expensive selling decision.

My biggest mistake

Why did I sell in 2019?

In 2018, the entire Nordic insurance market – including Protector – hit a wall. Fierce competition had pushed premiums down, and a sudden spike in claims caused combined ratios to surge above 100. The whole industry entered a loss phase.

At that point, I correctly analyzed that the situation would eventually normalize. Premiums would rise and profitability would return. However, I mistakenly concluded that recovery would take years.

So, I sold. But the issue was operational, not systemic. Protector's excellent management fixed the problem much faster than I anticipated. Within twelve to eighteen months, profitability and growth were restored.

Worse, I didn't re-enter the investment when it became clear that I had misjudged the situation. I can't offer a good explanation for that lapse in judgement.

Lessons from the investment case

- Never sell a great business with excellent management just because of short-term challenges.
- When a company faces problems, ask whether they're operational and solvable or systemic and enduring.
- You can't undo a mistake, but you can learn from it and make sure you don't repeat it.

38.

Case 5: A Great Jockey on a Slow Horse Is Not a Race Winner!

Introduction

This is one of my poorest performances as a business analyst. As the CEO and the situation have not really changed since, I have found it fair to write about the company but without exposing the names.

It's not uncommon for a mediocre company to experience a short-lived period of impressive growth and earnings. But as the saying goes, 'One swallow does not make a summer.' Conversely, companies that have underperformed for years due to poor management can sometimes be transformed under new leadership. A top-tier racehorse (a great business) can still win with a mediocre jockey (management), but even the best jockey can't win with an old, slow horse. Paying a premium for a slow horse – even with a world-class jockey – can be a costly mistake.

Business description

This company is a leading Nordic player in the building-materials industry and has its headquarters in Denmark. It produces and sells quality products in the Nordic countries and selected European markets. The market is mature and slow-moving, with demand growing modestly in line with the economy. Market shares shift slowly, resulting in some consolidation and mergers and acquisitions activity over time.

Great businesses can certainly exist in a mature industry with stable market structures. But the opposite is also true: companies can gradually lose earning power due to complacency or poor operational execution. Long-term profitability suffers when management becomes distracted by expansion into new markets or industries, or pursues misguided acquisitions.

Eventually, after years of declining earnings and lower returns on invested capital, owners may recognize the need for change. At that point, new leadership can act as a catalyst – refocusing on core operations, restoring profitability and pursuing rational capital allocation. For shareholders, this return to fundamentals can be the start of a profitable journey.

Such a return to core business and refocus on operational earnings was the basis of my investment thesis when I invested in this company in 2020.

Research

The company has been listed on OMX Nasdaq for many years, and during my time at PROSPECT I had met several times with its former executive team. I also worked with other Nordic companies in the same industry. I had followed this company for years and understood its business model well.

Inside my circle of competence?

Generally, companies in the building-materials sector have simple, straight-forward business models. Some are focused solely on new construction, while others – like this company – also benefit from the maintenance and renovation of existing buildings.

During my fifteen years at PROSPECT, I gained extensive experience analyzing businesses in simple industries, including several in the building-materials space. This gave me confidence that the company's model was well within my circle of competence.

Great business?

My analysis of the company's historical performance led me to conclude that it had been poorly managed for many years. Operational inefficiencies were evident, and capital-allocation decisions had been consistently poor.

Looking at long-term profitability, the deterioration in the EBIT margin stood out. Before the 2008–09 financial crisis, the EBIT margin was around 10%. By 2015–16, it had dropped to just 1.1%. ROE had similarly declined from 17–19% pre-crisis to only 1.6% in the same period.

Eventually, the owners decided a change was necessary, and new management was brought in with a strategy to restore profitability. This caught my attention.

After reviewing the company's fundamentals and management history, I concluded that the core business was solid and sustainable, operating in a stable market with relatively fixed market shares. If the new leadership could restore earnings and implement rational capital allocation – particularly by improving the capital structure through share buybacks – the business could become attractive.

Excellent management?

When the new CEO took over in the summer of 2016, efficiency measures were quickly introduced. By the 2016–17 financial year, EBIT had doubled (albeit from a very low base), and the EBIT margin had improved from 1.1% to 2.4%. My interest grew further, though I recognized that it would take time to fully turn the company around. At that point, I had not seen any changes in the capital structure so was in no rush – but I was increasingly confident in the new management's competence.

Hurdle rate and valuation?

This was a textbook case of a mature company with low revenue growth, roughly in line with growth in GDP. However, management had an opportunity to significantly improve profitability and reduce the share count through aggressive buybacks, setting the stage for strong growth in earnings per share. An improved capital structure would also lift return on invested capital.

I applied Buffett's hurdle rate for normal growth, requiring a 10% pre-tax real return, which translates to 7.8% after tax (assuming a 22% tax rate).

By the 2019–20 financial year, the EBIT margin had risen to 4.4% and return on capital kept improving. Then came a turning point: in August 2020, the company announced that earnings for the 2020–21 financial year would be significantly higher, despite only modest revenue growth of around 5%. This suggested that the turnaround was working, and profitability was returning.

At the time, earnings per share were around DKK 36. Using my required 7.8% return, I calculated an acceptable purchase price of about DKK 460. The market price was just DKK 360 – implying a potential return of 10% (36/360) plus 5% growth = 15% Day-1 return. Further operational improvements and share buybacks could lift EPS even more. Additionally, return on capital was suppressed by very high working capital and too much equity – including a lot of cash in the bank. In other words, there were plenty of opportunities to improve financial discipline. I decided to invest a meaningful portion of my capital.

"No name" A/S	2020
Metric	Growth/Percentage
Revenue	≈4-5%
Earnings	>10%
Earnings per share (EPS)	≈DKK 36
ROIC (average)	≈10%
ROUNTA (average)	≈12%
Purchase price	DKK 360
P/E ratio at purchase	10

Always remember that the metrics you calculate represent a 'snapshot in time. The company's financial situation at this very moment is not what matters. The key is to understand the underlying dynamics and to be able to form a well-informed view of how the situation is likely to evolve over the next five, ten or twenty years.

Over the following month, it became apparent that other investors had begun to see the same opportunities.

Working as a co-owner

After investing, I reached out to management to discuss capital allocation – specifically share buybacks and optimizing the capital structure. While they welcomed the dialogue, it became clear that their priority was growth and expansion, not returning capital to shareholders. Despite holding large cash reserves and no debt, management chose not to pursue buybacks. However, they remained fully focused on improving operational efficiency.

How did the investment work out?

Following my investment, other investors began recognizing the opportunity and the share price rose. Multiple profit upgrades followed, and it appeared that the turnaround strategy was working. Profitability improved and the return on capital increased.

But my analysis turned out to be flawed. This case became a perfect example of how you can believe you've conducted thorough research only to discover that you've overlooked a critical detail that changes everything.

This investment also illustrates the importance of having a margin of safety to protect against analytical errors. In this case, my margin of safety saved me from a significant loss despite my initial thesis being incorrect.

The key detail I had missed was the massive tailwind from the COVID-19 pandemic, which temporarily boosted demand for home-improvement products and materials and coincided with the arrival of the new management team and the change in fortunes. Consumers who were unable to travel or dine out had spent much more on home improvements. But that demand was unsustainable – home renovations are cyclical, not annual.

After the pandemic subsided and consumer behavior normalized, demand fell below typical levels. I had failed to properly account for the artificially inflated earnings. Not normalizing earnings is one of the most common investment mistakes – and one that every investor is likely to make at some point.

Ultimately, the company turned out to be a mediocre business – nothing more, nothing less. I also observed that instead of spending capital on share buybacks, management spent a lot of money on an expensive expansion into Eastern Europe.

When I realized my error in 2022, I was able to sell my shares close to my original purchase price. But this outcome was misleading, and it was my margin of safety that saved me. Without it, my investment could easily have been halved.

Today, more than three years later, the share price remains below my selling price.

Lessons from the investment case

- Always normalize earnings. Don't let a single year of high profitability distort your judgement if long-term performance tells a different story.
- Turnarounds rarely turn unless the underlying business has strong fundamentals and a defendable moat.
- If management refuses to allocate capital rationally, it's best to walk away.
- When you realize you've made a mistake, act immediately. Delay only compounds the problem.

39.

Case 6: When Everything Goes Wrong – and There's Nobody to Blame but Yourself!

Introduction

Almost every investor – even the best – has experienced a scenario where an investment goes completely wrong. By this, I mean that a company they believed was a good investment becomes virtually worthless.

As an investor, it's your responsibility to assess the risks a company faces and to evaluate the likelihood of various future outcomes. You need to develop a balanced view of how the company is expected to perform over time. Without this, there's no rational foundation for valuing the business or determining whether the investment is sound and attractive.

Typically, there are three main reasons why a company can become almost worthless in a short period of time, wiping out its shareholders:

- The market disappears. Sometimes a company's entire value evaporates because demand for its product simply vanishes. Think of VHS rentals, analogue photography (film, cameras and development), printed encyclopedias, or physical road maps that once had a place in every car. The list is long. Eventually, most companies see the foundation of their original business model disappear.

- Excessive debt. A company burdened with too much debt can end up costing its shareholders everything. There are countless examples where management, driven by aggressive growth ambitions, overloaded the company with debt to expand very fast or just acquire other businesses – often at wildly inflated prices. When it becomes clear that the acquisitions don't deliver the expected value or earnings, banks and lenders lose confidence. Credit dries up, the business falters and shareholders are left holding the bag. The company may survive through a bailout with new money and investors, but the original owners' capital is typically wiped out.

- The value was never real. This is often seen in highly speculative situations – startups and venture-backed companies where valuations rise each time new funding is needed, despite the business having no real earnings to support it. These companies sometimes go public after a series of funding rounds at ever-increasing valuations. Eventually – no one knows exactly when – the market value meets the true value; and that rendezvous always happens where the true value resides. Many of these companies never generate a profit; some don't even get to show revenue; and the sky-high valuations – often in the billions – turn out to be pure illusions at the end of the day.

The best way to avoid ending up in such situations is frankly simple: don't invest in those types of companies. In this case, I should have followed my own advice.

Business description and circle of competence?

In 2020, I ignored my own principles. I drifted. DecideAct, a SaaS company offering a management platform for businesses, appeared to fall within my circle of competence. I understood the business model and the value proposition, as we had used several SaaS products in my own business and I knew firsthand how sticky these services could be. We also had several listed software companies as clients in my company, so I felt comfortable that DecideAct was inside my circle of competence.

The software was designed to help management execute their strategic goals and related projects. Essentially, it was a kind of accounting system but for strategy execution rather than finances – offering oversight and control of strategic implementation.

The challenge was that both the software and the company were in the early stages. The product was not fully developed and the company had only a handful of customers. Still, the concept was compelling. It made sense that companies would need a tool to track and execute their strategy more effectively.

But in this case, I underestimated the human factor.

Great company and excellent management?

As the company did not yet make a profit it was not yet a great company. But I saw the need for the product and I knew that the business model was very profitable; and I figured that the company could grow revenue steadily over the next two to three years.

I knew the investment was risky, but it comforted me that the founders had strong backgrounds in strategic consulting and held significant equity stakes in the business.

I was in the same boat as the founders.

How did the investment work out?

I made a small investment during a pre-IPO funding round at what seemed like a reasonable valuation – especially considering the company's 'potential'. In early 2021, the company went public at a slightly higher valuation and attracted a lot of new investors. I participated in the IPO as well. Management claimed that the combined proceeds from these two rounds would be enough to take the company to cash-flow breakeven (where the cash inflows and outflows are equal) removing the need for further funding.

After the IPO, priced at DKK 8.15 per share, the company had 7,683,117 shares outstanding, for a market capitalization of just over DKK 62 million (roughly US$9 million). This wasn't a large IPO or an overly ambitious valuation – assuming, of course, that the company's long-term global potential could be realized.

But growth didn't materialize. Very soon, the company returned to selected investors to raise more capital. This happened repeatedly – almost every year – at progressively lower valuations and with increasing dilution for existing shareholders.

DecideAct A/S	2020
Metric	Growth/Percentage
Revenue (expected)	100%
Earnings	NEG
Earnings per share (EPS)	NEG
ROIC (average)	NEG
ROUNTA (average)	NEG
Purchase price	DKK 8.15
P/E ratio at purchase	NEG

A company with minimal revenue and negative earnings may possess a foundational business platform. However, misjudging its true potential can leave you with nothing. I have no excuse – I made a serious mistake and paid the price.

The latest capital raise, in September 2024, was done at DKK 2.75 per share – just 33% of the IPO price. Meanwhile, the number of outstanding shares had ballooned to 21,197,122, an increase of 176%. At this point, original investors owned only 36% of the company. The share price kept descending and nothing really started to improve businesswise. In late June 2025, the company filed for bankruptcy. Total market value: 0.

As an investor, this was obviously the poorest possible outcome. I never should have made this investment. Period.

Lessons from the investment case

- When a company has yet to prove itself and still runs an operational deficit, you are not only investing in the company – the most important investment factor is management and management's ability to unfold the company's potential.
- Look at the development in sales and earnings, not at the stock price.
- Don't invest in IPOs unless it is in a company where you can calculate its value and potential return on your investment based on the company's earnings.
- Accept that you will make mistakes – sometimes big ones – but make sure you don't make the same mistake twice.
- When you discover your analysis of the investment case was wrong, the time to act is now!

PART VIII:

How to Put It All Together

40.
Start Thinking Like a Business Owner

I hope you'll find motivation and encouragement in the fact that many of the wealthiest individuals in the world have built their fortunes by founding and owning a single company. It's equally inspiring to remember that even the largest corporations on the planet began as small businesses.

The common thread among these companies is that they were exceptional businesses led by outstanding management teams. If you can identify and invest in such companies while they're still relatively small, you won't need many investments. And if you have the discipline to hold onto them over the long term, they can make you extraordinarily wealthy – slowly but surely.

You may still be a student, or perhaps you work full time, and dedicate only a portion of your energy to investing (I certainly hope you have other meaningful pursuits in your life). Or maybe you're retired and now have the time and desire to give more focus to managing your capital. Whatever your situation, one thing remains true: when you own stocks, you are a business owner and a business investor.

One of the most effective ways I've found to reinforce this mindset is by creating a pro forma company – an imaginary business that reflects your actual holdings. You build this by aggregating your proportional share of each company's revenue, operational earnings (EBIT), net earnings, free cash flow, net cash position and dividends. This composite snapshot allows you to think and act like the owner of a single, well-structured business – which in essence is exactly what you are.

On the following page, it could look like this:

My Group (US$)	Company 1	Company 2	Company 3	Company 4	Company 5	Company 6	Total
Revenue	618,212	1,005,702	241,920	1,432,373	3,164,179	1,302,894	7,765,280
EBIT	155,115	235,248	60,001	332,282	161,304	109,944	1,053,894
Net earnings	117,090	181,934	44,954	257,266	123,897	84,197	809,337
Free cash flow	112,086	157,235	47,557	261,256	110,267	75,264	763,665
Net cash position	34,439	271,178	-50,174	775,269	174,993	-91,876	1,113,829
Dividends	60,560	131,308	13,440	225,232	84,665	0	515,205

When reviewing 'My Group', keep in mind that each of your companies generates wealth for you in multiple ways. First, each company produces earnings, of which you own a share. While not all earnings are distributed as dividends each year, a portion is often reinvested back into the company or allocated to new ventures. You also build wealth through the growth of your companies, as they generate increasing profits over time, assuming operations go well. Finally, you receive dividends that provide a steady stream of income, which you can either reinvest or use as you see fit. Note: for a description of all the relevant figures and calculations, see the Appendix.

Let's evaluate the thinking behind establishing 'My Group'. You start by taking your share of the company's revenue. You do that by taking your number of shares in the company and dividing it by the total number of outstanding shares and then multiplying it by the company's revenue. That will give you your share of the revenue. You do the same when it comes to EBIT, net earnings, free cash flow and net cash position. When it comes to dividends, you take the dividend per share and multiply it by the number of shares you have.

Once you've followed the same process for all your companies and added the figures together, you'll have a picture of your pro forma company, My Group.

In this example, the investor is a co-owner of six companies, and his pro forma company has a revenue of over US$7.7 million and net earnings of over US$800,000. We can conclude that My Group is relatively conservatively financed, with an aggregated net cash position of over US$1.1 million. The investor can also see that his group pays an annual dividend of more than half a million US$.

Now, it is obvious that each company is in reality operating independently and has its own life. But as an investor it is important that you think of your companies as a group of business that each have a stream of earnings and dividends that flow to you.

At the end of the day, you should focus on making the earnings of My Group as large as possible in ten to twenty years. If you do that, you can be sure that the valuation of My Group will follow.

Let's say you succeed in quadrupling earnings over the next ten years – from US$809,000 to US$3.2 million. That would represent an average increase in earnings of approximately 15%. In such a scenario, you could be confident that the value of My Group had increased more or less proportionally.

Meanwhile, you'll also have benefited from the dividends distributed along the way – an important part of your total investment return.

41.
Discipline and Structure Your Investment Work

At the outset of this book, we explored why it's so challenging to consistently outperform the stock market over the long term.

Two fundamental dynamics inform our conclusions.

First, most investors are primarily focused on stock prices and tend to be impatient in their pursuit of returns. Second, nearly every other participant in the market – including brokers, analysts, media and fund managers – profits from trading activity. The more trades investors make, the better it is for them.

These dynamics fuel a massive amount of short-term activity and contribute to significant market volatility. These forces are often self-reinforcing: volatility drives emotional reactions, which drive trading, which drives more volatility.

In this environment of constant noise, dramatic price swings and a media landscape where so-called experts compete to be the loudest voice in the room, the only rational response is to adopt a disciplined, structured and long-term approach to investing.

USE THE INVESTMENT PRINCIPLES

Start by implementing the three core investment principles. If you always remember to think like a business owner, you can use Mr. Market to serve rather than guide you and you can invest with a solid margin of safety.

This might sound simple, but it is not always easy to do. Thinking like a business owner means that you stop looking at stock prices every day and focus instead on the company's financial performance. And letting

Mr. Market serve you means that you really handle it with calmness when the stock market plummets 10–20% while everyone else begins to panic.

Investing with a margin of safety likewise sounds straightforward but is not always easy to do – especially when you have high-growth companies with an impressive stock-price development tempting you to jump on the train like everybody else. Always investing with a margin of safety takes discipline.

INVEST IN GREAT COMPANIES – RUN BY EXCELLENT MANAGEMENT

On top of the three principles, you invest in great companies – run by excellent management. As a matter of fact, finding great companies and ensuring they are run by excellent management is not that difficult. Look at the financial performance of the company. Examine how much of the revenue is converted into profit (the EBIT margin) to assess how profitable the business is. Look at the growth rate and then evaluate the return on capital. The numbers and financial trajectory will give you the answer. Your job – and this is the real challenge – is to determine what the company's moat is, and whether that competitive advantage is sustainable over the next ten years, so the company can continue being great. When you study a company's management, it's also quite possible to assess whether their performance is poor, average, or excellent. Look at how management focuses on operational efficiency, how it compares to the competitors and how (and whether!) capital allocation is explained!

Take a close look at acquisitions and whether the trade-off between share buybacks and dividend payments is clearly justified. Put it all together, and you'll have a solid analysis of management's performance.

USE BUFFETT'S HURDLE RATE OR THE FUTURE VALUATION METHOD

We discussed our investment hurdle rate in detail in Part V. You use the hurdle rate when you are sure you're looking at a great company, run by excellent management, within your circle of competence and you are confident that earnings growth will at least outpace inflation over time.

If it is a normal-growth company with 5–6% growth, you aim to achieve a 10% return on your investment based on the company's current (normalized) earnings before tax – or a 7.8% return after tax, assuming a corporate tax rate of 22%. This corresponds to a P/E ratio of 10 on pre-tax earnings and a P/E ratio of approximately 13 on after-tax earnings.

For high-growth companies within your circle of competence, you must first ensure the growth is strong and sustainable – sufficiently that the company's sales and earnings are likely to double in the foreseeable future. In these cases, you invest when you can expect a 15% pre-tax return on your capital based on the company's earnings after it has doubled in size, or 11.7% after tax (15% × (1 – 22%) = 11.7%).

The target return after the company has doubled translates into a 7.5% return on today's normalized pre-tax earnings, or approximately 6% after tax. That implies a P/E ratio of 13.33 on today's pre-tax numbers and about 17 on today's after-tax numbers.

Here's a simple table to summarize the hurdle rates:

Scenario	Pre-tax return	After-tax return (22%)	Implied P/E (pre-tax)	Implied P/E (after-tax)
Normal growth	10%	7.8%	10	12.82 ≈ 13
High growth (today's basis)	7.5%	5.85% ≈ 6%	13.33	17.1 ≈ 17

As Warren Buffett says, 'Keep it simple.' But it being simple doesn't necessarily mean it's easy!

These hurdle rates offer attractive return opportunities with a built-in margin of safety – provided you're operating within your circle of competence, conducting sound financial analysis and drawing the right conclusions about the business and its leadership.

You can also use the alternative to Buffett's classic hurdle rate focus – the inversion process, the future valuation standard we discussed. In this approach, you estimate the company's expected future value and compare it to today's valuation. This allows you to determine the expected annual return, to which you add the dividend yield to get your expected total annual return.

If you apply this method, I recommend using a five-year time horizon, a maximum growth rate of 10% and a capitalization factor between 10 and 25, depending on the company's quality. Conservative investors may prefer a lower maximum capitalization factor, such as 20.

My own preferred hurdle rate for investing is an expected annual return of 15%. Some investors may consider that too high and accept a lower target, perhaps 12% or even 10%.

Whatever valuation method and hurdle rate you adopt, the key is consistency. Nothing is more dangerous than 'mathematical drifting', where you constantly change your approach to valuation and investment decisions.

The evidence for this is straightforward: it is exactly what happens when you invest based on market sentiment. Mr. Market continuously shifts his perspective and priorities, offering different prices every day. At times, he and the average investor may be willing to pay 40 times earnings (P/E 40) for a company full of promise – only to value the same business at less than 15 times earnings a few months later. Remember, the intrinsic value of a company rarely changes significantly within a week, a month, or even a year. Adhering to your valuation standards and remaining patient is essential. Sooner or later, the right opportunity will present itself. Do not chase investments by lowering your hurdle rates.

Of course, from time to time, you may encounter opportunities with even higher potential returns. But more often than not you'll find that great companies – run by exceptional management – rarely meet your hurdle rates. That's perfectly fine. You don't need dozens of investments. You need just a few – but they must be the right ones.

Personally, I make only one or two investments per year, and I'm perfectly satisfied with that.

It's worth emphasizing a few key points for your future investment work.

Every time you're considering making an investment, ask yourself: 'What do I know about this company, its management and its future development that the broader market has overlooked or underappreciated – so much so that I want to become a part-owner of the business at this price level?'

The answer you should hope for is: 'This company will be worth significantly more in five, ten or twenty years than it is today.' The least compelling answer is: 'It's probably 10–20% undervalued compared to the current stock price.' Just because a company is 10-20% undervalued today doesn't mean it will be worth significantly more in the far future.

In short, be mindful of whether your reasoning is grounded in long-term fundamentals or is short-term and more speculative in nature.

As we begin to tie everything together, the second point worth remembering is that you cannot expect to find the best investment opportunities where everyone else is already looking. Nor should you expect others to direct your attention to the most attractive investments. In fact, the best investments are often found where very few people are looking.

And how could it be otherwise? It's hard to imagine that a large global company followed by thirty or forty equity analysts, owned by virtually every institutional investor and under constant media scrutiny hasn't already been thoroughly analyzed from every angle. Such situations are not typically where the best opportunities are found. In such cases, your only real edge lies in the possibility that the market and its participants are overly focused on the short term – failing to consider what the business might look like in five, ten or twenty years.

On the other hand, businesses that aren't followed by a dozen analysts, that have few or no institutional investors among their shareholders and that fly well below the media's radar can present some of the most compelling investment opportunities – especially if they are great businesses run by the founder and with a long runway for strong earnings growth.

STAY RATIONAL WHEN YOU SELL A COMPANY

As you gain experience, you'll discover that selling is, temperamentally and mentally, a very different discipline from buying.

It's important to remember that selling a great company is almost always a mistake – especially if the business is still growing and continues to generate high returns on capital. The only valid reason to sell a great company is that the reasons for your initial investment in it no longer hold true.

You should never sell simply because the share price has gone up, or because the broader market is experiencing panic and widespread fear-driven selling. In fact, these are often the best times to buy, not sell.

42.

Implement Good Habits – Get Rid of Bad Habits

With investing, there are habits you'll want to strengthen and habits you'll want to get rid of because they distract your investment work.

ADAPT YOUR INVESTMENT WORK TO FIT YOUR EVERYDAY LIFE

You need to adapt your investment work to fit your life and the time you can realistically dedicate each week to such work. The key isn't how many hours you put in as an investor, but how effectively you use them.

When you feel pressed for time as a business owner, take comfort in this simple truth: it is your company, not you, that generates your wealth. Never forget that your company continues to work for you, every single day; while you're busy doing other things, your company is selling products or services and generating income on your behalf.

BECOME A LIFELONG LEARNER

Dedicate as much time as you can reading and learning. A typical publicly traded company releases an annual report, four quarterly updates and several announcements each year. Additionally, there is usually an online investor presentation each quarter, along with various statements from management in the media when significant events occur. Overall, I estimate it takes about ten hours per year to read the company's reports and stay updated on its developments. None of these hours need to be found precisely when the company releases its reports and updates.

You can, even to your great advantage, read the relevant material in the evening, at weekends, or at any other time that fits into your schedule and life. The most important thing is that you concentrate and think carefully about the information you're reading and what it means for your company and its moat – how it influences the company's position ten years from now.

As an investor, you should remain curious and strive to learn as much as possible. An ongoing learning process that continues throughout your life forms a solid foundation for your investment work.

Some days will allow you more time to read and absorb knowledge than others; that's a simple fact of life. But you shouldn't panic if you can't follow your company for a few days – it will do just fine. Just keep learning and make sure you go to bed every night with a little more insight than you woke up with that morning.

KEEP TRACK OF YOUR PERFORMANCE

Routinely studying how your investments would have performed if you had made no changes over the years is one of the most insightful habits you can adopt. This will help you understand the value you personally contribute as an investor versus the value generated by the companies' business development and earnings growth.

For example, take a look at your portfolio as it was five years ago – your 'five-year portfolio'. Update the stock prices to their current values and compare the total value of this five-year portfolio to the value of your current portfolio. This comparison will provide a clear picture of the value you have personally added during this period.

If your five-year portfolio is worth more than your current portfolio, you'll know that leaving your investments untouched while you spent time on something else would have made better financial sense. On the other hand, if your current portfolio is worth more than the updated value of the five-year portfolio, you'll know that you have indeed contributed value as an investor.

I expect that the results will not only surprise you but will also confirm that it is the companies in your portfolio that are making you wealthier over time and not you. This is why many people become quite wealthy by simply buying shares and then doing nothing until retirement.

Let the companies work for you while you remain relatively passive. That's the name of the game!

AVOID CHECKING STOCK PRICES EVERY DAY

Any routine that shifts your focus away from daily stock-price fluctuations and towards a company's operations and long-term earnings will improve your chances of outperforming the market.

Constantly checking stock prices does not enhance your ability to think like a business owner. If you find yourself eagerly waiting for the stock market to open each morning and feel the urge to check prices as soon as trading begins, you are focusing on the wrong thing. You have neither lost nor gained anything simply because stock prices move up or down – they do that every day.

If you want to talk about 'gains' or 'losses', you must evaluate the company's future earnings potential. Only when a company releases an announcement that significantly changes its long-term profitability – whether positively or negatively – does it make sense to reassess your investment case and consider the stock price.

Establish a routine where you check prices only once a week or even once a month. However, make sure you automatically receive all company announcements, so you remain informed about what truly matters: the company's future earnings power.

STAY PUT DURING TRADING HOURS

Another useful routine is to avoid making quick investment decisions during trading hours. Decisions about buying or selling should be made when the market is closed. Take time in the evening to thoroughly review a company and make your investment decision before you go to bed. You can then execute it with a clear mind the following morning.

The only time it is necessary to make investment decisions during trading hours is when something significant happens that might fundamentally change your investment case, or when the market experiences a sharp decline, making some of your prospects cheap enough to meet your required returns according to your hurdle rate.

AVOID LOAN-BASED INVESTMENTS IN STOCKS

Never borrow money to rapidly expand your investments.

Debt-financed investments carry significant financial risk, which becomes especially evident during major market downturns. In such situations, lenders may require you to liquidate your investments if there is insufficient collateral to cover the loans. Borrowing to invest also undermines patience, composure and the mindset necessary to think like a long-term business owner.

FORGET MACRO

As a business owner, you recognize that your company is influenced by both national and global economic and political developments. However, no business owner would consider selling part of their ownership stake simply because economists or financial experts predict certain macroeconomic changes – whether it's a slight interest-rate adjustment by the Federal Reserve, a minor shift in inflation, or fluctuating oil prices. So why should you allow your investment decisions to be dictated by macroeconomic trends or expert forecasts about what might happen to the economy in the near term? Instead, stay focused on your companies and trust that the stock market tends to rise over the long term and that your wealth will too, if you follow the principles and guidelines in this book. Step by step, you will become richer and get closer to financial freedom.

That does not mean you should ignore how the market as such is valued. Investing in a market that is generally undervalued or overvalued can make a heck of a difference to your long-term performance.

Again, I use Warren Buffett's favorite metric of the market valuation. Warren Buffett has said several times that he considers the best indicator to be the market cap compared with the US GDP (Gross Domestic Product) as the best indicator. In other words, he looks at the value of all listed companies compared with the US GDP. For practical reasons, I use the Wilshire 5000 to GDP ratio. As you can see from the chart below, the market has never been more expensive than it is currently (late 2025). Over the long term, the stock market is valued at something like 80–85% of the GDP on average; yet as I write it is valued at more than 220% of the GDP.

The relationship between the 'Total Value of All Publicly Traded Stocks and US GDP' is Warren Buffett's preferred indicator for assessing whether the stock market is overvalued or undervalued. As the chart shows, the market has never been more expensive, which is why it's no coincidence that Warren Buffett's company, Berkshire Hathaway, at the end of 2025 held the largest cash reserve ever, with hundreds of billions of dollars waiting to be invested at a more attractive time.

43.
Building Your Portfolio

It goes without saying that the composition of your portfolio should differ significantly from the structure of a theoretical 'optimal' investment portfolio. After all, you cannot expect to achieve different results than the market if you invest exactly like the market does.

One of the most common portfolio models suggests that investors allocate roughly half of their savings to stocks and the other half to bonds. The rationale is that bond returns tend to be more stable than stock returns, albeit lower in the long term. This allocation aims to produce a smoother progression of portfolio value over time.

Historically, long-term returns on US Treasury Bonds have averaged around 5% annually, depending on the type. By contrast, the long-term return on US stocks, as measured by the S&P 500 Index, has been approximately 8–10% per year.

Let's run those facts through our 'rationale filter'.

If you're a long-term investor, then short-term fluctuations should not influence your investment decisions. What matters most is not the annual stability of returns, but the final outcome.

Now, imagine you invest 50% of your portfolio in bonds yielding 5% annually and 50% in stocks earning 10% annually. You also maintain this allocation consistently over time. Your average annual return would be 7.5%, compared with 10% if you invested solely in the S&P 500. In other words, you're sacrificing 2.5% in annual returns in exchange for a more stable but ultimately lower long-term growth trajectory – because half your capital is earning the lower bond yield.

Let's put that into perspective with an example.

Assume you're twenty-five years old and inherit US$10,000 from your great-grandmother. You decide to invest the entire amount until you retire aged sixty-five, forty years from now. Ignoring taxes and other costs for simplicity, your result would be:

Portfolio allocation	Annual return	Value after forty years
50% bonds/50% stocks	7.5%	US$180,442
100% stocks	10%	US$452,593

The difference is striking. By choosing a portfolio balanced between stocks and bonds, you would end up with less than half the wealth compared with investing entirely in stocks. The key takeaway is clear: as a long-term investor, maximizing your return matters more than minimizing short-term volatility.

HOW MANY STOCKS SHOULD YOUR PORTFOLIO CONTAIN?

Assuming you accept the long-term advantages of investing in stocks, the next logical question is how many companies you should invest in and how you should allocate your savings among them.

According to Warren Buffett, you don't need a large number of different stocks in your portfolio. As a young investor, he was willing to allocate up to 25% of his capital to the single company he believed had the best prospects. In total, Buffett considers a portfolio of about six companies to be sufficient.

His late partner Charlie Munger went even further, suggesting that as few as three companies could suffice, assuming each meets your required standards.

On the other hand, it's common practice among professional asset managers to hold significantly more diversified portfolios, sometimes containing thirty to fifty companies or more.

Naturally, the more companies you hold, the smaller the share each one occupies in your portfolio. This diversification leads your returns to mirror the broader market. But mimicking the market won't help you achieve your goal if your goal is to outperform it.

USE A '10 X 10' PORTFOLIO AS YOUR STARTING POINT

Of course, managing your own money is fundamentally different than managing money on behalf of others. This book does not attempt to review every portfolio strategy or weigh their respective pros and cons. Instead, I'll outline a simple yet effective portfolio approach that offers key advantages without introducing excessive long-term risk – provided you follow the investment guidelines discussed.

The '10 x 10' model is a sensible strategy. Let's explore why it makes intuitive sense, while recognizing that it should be viewed only as a guiding principle – a kind of North Star.

If an investor allocates capital to what are expected to be the ten most attractive companies – in terms of both quality and valuation – the portfolio will naturally consist of businesses that are above average on both dimensions and carry higher-than-average return potential.

Furthermore, by focusing exclusively on the ten highest-quality and most attractively valued companies, one should, all else being equal, expect long-term returns to exceed those of a portfolio diversified across twenty companies instead of ten. In other words, the ten most attractive investments are expected to outperform those ranked eleven through twenty.

At the same time, holding ten companies diversified across different industries – and with as little correlation as possible – while still remaining within the investor's *circle of competence,* is sufficient to achieve meaningful risk diversification.

When you start investing your money, you might place a bit more in your highest-conviction ideas and a bit less in the rest.

Then, let your investments grow. Each time you have additional capital to invest, look for the most attractive opportunity. If one of your top choices is a company you already own, simply add more to that position.

The most important principle, however, is not how you allocate new funds but that you avoid prematurely selling your 'winners' just because they've appreciated and now represent more than 10% of your portfolio. Selling a successful investment simply because it has grown may cost you dearly. You could be cutting short your ownership in what might become the next Walmart, Amazon, Berkshire Hathaway, or Apple – foregoing millions of dollars in future wealth.

44.

The Power of Your Checklist

The checklist helps ensure that your investment process – from mindset to methodology – remains structured and focused on the business fundamentals that drive long-term value creation in your portfolio companies.

When you read an annual report or a quarterly report from the company you own or follow, use the check list to ensure that you keep yourself updated about all the important issues in the business and compare the performance to its competitors.

The following extract from my own general checklist should provide you with a template to start with.

Company name
Company profile
- Moat (description)
- The biggest risks
- Megatrends (industry/company)
- The most important success factors for the company

Earnings and growth
Earnings growth (the platform):
- Market share – size of the industry
- Existing growth level
- Long runway?

Why are earnings growing?
- Expansion into new market with existing products/services
- Sell more of existing products/services in present markets

- Raise prices
- Reduce costs
- Get rid of losing operations/activities
- Start selling new products/services

Profits and hurdle rate

How does the adjusted net profit over time compare with FCF?
Return on my investment:

- Adjusted net profit / stock price
- Expected growth rate
- Dividends and/or buybacks

Return on capital

- Return on operational assets
- ROIC
- ROUNTA
- ROE

- Allocation of capital
- Incremental investments in existing business
- Acquisitions
- Reduce debt/save up cash
- Dividends
- Buyback stocks

Shareholder structure

- Founders
- Institutional investors
- Professional private investors
- Private investors in general

The checklist is a simple tool that allows you to periodically review the investment case for the companies you co-own, ensuring that you consider all angles before making a new investment. There is no standard model for the 'perfect' checklist, and mine has evolved over the years. In my experience, it's not the number of items that makes a checklist effective but its ability to provoke you to ask the right 'Why?' questions.

Over time, you will refine your checklist and come to realize that some factors play a greater role than others. The key drivers will also vary depending on the industry in which a company operates. In my experience, regardless of the sector or business model, there are usually two or three critical factors that ultimately determine a company's long-term ability to create value.

These are typically the elements that enable a company to sustain its moat, generate high returns on invested capital, and maintain healthy, sustainable growth. When these fundamentals are in place – and when management is also capable of running the business efficiently and allocating capital rationally – the foundation for long-term value creation is solid.

Monitoring how these factors evolve over time is a central part of any investor's long-term discipline – and soon, you will experience the power of your checklist.

45.

Plan B: if You Want to Invest Rationally but Don't Have the Time

This book would be incomplete if it didn't offer a solution for people who wish to invest rationally but simply don't have the time to engage in the work of being an active investor.

Naturally, anyone can save and invest rationally – it just requires rational thinking.

If you don't have the time to actively manage your investments, the rational solution – your Plan B – is to gradually invest in index funds as and when you have money available, choosing the index that best fits your market. For American investors, this typically means investing in S&P 500 index funds. If you're a German investor, you would invest in funds that follow the DAX index; and for a UK investor, the FTSE index would be the logical choice.

It's important to select index funds with the lowest possible management fees.

By investing in index funds that mirror the overall market, your investment returns will naturally track the performance of that market. This approach means you will not outperform the index – but that's entirely acceptable when you consider that the S&P 500, for example, has historically delivered an average annual return of around 10% with dividends reinvested.

To put this into perspective: imagine you invest the equivalent of US$10,000 per year for forty years, and that you increase that amount annually by 3% to account for inflation. Over that period, you will have invested a total of approximately US$787,000. However, because the S&P 500 grows by an average of 10% per year, the value of your investments would compound to about US$6 million over forty years.

Plan B also gives you the opportunity to achieve financial freedom at a certain age.

46.

A Final Word

It is my hope that this structured exploration of a rational, independent foundation for achieving attractive returns and long-term wealth through stock investing has offered you both insight and inspiration to develop and refine your own investment journey. If this book helps you grow your savings more than you otherwise might have, then it will have fulfilled its purpose. And if it has guided you away from blindly following markets or so-called experts – and towards more independent thinking – then it will have achieved even more.

On a personal level, I've fulfilled a lifelong objective: to try my best to make a difference for potentially millions of people around the world who wish to work hard and aim to save, invest and gradually improve their financial future – perhaps even to the point of achieving financial freedom.

If you've found value in this book, I hope you'll offer a quiet thank you to Warren Buffett. Without his unmatched wisdom and insight, countless investors – me included – would never have built the kind of wealth and security they now enjoy.

Writing this book has been challenging but deeply rewarding and I am grateful. As a former journalist, I know the power of putting thoughts clearly into words. Behind these pages lie my years of experience: as a journalist and business editor, as a company owner and advisor to boards and executives of public companies and private-equity firms across the Nordics, and as an investor for over fifty years – fifteen of them as a full-time professional. I've read and reread over 200 books on business and investing and have reviewed more than 7,000 pages of notes and clippings, all before even putting pen to paper.

If I could leave you with just one final piece of investment advice after all these years and all this work, it would be this: become a long-term owner of a few truly great businesses – and be extraordinarily patient.

Use your time to learn and prepare, not just in investing, so that you're ready when opportunities arise. Observe your surroundings, work with great people, and always focus on building strength from the inside.

Wishing you success and all the best on your journey.

Peter Gustafson

Key takeaways from Part VIII

- Start by implementing the three core investment principles:
- Think like a business owner
- Take advantage of Mr. Market
- Invest with a margin of safety
- Discipline and structure your investment work so it fits naturally into your life.
- Invest:
- In great companies
- In excellent management
- Using Buffett's hurdle rates
- According to your circle of competence and your investor profile
- Implement sound and good habits.
- Get rid of bad habits.
- Stop following the stock prices every day.
- Build your portfolio as a '10 x 10' – invest 10% of your money in the ten most attractive companies by both quality and price.
- Filter in new money when you have free savings.
- Don't sell a company just because the stock price has gone up and it represents more than 10% of your portfolio.

- Always compare a potential new investment with the best investment you already have in your portfolio.
- If you don't have the time to do investment work, go to the rational Plan B.
- Following Plan B, you invest your savings in a low-cost stock-index fund and just do nothing.

Appendix

47.

Getting the Most Important Numbers Right

Naturally, numbers will play a significant role in your work as a business investor. The stock price is a number, price changes are percentages, a company's revenue and profit are numbers, the return on invested capital is a percentage and the return on your portfolio is a number.

But having the ability to calculate all sorts of key figures for the company and being able to understand the most obscure representations of how asset managers always outperform the index they compare themselves to, should not lead you to believe that only numbers are important to your development as a successful investor. Understanding business and how the human incentive system works and drives management decisions always come first. When you can master those ideas within your own circle of competence, then you have gone a long way; but you'll still need to understand business numbers and financial statements to get the picture in full color.

Let me be clear: it is essential that you understand the most necessary financial figures and how to calculate the key ratios, such as the ROUNTA or the ROIC, which is some of the most important indicators of whether a business is a great business and management is doing a good job allocating capital.

But you need only master the basic arithmetic. All those formulas with Greek letters taught at business schools around the world are practically worthless. How can it be otherwise? You're working towards finding a small number of great businesses with a long runway so that profits can grow for many, many years while ensuring that the company is run by excellent management. If you can find such companies, and are sure you've invested according to your hurdle rate, then the most important skill to master is patience. If you can do that, as few as two or three such investments will be sufficient for you and your family to achieve financial freedom. You don't need to know Greek letters or sophisticated formulas to realize that.

But it is crucial that you understand the most central numbers and can examine the company's performance over the last five to ten years to get an idea of how the business is developing. You must study the income statement to figure out how well the business is doing and how much it is growing in sales and earnings. In the balance sheet, you will discover which assets the company uses to produce the sales and profits; and on the liability side you'll see how much equity and debt the company has used to finance its assets. Last but not least, when you view the cash-flow statement you'll understand whether the company's activities are producing a solid free cash flow.

As you gain experience, you'll find it easier to understand the numbers and how to calculate the different key metrics like earnings per share and return on invested capital. If you are in doubt, you can get help at many online sites that offer explanations of accounting numbers and financial measures free of charge. As an example, www.investopedia.com offers hundreds of free financial and accounting explanations and advice on calculating the numbers.

It is well beyond the scope of this book to provide a thorough explanation of all the numbers and calculations you'll need; but over the years you will develop a better understanding of accounting – the language of business. I can only advise you to spend time improving your circle of competence within accounting and financial numbers.

Let's focus on a general understanding of what you'll need to begin investing.

48.

The Income Statement

The income statement is where the company provides the numbers related to revenue and operating costs. This leads to an operating profit, which is a very important figure to track. Unfortunately, there are several ways to calculate operating profit and different costs that may or may not be included. Out of the operating profit, the company must pay for financial costs from loans and currency transactions. After these payments, the company can observe how much it earns before taxes – the number Warren Buffett refers to when he speaks about his investment hurdle rate. Once taxes are paid, the company is left with its net earnings – sometimes called net profit. If you divide the net earnings by the number of shares outstanding (some of which might be owned by you), you get the earnings per share (EPS). EPS is often used to calculate the most popular key metric on the stock market, the price/earnings (P/E) ratio. The P/E ratio simply tells you how much you need to pay (the stock price) to receive the earnings (per share). The challenge is that individual companies can choose to present different numbers in the income statement and in different ways – especially operating earnings. So, let's go through the income statement step by step, and I will explain how to read and interpret the different figures.

MICROSOFT CORPORATION

INCOME STATEMENT	Fiscal year ended June 30,		
(US$ millions)	2025	2024	2023
REVENUE:			
Product	63.946	64.773	64.699
Service and other	217.778	180.349	147.216
Total revenue	281.724	245.122	211.915
COST OF REVENUE			
Product	13.501	15.272	17.804
Service and other	74.330	58.842	48.059
Total cost of revenue	87.831	74.114	65.863
Gross margin	193.893	171.008	146.052
Research and development	32.488	29.510	27.195
Sales and marketing	25.654	24.456	22.759
General and administration	7.223	7.609	7.575
Operating income	128.528	109.433	88.523
Other income (expenses), net	-4.901	-1.646	788
Income before income taxes	123.627	107.787	89.311
Provision for income taxes	21.795	19.651	16.950
Net income	101.832	88.136	72.361
Shares outstanding (millions)			
Basic	7.433	7.431	7.446
Diluted	7.465	7.469	7.472
Earnings per share (US$)			
Basic	13.70	11.86	9.72
Diluted	13.64	11.80	9.68

(see explanation on the next page)

REVENUE – OR SALES

The revenue is the sales number and tells you how much the company has invoiced its customers over the year.

revenue = invoiced sales

Management can choose to make the revenue number look larger or smaller by using different accounting techniques, so you need to know how the figure is generated. The revenue number is used to show how much the company has grown its sales from year to year. When you read or hear that a company has grown by 8%, this most likely refers to how much the company's revenue has increased compared with last year. Of course, it's important that the company has grown its revenue by 8%; but your job is to ensure that it's not only revenue that management has been able to grow. For you as an owner or investor, the long-term growth in earnings is what truly matters. Remember: stocks follow earnings per share. Unfortunately, it's very common to see management happy and proud because revenue is growing, while ignoring the fact that earnings per share are stagnating or even decreasing. In such cases, the company's value (the stock price) at best doesn't increase and may even decline.

As shown on page 256, in Microsoft's income statement, it is an exceptionally profitable company, with an EBIT margin (US$128,528 million / US$281,724 million) of nearly 46% and a net income margin of approximately 36% (US$101,832 million / US$281,724 million) of revenue in 2025. A company achieves such margins on a sustainable basis only when its revenue and earnings are protected by an exceptionally strong moat.

WALMART INC.

INCOME STATEMENT	Years to 31 January		
(US$ millions)	2025	2024	2023
REVENUES:			
Net sales	674.538	642.637	605.881
Membership and other income	6.447	5.488	5.408
Total revenues	**680.985**	**648.125**	**611.289**
COSTS AND EXPENSES:			
Cost of sales	511.753	490.142	463.721
Operating, selling, general and administrative expenses	139.884	130.971	127.140
Operating income	**29.348**	**27.012**	**20.428**
INTEREST:			
Debt	2.249	2.259	1.787
Finance lease	479	424	341
Interest income	-483	-546	-254
Interest, net	2.245	2.137	1.874
Other (gains) and losses	794	3.027	1.538
Income before income taxes	**26.309**	**21.848**	**17.016**
Provision for income taxes	6.152	5.578	5.724
Consolidated net income	**20.157**	**16.270**	**11.292**
Consolidated net (income) loss attributable to noncontrolling interest	-721	-759	388
Consolidated net income attributable to Walmart	**19.436**	**15.511**	**11.680**
Weighted-average common shares outstanding: *millions*			
Basic	8.041	8.077	8.171
Diluted	8.081	8.108	8.202
Net income per common share: US$			
Basic net income per common share attributable to Walmart	2.42	1.92	1.43
Diluted net income per common share attributable to Walmart	2.41	1.91	1.42
Dividends declared per common share US$	0.8300	0.7600	0.7467

(see explanation on the next page)

COSTS

A company has many different types of costs, but operating costs can generally be divided into two main categories. The first is the cost of sales or cost of goods sold. These are the direct costs associated with producing the product or service sold. The second includes all costs related to running the operation. When the company deducts the cost of sales from revenue, the result is a figure for gross profit:

$$\textbf{gross profit = revenue} \div \textbf{cost of sales}$$
$$\textbf{[also called costs of goods sold]}$$

$$\textbf{gross margin = gross profit / revenue}$$

Few analysts and financial experts pay much attention to gross profit and gross margin. But these figures can provide very important insights about a company if you take the time to analyze them.

Gross profit and gross margin represent what's left after the cost of production is covered. The higher the gross margin, the more the company retains to cover other expenses. Let's explore this idea and use it to illustrate some interesting points.

If a product is sold for US$10 and the company has a gross profit of US$2 – or a gross margin of 20% – that means it costs US$8 to produce the product. Now, suppose the company operates in a highly competitive industry and has no moat to protect its earnings. Consequently, it cannot raise its prices when inflation hits and increases the production cost by 12.5%, pushing it from US$8 to US$9.

As shown on page 258, Walmart is a completely different type of company than Microsoft. Walmart generates more than twice the revenue of Microsoft (US$680 billion versus US$282 billion), but it operates with an EBIT margin of only 4.3% (US$29,348 million / US$680,985 million) compared to Microsoft's 46%. As we saw on the 'Moat Map', being the lowest-cost producer is the only viable strategy when there are many competitors – which is certainly the case in the grocery industry. As a result, Walmart is able to earn only about 20% of what Microsoft earns in net profit, even though its revenue is more than twice as large.

This reduces the gross profit from US$2 to US$1 – a 50% decrease. The gross margin also falls from 20% to 10%. In other words, the business's profitability is cut in half, leaving the company with only half as much money to cover all its other expenses. In many cases, a company in this position will need to cut operating expenses to an absolute minimum just to stay profitable, or else it may end up running at a loss. As an investor, you'd likely conclude that such a company will never become a great business.

Now let's take the opposite scenario. This company sells its product for US$10 but incurs only US$2 in production costs, resulting in a gross profit of US$8 and a gross margin of 80%. When inflation of 12.5% raises production costs to US$2.25, the company still retains a gross profit of US$7.75 – or a gross margin of 77.5%. It's likely that management could cut other costs by 2.5% to offset this increase, leaving earnings unaffected. It's also likely that the high gross margin indicates the presence of a protective moat, giving management the ability to raise prices without losing customers.

The higher the gross margin, the more protected the earnings are – and the more likely that management has built a moat around the company. So, high gross margins are something to look for when you're analyzing the income statement.

The second group of costs includes operating expenses such as sales, distribution, marketing, administrative expenses, employee salaries and research and development. These costs vary widely between companies and should be studied individually. It's important to understand that the efficiency with which these operating expenses are managed can differ greatly from one management team to another.

Quite often, operational costs balloon during good years. You may also find that when a company has run into trouble and new management has taken over, they are able to significantly reduce operating costs without serious consequences. The best way to evaluate a company's operating expenses is to compare them with competitors and to pay close attention to what management says or writes about cost control.

DEPRECIATION AND AMORTIZATION

Depreciation and amortization represent the final category of costs related to operations and assets. This is an important area, and many companies, analysts and financial experts manipulate depreciation and amortization expenses to present the company as more profitable than it really is.

Depreciation

Some companies report earnings before depreciation and amortization, using a metric known as **earnings before interest, taxes, depreciation and amortization (EBITDA)**, which has become very popular in the financial world. But the truth is that interest, taxes, depreciation and (some) amortization are real costs and must be paid by the company.

Despite EBITDA's widespread use in the financial sector, it is my strong advice that you never use it to value a company or evaluate its earnings. Instead, I recommend following Warren Buffett's approach to depreciation and amortization and calculating your earnings figure accordingly.

Let's first understand what depreciation is and how it affects the income statement. Depreciation is a standard accounting method that allows a company to spread the cost of acquiring a physical (tangible) asset – such as a factory, machinery, or equipment – over the asset's expected useful life.

For example, if a company buys a machine for US$10 million and expects it to last ten years, then it will record US$1 million in depreciation each year for ten years. As a result, the income statement will reflect a US$1 million depreciation expense annually.

Without depreciation accounting, the full US$10 million cost would have to be recorded in the year the machine was purchased. This would dramatically reduce earnings in the purchase year, while overstating profits in the following nine.

The key takeaway is that purchasing the machine is a US$10 million cost to the company – and that cost must be accounted for. Depreciation is not an accounting trick; it reflects the reality that physical assets lose value over time through use and obsolescence.

Therefore, we should always include depreciation when evaluating a company's earnings and future earning power.

Amortization

Just as depreciation spreads the cost of physical (tangible) assets over time, amortization spreads out the cost of non-physical (intangible) assets. These can include goodwill, patents, trademarks, customer relationships, product rights, software and capitalized development costs.

Amortization is also recorded in the income statement as an annual expense. So far, so good. However, there's a challenge: not all amortization expenses reflect real economic costs – they may exist only for accounting purposes.

Here's a simple example. Suppose a company acquires another business for US$100 million. If the buyer receives only US$20 million in tangible assets, the remaining US$80 million must be recorded as intangible assets like goodwill and customer relationships.

In the years following the acquisition, that US$80 million will typically be amortized – even though the value of those intangible assets may not have changed at all. Unlike physical machinery, these intangible assets don't necessarily lose value, yet the income statement still absorbs amortization charges.

Of course, some amortization – such as for software development or new product research and development – does reflect real economic cost. But other amortization is purely theoretical, leading to a distorted picture of a company's actual costs and earnings.

The fix is simple but requires some effort. You'll need to adjust the company's earnings by adding back any amortization of intangible assets that don't reflect real economic loss. In general, you should add the after-tax amortization of these intangibles to net profit to get a more accurate picture of true earnings. For that reason, many companies and investors prefer the EBITA number as a more accurate estimate of the company's operating performance.

However, as a business investor you must bear in mind that the company must still pay interest on its financial obligations and tax. It should come as no surprise, therefore, that Warren Buffett has often emphasized that adding back the amortization of intangible assets to reported earnings (net profit) usually gives a better view of a company's real earning power. In other words, Buffett does not leave the interest payments and tax hanging in the air because those costs are just as real as any other costs except amortization of intangible assets. I strongly recommend you do the same.

So, add back the amortization of the intangible assets not used in the operating business adjusted for tax, and then you have the number you could call 'net profit + tax-adjusted amortization of intangible assets', which is a very close approximation to the actual earnings of the company. Just remember to carefully examine which intangible assets are being amortized – and adjust only for those that truly don't decline in value.

OPERATING PROFIT

After all costs but interest and taxes have been paid, including depreciation and properly adjusted amortization, the result is the operating profit. This is an important figure, as it shows how much profit the company can generate from its sales and assets.

You will recall that in financial terms, operating profit is also known as earnings before interest and taxes (EBIT).

operating earnings (EBIT) = gross profit – operating costs – depreciation – adj. amortization

EBIT margin = EBIT / revenue

We will discuss operating profit further when we examine the important topic of return on invested capital.

For now, it's important to note that, generally speaking – and with a few exceptions – the higher the EBIT margin, the better the business. It should seem obvious that the more a company earns from each dollar of sales, the more profitable it is. A very high sustainable EBIT margin is often a strong indication that the company's earnings are protected by a competitive moat.

FINANCIAL COSTS

In the income statement, the company must report financial costs related to interest payments on debt and, if applicable, expenses related to currency. It's clear that the more debt a company uses to finance its operations, the higher the financial costs – and vice versa.

Generally speaking, great companies are so profitable that they don't need to use debt and very often have none. In fact, great companies are quite often able to report a positive income under financial costs, reflecting the company's cash holding and little or no debt.

At the other end of the 'quality-meter', some companies struggle just to produce profits. That profit can generate a reasonable return for the company's owners only if the company relies heavily on debt instead of equity. This is not necessarily a problem in the short term; but over time it can leave the company vulnerable if interest rates suddenly rise or financial markets freeze, making it difficult for the debt-laden company to refinance its loans.

PROFIT BEFORE TAX

After paying financial costs, the company's income statement shows how much it has earned before tax. Profit before tax is the number Warren Buffett uses in his investment hurdle rate. As previously described, Buffett requires that the profit before tax delivers at least a 10% return on his investment. Additionally, profit before tax must grow at a rate equal to or faster than the rate of inflation.

The reason Buffett uses profit before tax – and not the more popular profit after tax (also called net profit) – is because he pays taxes on all his companies at an aggregated level. In other words, it's not relevant for Buffett to look at after-tax profits at individual-company level.

PROFIT AFTER TAX – OR NET PROFITS

The corporate tax rate can vary from country to country but is typically around 20–25%. After taxes are paid, you are left with the company's profit after tax, also very often called earnings or net earnings. This is usually the simple number many investors use as the denominator when calculating P/E, the most common financial metric in discussing the price of a stock. But, as already outlined, it often requires some adjustments to show the real earnings of the company. And to follow Buffett's thinking, you must add the tax-adjusted amortization of intangible assets.

Buffett calls reported earnings + amortization of (some) intangible assets a very good representation of the company's real earnings. And if you follow his advice, you should use this number to calculate your return in relation to your investment hurdle rate.

Buffett's earnings number = adjusted net profit ≈ reported profit after tax (net profit) + adjusted amortization of intangibles

In some cases, you don't need to adjust for the amortization of intangibles, as there is little or no amortization. In other situations, the company reports significant amortization of intangibles, and some of that is not a real cost and should be added back to earnings. Remember to adjust any amortization you add back for the tax effect.

Now that we've reviewed the income statement at a high level and determined how to calculate the earnings figure we need – the reported earnings plus amortization of the intangible assets – for our investment hurdle rate and return calculations, let's look at the balance sheet, how the company reports assets and liabilities and which items should be closely examined.

49.

The Balance Sheet

While the income statement provides an overview of how much the company has generated in revenue, what expenses were incurred and the resulting profit, the balance sheet first reveals the assets the company uses to generate that revenue and profit and then shows the liabilities used to finance the assets.

In other words, the balance sheet gives us a look under the hood, allowing us to examine the company's assets and understand how management has chosen to finance them through liabilities.

From an analytical perspective, there's no doubt that the balance sheet offers much deeper insight into a company than the income statement does. Yet, investors and analysts almost exclusively focus on the income statement when evaluating company performance. This is likely because it includes the earnings figures used to estimate the company's current value – and, by extension, what its stock price should be.

However, without paying attention to the balance sheet and the capital invested in the business, one risks overlooking the most critical metrics of all: return on unlevered net tangible assets (ROUNTA) and return on invested capital (ROIC). As we discussed, ROUNTA is the key figure to indicate the quality of the company and ROIC is the indicator of how well management has allocated capital. And without analyzing the assets themselves, it becomes difficult to judge whether that return is sustainable.

Before we go through each item, here's a quick insight. When you look at the figures in the balance sheet, where the most recent numbers are usually shown in one column and the numbers from the same time last year are shown beside them, start by comparing where the biggest changes have occurred. This gives you a good indication of where to focus your attention.

BALANCE SHEET: ASSETS

The structure of the assets in the balance sheet varies from country to country. In the United States, current assets are listed first, followed by non-current assets. In Europe, the order is reversed. Don't let this confuse you – it doesn't change the overall picture or the individual asset items.

Current assets

Under current assets, you'll find figures for how much the company has in cash, inventory and accounts receivable (unpaid customer invoices). There is usually also a line item labeled 'other current assets'.

Current assets are part of the working capital the company operates with, and a key characteristic is that these items change continuously. Customers pay their invoices, new invoices are issued, the cash balance rises and falls and the same goes for the inventory.

Your task is to keep an eye on whether the cash balance is larger than necessary – and if it is, ask yourself why. The same applies to the inventory and accounts receivable. The larger the inventory, and the more unpaid invoices the company has issued, the more capital is tied up in the business, which puts pressure on the return on invested capital. So, the development in current assets tells you something about how efficiently management is using capital – and whether you're dealing with excellent management.

Non-current assets

Under non-current assets, you'll find all the items that are more or less fixed and unchanged from month to month. These are usually divided into two categories: tangible assets and intangible assets – in other words, physical and non-physical assets.

Tangible assets

Under tangible assets, depending on the industry, you'll find an overview of factories, machinery and other physical equipment such as trucks. For an

IT company that sells software, tangible assets may be minimal, whereas industrial or transportation companies may have significant tangible assets. These could be owned equipment or leased equipment, where the value of lease contracts is included as part of tangible assets.

In relation to our earlier discussion of depreciation in the income statement, you can find in the notes to the financial statements how much the company has depreciated its tangible assets over the reporting period.

Intangible assets

It's fair to say that intangible assets are often 'messier' than tangible ones – especially when it comes to analyzing the operational assets the company relies on to generate revenue and profit.

This is because intangible assets often include items recorded purely for accounting purposes. The company itself is not even aware that it 'owns' these intangible assets; and they are in no way used to produce the products or services sold to customers.

These non-productive intangible assets include goodwill and, for example, customer relationships. These items typically arise when a company acquires another business for a price exceeding the value of its physical assets. According to accounting rules, this excess amount must be recorded – often as goodwill. But for analyzing the operational assets driving revenue and profit, goodwill and similar items are irrelevant.

On the other hand, some intangible assets are highly relevant when it comes to understanding a company's revenue and earnings. Take, for instance, a patent in a pharmaceutical company. Without the patent, competitors would be free to copy the company's medicine and the patent would no longer protect the company from competition – causing revenue and earnings to collapse.

Similarly, for an IT company, software listed as intangible assets plays a central role in generating revenue and earnings.

Total assets

As you analyze more companies, you'll discover that some businesses require very few operational assets – whether tangible or intangible – to operate. These are often the companies you'll identify as great businesses, because they require little capital to finance the operating assets. As a result, return on invested capital tends to be high and attractive.

Other businesses require a large number of operational assets – and thus more capital – to operate, which leads to a lower and less attractive return on invested capital.

MICROSOFT CORPORATION
BALANCE SHEETS

(US$ millions)	June 30,	
ASSETS	2025	2024
Current assets:		
Cash and cash equivalents	30.242	18.315
Short-term investments	64.323	57.228
Total cash and short-term investments	**94.565**	**75.543**
Accounts receivable	69.905	56.924
Inventories	938	1.246
Other current assets	25.723	26.021
Total current assets	**191.131**	**159.734**
Non-current assets:		
Property and equipment	204.966	135.591
Operating lease right-of-use assets	24.823	18.961
Equity and other investments	15.405	14.600
Goodwill	119.509	119.220
Intangible assets, net	22.604	27.597
Other long-term assets	40.565	36.460
Total non-current assets	**427.872**	**352.429**
Total assets	**619.003**	**512.163**

LIABILITIES AND SHAREHOLDERS' EQUITY		
Current liabilities:		
Accounts payable	27.724	21.996
Short-term debt	0	6.693
Current portion of long-term debt	2.999	2.249
Accrued compensation	13.709	12.564
Short-term income taxes	7.211	5.017
Short-term unearned revenue	64.555	57.582
Other current liabilities	25.02	19.185
Total current liabilities	**141.218**	**125.286**
Non-current liabilities:		
Long-term debt	40.152	42.688
Long-term income taxes	25.986	27.931
Long-term unearned revenue	2.710	2.602
Deferred income taxes	2.835	2.618
Operating lease liabilities	17.437	15.497
Other long-term liabilities	45.186	27.064
Total non-current liabilities	**134.306**	**118.400**
Total liabilities	**275.524**	**243.686**
SHAREHOLDERS' EQUITY		
Common stock and paid-in capital	109.095	100.923
Retained earnings	237.731	173.144
Accumulated and other comprehensive loss	-3.347	-5.590
Total stockholders' equity	**343.479**	**268.477**
Total liabilities and stockholders' equity	**619.003**	**512.163**

The most striking feature of Microsoft's balance sheet is that the company holds cash and short-term investments totaling US$94,565 million. Looking at the 'Liabilities' under non-current liabilities, we see that debt amounts to only US$40,152 million – in other words, the company has no net debt and a substantial cash position. This aligns perfectly with the profile of 'a great business' with a strong moat.

WALMART INC.

BALANCE SHEET

(US$ millions)	Year to 31 January	
ASSETS	2025	2024
Current assets:		
Cash and cash equivalents	9.037	9.867
Receivables, net	9.975	8.796
Inventories	56.435	54.892
Prepaid expenses and other	4.011	3.322
Total current assets	**79.458**	**76.877**
Non-current assets:		
Property and equipment, net	119.993	110.810
Operating lease right-of-use assets	13.599	13.673
Finance lease right-of-use assets, net	6.112	5.855
Goodwill	28.792	28.113
Other long-term assets	12.869	17.071
Total non-current assets	**181.365**	**175.522**
Total assets	**260.823**	**252.399**

LIABILITIES, REDEEMABLE NON-CONTROLLING INTEREST, AND SHAREHOLDERS' EQUITY		
Current liabilities:	3.068	878
Short-term borrowings	58.666	56.812
Accounts payable	29.345	28.759
Accrued liabilities	608	307
Accrued income taxes	2.598	3.447
Long-term debt due within one year	1.499	1.487
Finance lease obligations due within one year	800	725
Total current liabilities	**96.584**	**92.415**

Non-current liabilities:		
Long-term debt	33.401	36.132
Long-term operating lease obligations	12.825	12.943
Long-term finance lease obligations	5.923	5.709
Deferred income taxes and other	14.398	14.629
Redeemable noncontrolling interest	271	222
Total non-current liabilities	**66.818**	**69.635**
Total liabilities	**163.402**	**162.050**
SHAREHOLDERS' EQUITY		
Common stock	802	805
Capital in excess of par value	5.503	4.544
Retained earnings	98.313	89.814
Accumulated other comprehensive loss	-13.605	-11.302
Total Walmart shareholders' equity	**91.013**	**83.861**
Nonredeemable noncontrolling interest	6.408	6.488
Total shareholders' equity	**97.421**	**90.349**
Total liabilities, redeemable noncontrolling interest, and shareholders' equity	**260.823**	**252.399**

Looking at Walmart's balance sheet, the company holds only about US$9 billion in cash, while its short-term and long-term debt totals US$92 billion (58,666 + 33,401). In other words, Walmart relies heavily on debt to finance its operations. We also see that Walmart can have its suppliers ('Accounts payable') finance a significant portion of its inventory.

BALANCE SHEET: LIABILITIES

On the liability side of the balance sheet, the company reports how its assets are financed and what types of capital have been used. Again, the structure of the liabilities section varies depending on the country. Companies in the United States typically list current liabilities first, followed by non-current liabilities and finally equity – the capital invested by the owners. In Europe, the order is reversed; but again, there's no need to be confused by this – it doesn't affect the overall understanding.

The consequences of using different types of capital to finance assets vary widely. For example, a company has liabilities to its suppliers in the form of payables, or unpaid bills. This kind of 'loan' is often free of charge, if the company pays its bills according to the agreed payment terms.

Similarly, some companies benefit from customers prepaying for products or services. This might include subscription payments, insurance premiums, or airline tickets purchased for future travel. This type of capital also functions as an interest-free loan.

The more capital a company can borrow for free from its suppliers and customers, the less its need to invest expensive capital in the business in the form of bank loans, other forms of credit, or equity from the owners – and the higher the return on invested capital.

Current liabilities

Current liabilities consist of short-term obligations that change continuously. As mentioned above, liabilities to suppliers and prepayments from customers are examples of such short-term items. Similarly, short-term loans (with a maturity of less than twelve months) are included in current liabilities, along with the portion of long-term debt that is due within the next year.

Leasing obligations, if the company has any, that require payment within the next twelve months are also classified as current liabilities.

Working capital

An important key figure is the company's working capital, which is calculated as:

working capital = current assets minus current liabilities

Current assets should be sufficient to cover short-term obligations for the company's short-term financing to be considered healthy. In other words, working capital measures a company's liquidity and short-term financial situation and indicates its ability to fund operations for the next twelve months.

When current liabilities exceed current assets, this may signal that the company is heading towards liquidity problems, so investors should always keep an eye on the working capital and make sure it is positive and healthy. If the company has negative working capital, it is important to understand why and whether this is or could become an issue. If the working capital is negative and the issue is related to short-term debt included in current liabilities, there is good reason to be extra cautious – especially if the company relies heavily on debt to finance its operations. In such cases, there is a real risk that the company could enter a full-blown liquidity crisis, and the warning sign of negative working capital may be just the tip of the iceberg.

Non-current liabilities

Just as non-current assets refer to long-term assets that do not change over a short period of time, non-current liabilities refer to the company's long-term payment obligations. Typical non-current liabilities include long-term debt, deferred tax liabilities and long-term lease obligations. In addition, the company may have other long-term obligations such as pension liabilities or similar commitments.

It's important for investors to identify and distinguish between interest-bearing long-term liabilities – which come at a cost and are therefore part of the invested capital – and non-interest-bearing non-current liabilities, which represent 'free' capital.

Equity

The final component of the company's capital structure is the equity provided by the owners. Equity consists of the paid-in share capital plus, broadly speaking, the retained earnings that the owners have allowed to remain in the company. In some cases, the company may also have repurchased some of its own shares from former shareholders. These repurchased shares are included in equity as a negative amount, as the company used equity to buy them back.

Total equity and liabilities

Altogether, a company's equity and liabilities equal the exact same amount as its total assets. In other words, the balance sheet shows how the company's assets are allocated and how those assets are financed – dollar for dollar.

50.

Return on Capital

A company's return on capital is central to the strength of the long-term investment one can expect as an investor.

No one has said it more precisely than Charlie Munger and this is worth repeating again:

'Over the long term, it is hard for a stock to earn a much better return than the business, which underlies its earnings. If the business earns 6% on capital over 40 years and you hold it for 40 years, you are not going to make much different than a 6% return – even if you originally buy it at a huge discount. Conversely, if a business earns 18% on capital over 20 or 30 years, even if you pay an expensive price, you end up with one hell of a result.'[12]

In other words, we are looking for companies with a consistently high return on invested capital.

It's important to keep in mind what the capital is actually invested in when you're analyzing a company's return on invested capital and trying to determine whether it's a great business.

As we have discussed, there is a distinction between the capital the company needs to finance its operational activities and the total capital invested. For example, in connection with an acquisition, management may have paid a significant amount in the form of goodwill to the seller. This goodwill appears under intangible assets on the balance sheet, but the

---

12 Munger, 1994.

investment in goodwill is entirely irrelevant to the company's operations and earnings.

Nevertheless, management did pay the total amount when buying the company and management must be measured on the return on total invested capital.

RETURN ON OPERATIONAL ASSETS

Let's begin by analyzing the return on operational assets – that is, the physical and operational intangible assets the company needs to generate revenue and earnings. In other words, these are the assets the company uses to generate sales and profits no matter how the company is financed.

On the balance sheet, we include non-current tangible assets as well as current assets. However, we do not include intangible assets that are unnecessary for the generation of revenue and earnings, such as goodwill. That said, we do include intangible assets that are operational essential to the business. For IT companies, this may include software, while for pharmaceutical companies it typically involves patents.

return on operational assets = NOPAT / (non-current assets – non-operational intangible assets + current assets)

The return on operational assets is simply calculated and provides a clear picture of the company's profitability no matter how the assets are financed. The higher the return on operational assets, and the more sustainable that return is over the long term, the greater the business.

As a benchmark for when a company can be considered 'great' independent of how it is financed, my experience suggests that if return on operational assets is below 15% (with a few exceptions), it is not a great business – and if the figure is below 10%, the company is almost certainly mediocre.

On the other hand, there are companies that manage to deliver returns on operational assets above 50%. These are typically truly great businesses – especially if such returns are sustainable over many years. Such companies are extremely valuable, but difficult to find, and it is very rare to be able to invest in them at an attractive price.

Let's use Microsoft and Walmart as examples and calculate the return on operational assets and invested capital for both companies in 2024 and 2025. For almost all companies, there will be opportunities to fine-tune the individual figures that go into calculating the return on invested capital. However, in my experience, it is most useful at the outset to develop a basic understanding of the company's profitability and the level of return on its operating assets and invested capital.

If these figures clearly indicate that the returns are unattractive, there is no reason to spend additional time on the company – you should move on to the next one. Conversely, if the calculations suggest high returns, it is worth diving deeper and carefully reviewing the company's financial statement notes and other disclosures to ensure that you, as an investor, are getting a precise and accurate picture.

It is also important to calculate the figures over a period of several years, to confirm whether the current situation is actually extraordinary and whether the company's long-term normalized earnings and return patterns differ significantly.

Microsoft

Looking first at Microsoft – which, as a software company, is characterized by high profitability and relatively few operational assets – we can see that in 2025 the company reported non-current assets of US$427,872 million. Of this amount, US$119,509 million was goodwill, which is excluded. The company also reports 'equity and other investments', which must be reviewed to determine whether they are used in core operations. We will choose to include them. Thus, total non-current operational assets amount to: US$427,872 million – US$119,509 million = US$308,363 million.

Next, Microsoft's current assets in 2025 totaled US$191,131 million, but a large portion of this comprises cash and short-term investments that are not required for operations and should therefore be deducted. As such, Microsoft's current operational assets total: US$191,131 million – US$94,565 million = US$96,566 million.

Thus, Microsoft's total operational assets in 2025 amounted to: US$308,363 million + US$96,566 million = US$404,929 million.

Choosing the appropriate tax rate for calculating NOPAT always involves some judgment, but the simplest method is to calculate the company's effective tax rate for the year and apply that rate to NOPAT.

From the income statement, we can see that Microsoft reported a pre-tax profit of US$123,627 million and an after-tax profit of US$101,832 million. In other words, the effective tax rate was US$21,795 million / US$123,627 million = 17.6%.

Microsoft's income statement shows operating income of US$128,528 million in 2025, so NOPAT is US$128,528 million × (1 − 17.6%) = US$105,907 million.

We can therefore calculate Microsoft's return on operational assets as: US$105,907 million / US$404,929 million = 26.2%.

Calculating the same figure for 2024 shows that Microsoft had a return on operational assets of 28.2%.

In other words, Microsoft demonstrates very high profitability on the assets used in its operations, regardless of how those assets are financed.

Walmart

Let's now look at Walmart, which is of course a very different type of company. Grocery retailing requires substantial assets in both buildings and inventory, and consequently profit margins are naturally much lower – customers can always shop at a competing supermarket.

In 2025, Walmart reported operating income of US$29,348 million and an effective tax rate of 23.4%, giving NOPAT of US$29,348 million × (1 − 23.4%) = US$22,481 million.

Walmart's 2025 balance sheet shows current assets of US$79,458 million, of which US$9,037 million are cash and cash equivalents. The cash position is therefore much smaller than Microsoft's, raising the question of whether cash should reasonably be viewed as part of operational assets. For comparability, we choose to deduct cash so that the figures for Microsoft and Walmart are calculated on the same basis. Walmart's current operational assets therefore amount to: US$79,458 million – US$9,037 million = US$70,421 million.

For non-current assets, we adjust only for goodwill, resulting in: US$181,365 million – US$28,792 million = US$152,573 million. Walmart's total operational assets in 2025 therefore amount to: US$70,421 million + US$152,573 million = US$222,994 million. The company's return on operational assets is: US$22,481 million / US$222,994 million = 10.1%.

Calculating the same figure for 2024 shows that Walmart had a return on operational assets of 9.4%.

We can therefore conclude that Walmart's return on operational assets does not appear particularly impressive. In other words, we should expect that Walmart will need to employ a more aggressive financing structure than Microsoft in order to deliver the highest possible returns to its shareholders.

RETURN ON INVESTED CAPITAL (ROIC)

Now, let's look at the company's return on total invested capital. This is the amount of capital that management has decided to invest in the business. As soon as we do that, we shift our focus from the asset side of the balance sheet – what the company earns on its operational assets – to what the company earns on the capital (equity and debt) that management has chosen to invest.

In other words, we begin to evaluate the consequences of management's capital-allocation decisions. ROIC tells us how effectively the company generates profit from the capital management has invested to finance its assets.

When calculating ROIC, we cannot disregard goodwill on the balance sheet. Management is, after all, deploying capital when acquiring another company; and while part of that capital often ends up classified as goodwill it is still invested capital.

The ROIC is not difficult to calculate.

ROIC = NOPAT / (equity + debt (including leasing liabilities) – excess of cash)

If the company holds a large cash position, it is reasonable to reduce the denominator by the sum of the excess cash, since management could use that cash to pay down debt and thereby improve the ROIC.

As for a benchmark of whether a company's ROIC is attractive, you can rely on Charlie Munger's definition: a return of 18% will deliver very attractive long-term returns; and a 6% return on invested capital is not worth pursuing. In my own work, I use 15% as an absolute minimum.

Again using Microsoft and Walmart as examples, when we calculate ROIC we quickly see that these two companies differ significantly in this area too.

Microsoft

We have already calculated Microsoft's 2025 NOPAT, which amounted to US$105,907 million. Looking at Microsoft's liabilities and equity, we can see that in 2025 the company had equity of US$343,479 million. Under non-current liabilities, we find long-term debt of US$40,152 million and operating lease liabilities of US$17,437 million. Under current liabilities, the current portion of long-term debt totals US$2,999 million. The total invested capital therefore amounts to: (343,479 + 40,152 + 17,437 + 2,999) = US$404,067 million.

However, we also know that Microsoft holds a very large cash balance of US$94,565 million, which should be deducted. The company's actual invested capital therefore is:

US$404,067 million – US$94,565 million = US$309,502 million.

Microsoft's ROIC in 2025 was thus: US$105,907 million / US$309,502 million = 34.2%. Calculating Microsoft's ROIC for 2024 yields 34.4%.

We can already conclude that Microsoft appears to be a great business and that management has allocated invested capital in an attractive and value-creating manner.

Walmart

Walmart's NOPAT for 2025 amounted to US$22,481 million. Based on the company's liabilities and equity, Walmart reported equity of

US$91,013 million. Under non-current liabilities, we find long-term debt of US$33,401 million, long-term operating lease obligations of US$12,825 million, and long-term finance lease obligations of US$5,923 million. Under current liabilities, we see short-term borrowings of US$58,666 million, long-term debt due within one year of US$1,499 million, and finance lease obligations due within one year of US$800 million. Finally, Walmart has a cash balance of US$9,037 million, which we choose to deduct.

Total invested capital therefore amounts to: (91,013 + 33,401 + 12,825 + 5,923 + 58,666 + 1,499 + 800 – 9,037) = US$195,090 million.

Walmart's ROIC in 2025 was therefore: US$22,481 million / US$195,090 million = 11.5%. Calculating Walmart's ROIC for 2024 yields 10.7%.

These results reinforce what we observed from the return on operational assets: Walmart is fundamentally unable to generate anything like the sort of returns on invested capital that Microsoft can. However, management must work with the circumstances they are given and take full advantage of the opportunities available to optimize the financing of invested capital.

Let's begin confirming our expectations by looking at ROUNTA.

RETURN ON UNLEVERED NET TANGIBLE ASSETS (ROUNTA)

As we know, ROUNTA is Warren Buffett's favorite metric for evaluating whether a company is by itself a great company or not. ROUNTA was created by Buffett himself and is not commonly used by analysts or financial experts. However, it's a highly effective metric because it shows the return on invested capital in operational assets.

According to Buffett, ROUNTA is the best metric to use when evaluating how great a business truly is and how much it earns on the capital invested in its operating assets – regardless of whether that capital comes from debt or equity.

Calculating ROUNTA is not very difficult. You start with the same capital calculation used for ROIC, and then subtract intangible assets.

Just to make thinking easier: ROUNTA = ROIC – intangible assets. The calculation is therefore as follows:

ROUNTA = NOPAT/ (equity + debt – goodwill [or other non-operational intangible assets] – excess of cash)

If the company holds excess cash under current assets, you should subtract that cash from the debt.

Here it is important to remember that if the company has no debt, NOPAT is more or less equal to net profit after tax, which is the term Buffett uses, when focusing on ROUNTA.

According to Buffett, a ROUNTA above 20–25% indicates a great business and you may even find businesses with a ROUNTA above 100%. Companies with a ROUNTA between 12% and 20% are considered acceptable or good businesses, while those below 12% are generally less attractive.

The very best businesses have a high – or even negative – ROUNTA and can grow significantly without needing additional capital to fund their expansion.

Microsoft

Microsoft's NOPAT for 2025 remains US$105,907 million. When we calculated Microsoft's 2025 ROIC, we found that the company had total invested capital minus cash of US$309,502 million. However, US$119,509 million of this was invested in goodwill; and since we are only interested in the capital invested in operational assets, that amount is deducted when calculating ROUNTA.

Microsoft's ROUNTA in 2025 is therefore: US$105,907 million / US$189,993 million = 55.7%. The corresponding figure for 2024 is 63.6%.

In other words, Microsoft is an exceptionally strong business and holds a substantial cash balance of US$94,565 million, which more than offsets its total debt.

Walmart

As noted earlier, Walmart's NOPAT for 2025 amounted to US$22,481 million. Total invested capital was US$195,090 million, from which we deduct the company's goodwill of US$28,792 million.

Walmart's ROUNTA in 2025 is therefore: US$22,481 million / US$166,298 million = 13.5%. The corresponding figure for 2024 is 12.6%.

Thus, with respect to returns on invested capital overall – and the capital invested specifically in operating assets – Walmart can be characterized as acceptable, but is certainly incapable of matching Microsoft.

*   *   *

Finally, let's look at the return on equity – that is, the capital invested by the owners, the shareholders – in the two companies and see whether the financing structure changes the overall picture.

RETURN ON EQUITY (ROE)

For a company's owners, it is of course also highly relevant to consider the direct return on the capital they have invested in the business, or the equity.

Return on equity (ROE) is quite simple to calculate:

return on equity = adjusted net profit / equity

ROE provides two important pieces of information. First, it shows how attractive it is for the owners to invest additional equity into the business as it grows. If a company is growing quickly and can reinvest all profits back into the business each year to finance that growth – and can do so at a ROE of 20% – it means that, as an owner, you're earning a 20% return on your existing investment as well as on any new capital that management reinvests into the operations.

A company that can compound equity at 20% annually is a very attractive business. Many companies have a ROE of 20%, which is certainly a strong performance, but in most cases are unable to deploy additional capital at that same rate.

On the other end of the performance spectrum are companies with low ROE, or those where ROE appears high and attractive until you realize that the company has taken on significant debt to achieve it, thereby increasing its financial risk. In such cases, the ROE might look strong but the ROIC – which also accounts for debt – is much lower. It's easy to understand that ROE and ROIC are more or less equal if the company has no debt.

Let's look at ROE for Microsoft and Walmart. For simplicity, we will use the net earnings figures reported by the companies in their income statements.

Microsoft

In 2025, Microsoft reported net profits of US$101,832 million, and the company's equity at year-end was US$343,479 million. ROE for 2025 is therefore:

US$101,832 million / US$343,479 million = 29.6%. The corresponding calculation for 2024 was: US$88,136 million / US$268,477 million = 32.8%.

It is worth noting that the company holds a substantial cash balance, which in principle could be distributed to shareholders, significantly reducing equity and increasing ROE from an already very high level. In short, Microsoft can be concluded to be a highly attractive business and a veritable money machine.

Walmart

Walmart's owners reported net profit in 2025 of US$19,436 million and equity of US$91,013 million. ROE for 2025 is therefore: US$19,436 million / US$91,013 million = 21.4%. The corresponding calculation for 2024 was: US$15,511 million / US$83,861 million = 18.5%.

We can see that by using debt and lease obligations, Walmart is able to reduce the need for equity such that returns on shareholder capital reach around 20%. A ROE of 20% is certainly satisfactory, but management can only achieve this return by employing a significant amount of debt. On the other hand, one can assume that Walmart is a stable company, making this level of debt generally manageable.

It is also clear that a ROE of 20% or higher is particularly attractive during a phase when a company like Walmart is undergoing rapid expansion, opening store after store. During this period, the company can reinvest its entire profit at a 20% return, thereby creating what we have previously described as a compounding machine.

Generally speaking, I prefer companies with little or no debt on the balance sheet. As we have seen, great businesses often don't need debt to operate effectively. Though they're few in number, there are some businesses that can run without any equity or debt at all.

51.

The Cash-Flow Statement

The total amount of free cash a company generates – from today until the day it ceases to exist – represents the company's value. Nothing more, nothing less. The only adjustment that needs to be made is for the timing of when the company's generated cash becomes available. That is exactly what the discounted cash flow (DCF) model accounts for.

The DCF is theoretically correct but – as we have discussed – unworkable in practice because it's nearly impossible to input exactly the right numbers. Consequently, the DCF will inevitably produce incorrect results.

However, that doesn't mean you shouldn't study a company's cash flow. There's a wealth of useful information in the cash-flow statement, so let's go through the key components and discuss what to look for.

The company's cash-flow statement is divided into three sections:

- Cash flow from operating activities
- Cash flow from investing activities
- Cash flow from financing activities

CASH FLOW FROM OPERATING ACTIVITIES

Unlike the income statement, the cash flow from operating activities focuses solely on recording what comes in as cash and what is used as cash in the company's operations.

MICROSOFT CORPORATION

CASH-FLOW STATEMENT	Fiscal year ended June 30,		
(US$ millions)	2025	2024	2023
OPERATIONS			
Net income	101.832	88.136	72.361
Adjustments to reconcile net income to net cash for operations:			
Depreciation, amortization and other	34.153	22.287	13.861
Stock-based compensation expenses	11.974	10.734	9.611
Net recognized losses on investment and derivatives	609	305	196
Deferred income taxes	-7.056	-4.738	-6.059
Changes in operating assets and liabilities:			
Accounts receivable	-10.581	-7.191	-4.087
Inventories	309	1.284	1.242
Other current assets	-3.044	-1.648	-1.991
Other long-term assets	-2.950	-6.817	-2.833
Accounts payable	569	3.545	-2.721
Unearned revenue	5.438	5.348	5.535
Income taxes	-38	1.687	-358
Other current liabilities	5.922	4.867	2.272
Other long-term liabilities	-975	749	553
Net cash from operations	**136.162**	**118.548**	**87.582**

FINANCING			
Proceeds from issuance of short-term debt	-5.746	5.250	0
Proceeds from issuance of debt	0	24.395	0
Repayment of debt	-3.216	-29.070	-2.750
Common stock issued	2.056	2.002	1.866
Common stock repurchased	-18.420	-17.254	-22.245
Common stock cash dividends paid	-24.082	-21.771	-19.800
Other, net	-2.291	-1.309	-1.006
Net cash used in financing	**-51.699**	**-37.757**	**-43.935**

INVESTING			
Additions to property and equipment	-64.551	-44.477	-28.107
Acquisitions of companies, net cash and divestitures and purchases of intangible and other assets	-5.978	-69.132	-1.670
Purchases of investments	-29.775	-17.732	-37.651
Maturities of investments	16.079	24.775	33.510
Sales of investments	9.309	10.894	14.354
Other, net	2.317	-1.298	-3.116
Net cash used in investing	**-72.599**	**-96.970**	**-22.680**

Effect of foreign exchange rates on cash and cash equivalents	63	-210	-194
Net change in cash and cash equivalents	**11.927**	**-16.389**	**20.773**
Cash and cash equvalents, beginning of period	18.315	34.704	13.931
Cash and cash equvalents, end of period	**30.242**	**18.315**	**34.704**

Microsoft's cash-flow statement demonstrates how cash-generative the business is, with net cash from operations of US$136 billion in 2025. However, if you look further under 'Investing' you will notice a significant increase in 'Additions to property and equipment', from US$28 billion in 2023 to US$64.5 billion in 2025. This increase mostly reflects the company's investments in data centers and AI.

WALMART INC.

CASH-FLOW STATEMENT	Year to 31 January		
(US$ millions)	2025	2024	2023
CASH FLOWS FROM OPERATING ACTIVITIES			
Consolidated net income	20.157	16.27	11.292
Adjustments to reconcile consolidated net income to net cash provided by operating activities			
Depreciation and amortization	12.973	11.853	10.945
Investment (gains) and losses, net	878	3.193	1.683
Deferred income taxes	-635	-175	449
Other operating activities	2.889	2.642	1.919
Changes in certain assets and liabilities, net of effects of acquisitions and dispositions			
Receivables, net	-1.106	-797	240
Inventories	-2.755	2.017	-528
Accounts payable	3.228	2.515	-1.425
Accrued liabilities	379	-1.324	4.393
Accrued income taxes	435	-468	-127
Net cash provided by operating activities	**36.443**	**35.726**	**28.841**

CASH FLOWS FROM INVESTING ACTIVITIES			
Payments for property and equipment	-23.783	-20.606	-16.857
Proceeds from the disposal of property and equipment	432	250	170
Proceeds from disposal of certain strategic investments	4.080	-	-
Payments for business acquisitions, net of cash acquired	-1.896	-9	-740
Other investing activities	-212	-922	-295
Net cash used in investing activities	**-21.379**	**-21.287**	**-17.722**

CASH FLOW FROM FINANCING ACTIVITIES			
Net change in short-term borrowings	2.212	512	-34
Proceeds from issuance of long-term debt	-	4.967	5.041
Repayments of long-term debt	-3.468	-4.217	-2.689
Dividends paid	-6.688	-6.140	-6.114
Purchase of company stock	-4.494	-2.779	-9.920
Dividends paid to noncontrolling interest	-576	-763	-444
Purchase of noncontrolling interest	-	-3.462	-827
Sale of subsidiary stock	362	716	66
Other financing activities	-2.170	-2.248	-2.118
Net cash used in financing activities	**-14.822**	**-13.414**	**-17.039**

Effect of exchange rates on cash, cash equivalents and restricted cash	-641	69	-73
Net increase (decrease) in cash, cash equivalents and restricted cash	**-399**	**1.094**	**-5.993**
Cash, cash equivalents and restricted cash at beginning of year	9.935	8.841	14.834
Cash, cash equivalents and restricted cash at end of year	**9.536**	**9.935**	**8.841**

Walmart's 2025 cash-flow statement is actually quite straightforward. The company generates US$36 billion in net cash from operating activities. Roughly speaking, it invests nearly US$24 billion of that in 'Payments for property and equipment'. Of the remaining US$12 billion, Walmart uses US$6.7 billion for dividends and US$4.5 billion for share repurchases (buybacks

Depreciation and amortization

As we've seen, in the income statement depreciation of property, plant and equipment is deducted because the value of these assets is written down over their expected lifetime for accounting purposes. Similarly, amortization expenses for intangible assets are also deducted in the income statement.

In the cash-flow statement, you generally start with the net result from the income statement and then adjust for actual changes in cash flow. Since depreciation and amortization are not paid out as cash but are recorded as accounting expenses in the income statement, these are added back in the cash-flow statement. In other words, depreciation and amortization often appear as large positive items in the cash-flow statement.

Change in working capital

Another important item to watch in the cash-flow statement is the change in cash related to working capital. We described working capital (current assets minus current liabilities) when reviewing the balance sheet, and changes in working capital can often be significant in the cash-flow statement. Working capital includes inventory, accounts receivable from customers and payables to suppliers. There can be substantial shifts in how much capital the company has tied up in working capital each year. A single year's change in working capital doesn't say much about the company's long-term capital needs, but a company that must tie up a large portion of its earnings in bigger inventories and more receivables year after year is consuming the owners' earnings. A company that must spend a lot of the earnings to finance an ever-increasing working capital need is highly unlikely to become a great business with a high return on capital.

So, pay attention to how much cash the company must tie up in working capital each year. The least attractive companies use almost all their profits to fund working capital. It might sound strange, but some of the best companies are able to operate with negative working capital because they don't need inventory and receive cash from customers before paying their suppliers. As the company grows, cash inflows from working capital also grow. From an accounting perspective, it may look like the company's liabilities are increasing, but in reality the company is being granted more and more free capital by its customers and suppliers. Since this capital is more or less permanent – providing the company continues to grow – it can to some extent be considered free permanent capital available to the owners.

Financial costs and income

Financial costs and income usually appear as 'finance costs paid' and 'finance costs received'. What's crucial is not necessarily the size of these items, but that they are included under cash flow from operating activities – not, as some companies would have it, under cash flow from financing activities.

The likely reason that some companies choose to place financing costs and income under financing activities instead of operating activities is that management wants the free cash flow – used in the DCF model – to appear as large as possible, thereby making the company seem more valuable (and in turn supporting the stock price as much as possible).

I've even seen companies that include finance income under cash flow from operating activities but place finance costs under cash flow from financing activities. This way, the costs don't directly impact the calculation of free cash flow – unless you notice and adjust for it. As I mentioned earlier, accounting is the language of business but it has many dialects!

CASH FLOW FROM INVESTING ACTIVITIES

In the statement of cash flows from investing activities, you will find three categories of investments.

The first is investment made in the company's operations. This is often divided into two parts: investment in tangible assets, such as property, plant and equipment, and investment in intangible assets, such as software and similar items.

Unfortunately, most companies do not distinguish between maintenance investments and growth investments. This makes it difficult for investors to assess how much is required to simply maintain the company's current operations, versus how much is being invested to support future growth. Still, it's clear that without these investments, the company would struggle to stay competitive over the long term and to grow the business.

The second category is business acquisitions – that is, purchases of other companies or subsidiaries. These investments can sometimes be significant, but they should not be included in the calculation of free cash flow, as acquisitions are discretionary management decisions and not directly tied to the ongoing operations of the existing business.

Finally, some companies invest excess cash in securities. The purchase and sale of these financial assets are considered investment activities and therefore appear in the 'cash flow from investing' section. However, it's important to remember that managing excess cash through investments in securities is not part of the core business – it is a management decision related to cash management and capital decisions.

FREE CASH FLOW (FCF)

After reviewing the cash flow from operating activities and investing activities, we can now calculate the free cash flow (FCF), which is the key input in a DCF model.

FCF represents the amount of cash a company generates after covering the expenses required to operate and maintain the assets that produce its income. It provides a correct picture of the company's financial earnings power. The challenge with using the FCF number is that it can fluctuate greatly from year to year.

FCF = cash flow from operating activities* – investments in property, plant and equipment and intangible assets
*Including financial costs and income and tax

My suggestion is that you use the FCF as an alternative to reported net profit plus amortization of intangibles when you're deciding whether your investment hurdle rate is met and calculating your return on investment. However, I must also emphasize the need for caution: a single year's FCF can be heavily influenced by changes in working capital or unusually large investments in production assets, whether physical or intangible. Handling this issue, it is my recommendation that you use FCF as a check point but 'normalize' the numbers by reviewing the figures over several years before drawing any conclusions about your company's normalized FCF earnings. The easiest way to do this is to calculate the last five to seven years of FCF as a percentage of revenue. This gives you an average FCF percentage of revenue that can be used to normalize the present FCF. Once again, remember to always think about why the numbers are what they are.

CASH FLOW FROM FINANCING ACTIVITIES

Financing activities include dividend payments, the purchase of treasury shares (share buybacks), proceeds from loans and borrowings, repayments of debt and repayments of lease obligations.

Cash flow from financing activities largely reflects management decisions and is not directly related to the company's core business operations unless the company has a lot of its assets financed by leasing contracts.

When analyzing financing activities in the cash-flow statement, I also review the liabilities section of the balance sheet to assess whether management has made any significant changes to the company's capital structure. I pay particular attention to the balance between dividends paid and share repurchases to evaluate whether capital is being allocated in a rational and shareholder-friendly way.

Acknowledgements

Let me begin by expressing my deep appreciation to Warren Buffett for his contribution to this book. Without his insights, annual letters, shareholder meetings, and remarkable investment track record, this book would never have come into being. Nor would I personally have had the opportunity to achieve the financial freedom and business understanding I enjoy today. I truly stand on the shoulders of a giant – and in doing so, I stand alongside thousands of other investors across the globe.

But Warren Buffett's influence extends far beyond the field of investing. For many thousands of lifelong learners around the world, he has provided inspiration, wisdom and a simple, rational way of understanding and navigating life's many complexities.

I owe nearly as great a debt of gratitude to my friend Robert P. Miles (Bob), who first encouraged me to write this book five years ago. His suggestion came after I delivered my first presentation at his annual seminar, *The Genius of Warren Buffett*, at the University of Nebraska at Omaha in the days leading up to the Berkshire Hathaway Annual Meeting.

Since then, my presentations in Omaha have evolved considerably, shaped by countless conversations between Bob and me – conversations aimed at continually improving participants' ability to understand not only Warren Buffett's mindset and methodology, but also themselves as investors. Bob's inspiration and perspective are therefore deeply woven into the new ideas and insights I believe this book contains. Thank you, Bob.

I made the final decision to write this book in September 2024, and for that I owe my thanks to Susanne M. Skov. On a warm, late-summer day, sitting on my balcony, I told Susanne that I had drafted a five-page synopsis for a possible book I was considering. She asked to read it. When she had finished, she looked at me and said, 'Then you'd better get started.' It was a defining moment for me. The book you're now holding in your hands is the result of Susanne's encouragement and the many months of work that followed.

Many people have supported and encouraged me throughout this project, helping me maintain momentum and push through to completion. In particular, I wish to thank my friends Oliver Müller (Mauritius), Andrew Coye (Dubai), Flavio Montenegro (Guatemala), Enrique Franco (Mexico), Rodrico Pastor (Brazil) and Shivam Kashan (USA) for reading the manuscript with great dedication and offering so many valuable suggestions for improvement. You have elevated this book to a level I could never have achieved without your feedback.

I also owe special thanks to my editor, Mike Jones, in England, who has been an extraordinary source of support and expertise in making the book more accessible and easier to understand. This contribution is far from insignificant – not least because my English is strong, but Danish is my native language. I did not know Mike before beginning this project, and nor was I familiar with the leading business editors in the US or the UK. So, I did what seemed most sensible: I simply asked ChatGPT, 'Who are the three best English-language business editors in the world for intellectually driven business and investment books?' Mike was among the three names returned, and after reviewing the work and personal approach of each candidate, I had no doubt that he was the right choice. After our first conversation about the project, my decision was fully confirmed. Working with him has been a privilege, and he is, without question, a first-class editor.

My thanks also go to Glen Edelstein for designing the cover, layout and all other graphic elements of the book. Although Glen divides his time between Mexico and New York, we have worked closely together from the start. He has offered valuable, experienced guidance on both the book's visual identity and the publishing process. It will not surprise you that I also found Glen through ChatGPT – and like Mike, he has proven to be truly world-class.

While Mike and Glen have shaped the major elements of the book, I would like to highlight the contribution of my proofreader, Monica

Hope, in England, whose meticulous work has been invaluable. She has carefully reviewed the manuscript, corrected errors and refined sentences that needed clarification.

Anyone who has written a book knows how solitary the process can be and how much time it demands. For me, it required roughly 2,200 hours of work over 15 months. I am immensely grateful to have had this time – but am also acutely aware that it could have been spent with family and close friends. The work and the necessary priorities have not been without cost; and, particularly as a first-time author, one quickly learns that there are consequences one cannot foresee.

Yet the support has been tremendous, and I want to extend my heartfelt thanks to my parents, my children, grandchildren, my sister and brother-in-law and my closest friends for their interest and encouragement. I hope this book offers current and future members of my family something of lasting value – something they may use constructively in their own lives.

To all those I have mentioned, I offer my sincere gratitude for your constructive contributions to this book and for whatever value and perspective it may bring to its readers. Should there be any errors, misunderstandings, or significant omissions, the responsibility is mine alone.

P.G.